PASTORAL
COUNSELING
WITH ADOLESCENTS
AND YOUNG ADULTS

PASTORAL COUNSELING WITH ADOLESCENTS AND YOUNG ADULTS

Charles M. Shelton

CROSSROAD • NEW YORK

1995

The Crossroad Publishing Company
370 Lexington Avenue, New York, NY 10017

Printed in the United States of America

Library of Congress Cataloging-in-Publication Data

Shelton, Charles M.
    Pastoral counseling with adolescents and young adults / Charles M.
Shelton.
        p.   cm.
    Includes bibliographical references and index.
    ISBN 0-8245-1486-6 (pbk.)
    1. Teenagers—Pastoral counseling of.   2. Church work with
teenagers.   3. Teenagers—Religious life.   4. Adolescent psychology.
I. Title.
BV4447.S48   1995
259'.23–dc20   94-45697
                                                                    CIP

For Harry Hoewischer —
Mentor, Brother, Friend

Contents

Preface

With this work I complete the third and final book in a series devoted to the ministry to the spiritual, moral, and mental health needs of adolescents and young adults. The first book in this series, *Adolescent Spirituality: Pastoral Ministry for High School and College Youth,*[1] set forth an overall pastoral theology for young people. In essence, my pastoral theology for adolescents incorporates the themes of compassionate care and loving challenge, touchstones for every pastoral ministry. In *Adolescent Spirituality* I applied these twin themes to various areas of the adolescent's experience (e.g., formation in faith, sexual development). This work focused on basic developmental patterns during adolescence and did not address, for the most part, mental health concerns.

In addition to spiritual development, our understanding of ourselves as moral persons is essential for human growth. Within the context of adolescent and young adult development, then, my second book in the series, *Morality and the Adolescent: A Pastoral Psychology Approach,*[2] explored youth's attempt to fashion and construct a moral self. The task for youth is to move from the question "Who am I?" to the related question, "What am I about?" As adults, our central focus must be aiding youth to respond maturely to this latter question. My own perspective for addressing youth's moral concerns focuses on the development of *conscience*. Indeed, as they mature, adolescents and young adults will utilize conscience for charting their life direction and making moral decisions. In *Morality and the Adolescent* I developed a seven-dimensional view of conscience that is holistic in considering adolescent development and living of the moral life, yet practical in helping adults to address youth's moral concerns.

In addition, though, we would be remiss if we concluded our discussion with an examination of only youth's spiritual and moral development. The current cultural climate and the ravaging of family life make it necessary to provide discussion of adolescent and young adult mental health. When giving workshops around the country, I am more and more struck by how many questions focus on mental health concerns. It is increasingly apparent that problems in young people's mental health influence their relationships with the Lord as well as their view of others and themselves.[3]

In the pages that follow I hope to offer a concise yet substantial overview of adolescent mental health in order to benefit adults working with high school and college age youth. By discussing both adolescents (high school) and young adults (college students) in the same book I do not mean to say we can equate their experience and worldviews. On the contrary, there are significant developmental differences between these two age periods. Yet any pastoral minister who works with college students is well aware that young adults bring to their college years a large number of early and middle adolescent issues. As a consequence, in order to minister in an effective manner with the college student, awareness of and attention to these issues is vital. I hope, then, my discussions of these two developmental periods are complementary. The adult working with junior and senior high students will benefit from discussion of the college years and utilize this information in ways to prepare the high school student for meeting and resolving future developmental tasks. On the other hand, the adult working with college students will benefit from the discussion of high school adolescents and utilize this information in helping the young adult acquire insight into his or her previous life experience. Our discussion will offer insights into the emotional functioning of adolescents and young adults and address concrete concerns that educators, youth ministers, and pastoral counselors encounter. When helpful, concrete suggestions will be offered.

One other limitation in this work is the focus on youth in educational and youth ministry settings. Since the vast majority of youth attend high school and a significant number acquire post-secondary school education, and since a majority of adults working with youth minister to young people in school, religious education, or youth ministry settings, I believe it appropriate to make these youth the focus of this work. I do not intend to slight high school dropouts, those young people who marry early, those who are seriously disturbed, or those who enter the job market while still in their teens or without a college education. I believe that most of the issues discussed in these pages are relevant to many of these young people as well. The reader might also profit from the extensive references and use these as a resource for further discussion of various issues. The adult working with "select" groups of adolescents such as the severely disturbed or dropouts will, of course, want to explore other resource materials in addition to this book.

On a more personal note, I am a clinical psychologist, and it is this perspective that I bring to the discussion. A counselor's orientation is significant. A counselor or therapist has certain views of human nature and behavior that invariably influence his or her style and analysis of a client's problem. For example, someone trained in behavioral therapy will focus on observed behavior and spend little time attempting to understand the client's internal psychic processes. I believe it important to be explicit regarding my own orientation. From reflection, reading, and clinical work, I have found the approach most helpful in working with clients to be a cognitive-dynamic approach. This integrative orientation incorporates recent insights from the cognitive school of psychology along with the well-seasoned insights of psychodynamic approaches. In other words, the cognitive-dynamic orientation blends the emphases on thinking patterns (self-statements) and significant affective bonding (relationships). I will say more about this in the pages ahead. For now, it is important that readers begin to think about their own views on human nature and how human behavior is best explained.

In summary, readers will find in the pages ahead a comprehensive view of adolescent mental health. For those beginning their work with youth, this book, I hope, will become a ready resource. For those more experienced, I offer these pages as a source for deepening insight and greater pastoral effectiveness. For both groups my intention is for this book to serve as a standard reference work on youth's mental health in the pastoral context and be an aid for adults whose pastoral work is ministry with youth.

CHAPTER ONE

Adolescent Pastoral Counseling:
Some Initial Considerations

Recently a concerned parent asked me if adolescents were really as troubled as the news media portrayed or are they "just being kids." I have often been asked this question over the past decade. In workshops and lectures I have given around the country one cannot help but notice the increased urgency with which parents and educators ask questions about the problems of youth today. Indeed, I have noticed that the questions have more and more been concerned with serious behavioral and emotional problems. One writer characterizes some children's home life and early experience as so problematic that it leads to the decline and impairment of conscience functioning.[1]

The adolescent's world today is far more complex, dangerous, and insecure than it was even a generation ago. One need only mention the word "AIDS" to understand the gravity of issues that today's youth must confront. Adults appear to accept the reality of young peoples' lives as more complex and dangerous than their own. A nationwide survey of one thousand adults reported that 72 percent of the adults surveyed believed that young people today experience more serious problems then they faced when they were young. Adults rated drug abuse as the most serious problem youth face. Other youth problems that were of serious concern included: alcohol abuse, negative peer pressure, unwanted pregnancy, child abuse, teen crime, depression, conflict with parents, suicide, and runaway behavior.[2] Writing in the preface for a report issued by the National Commission on Children, Sen. John D. Rockefeller noted:

> Too many of today's children and adolescents will reach adulthood unhealthy, illiterate, unemployable, lacking moral direction and a vision of a secure future. This is a personal tragedy for the young people involved and a staggering loss for the nation as a whole. We must begin today to place children and their families at the top of the national agenda. . . . Many young people believe they have little to lose by dropping out of school, having a baby as an unmarried teenager, using and selling dangerous drugs, and committing crimes. When they

1

lack a sense of hope and the opportunity to get a good job, support a family and become a part of mainstream adult society, teenagers are frequently not motivated to avoid dangerous or self-destructive behaviors. These youth can see few compelling reasons to avoid or delay activities that provide immediate gratification. Unfortunately, their actions often make their expectations a self-fulfilling prophecy.[3]

Statistics supporting the above statement provide a frightening glimpse of the trials and tribulations facing America's youth. Consider the following: In any given year, nearly one million teenagers drop out of school, and in many inner-city schools this dropout rate is above 50 percent. In 1987 1.8 million teens (under eighteen years of age) were arrested. By the age of seventeen half of all girls and two-thirds of all boys have had sexual intercourse.[4]

The Children's Defense Fund has published the following chilling findings. Every day in America:

- 8,441 teen become sexually active
- 2,756 teens become pregnant
- 248 children are arrested for violent crimes
- 176 children are arrested for drug abuse
- 427 children are arrested for alcohol abuse or drunk driving
- 10,988 public school students are suspended each school day
- 2,250 students ages sixteen to twenty-four drop out of school[5]

What makes these figures even more disconcerting is that the very fabric of society — its family structure — is increasingly under attack. One out of five American children lives in poverty; forty thousand children fail to see their first birthday; the U.S. has the highest divorce rate, teenage pregnancy rate, child poverty rate, and abortion rate in the Western world; nearly twelve million U.S. children go to bed every day either hungry or underfed; the teenage suicide rate has gone up 300 percent in the last thirty years; more than eight million children are without insurance; increasingly the homeless in our land are mothers and children.[6]

One clear indicator is that the "structure" of the American family is undergoing dramatic change.

There are, however, clear and potentially troublesome social indications that the "traditional" American family, which has been the model upon which notions of childrearing and adolescent development have been based, is disappearing as a result of changing patterns of marriage, divorce, childbearing, and parenting.[7]

In a large nationwide survey of over forty-five thousand sixth to twelfth graders a number of factors were listed that contributed to "positive teenage development."[8] These assets enabled teens to make maturing and thoughtful decisions that prepared them as productive adults. The assets were divided between "external assets" and "internal assets."

The "external assets" were:

1. family support
2. parent(s) as social resources
3. parent communication
4. other adult resources
5. other adult communication
6. parent involvement in schooling
7. positive school climate
8. parental standards
9. parental discipline
10. parental monitoring
11. time at home
12. positive peer influence
13. involvement in music
14. involvement in school extracurricular activities
15. involvement in community organizations or activities
16. involvement in church or synagogue[9]

The "internal assets" were the following.

1. achievement motivation
2. educational aspiration
3. school performance
4. homework
5. valuing helping people
6. concern about world hunger
7. caring about people's feelings
8. valuing sexual restraint
9. assertiveness skills
10. decision-making skills
11. friendship-making skills
12. planning skills
13. self-esteem
14. positive view of personal future

Unfortunately, the Search Institute survey reports that "the average student has only 50 percent of the external assets and 60 percent of the internal assets. As youth get older and face tougher choices, the number of assets tends to decrease in the key areas of positive values, control and social support."[10]

Surveys indicate that these conditions have led to "anxiety" among parents about American family life. "Americans are generally gloomy about the state of the family but feel better about what goes on in their own homes."[11] Even though many Americans report that there is adequate communication in their own families, the tenuous if not antagonistic state of American society leads most Americans to perceive American family life as being in a precarious state. There is, in other words, a negative bias in how Americans view family life. Indeed, "in one of every 10 families, parents worry 'a lot' that someone will shoot their children."[12]

Adolescence: A Definition

Adolescence is a time of significant biological, emotional, social, and intellectual changes. According to some researchers, recent historical events have made this period more challenging than ever before. Historical trends that have made adolescence more difficult include the following.

First, the time period for adolescence appears to be lengthening. "For many young people, the protracted period of adolescence introduces a high degree of uncertainty into their lives."[13]

Second, adolescents achieve biological maturity earlier than they achieve cognitive maturity and adequate life experience. Consequently, young people are faced with numerous and significant choices before they are developmentally prepared to make such decisions.

Third, youth today appear to be confused about adult roles they will undertake and also the future they will inherit. In stark contrast to earlier times, young people today lack the extensive time needed with adults that enables them to learn adult roles.

Fourth, unlike youth of earlier periods who could count on close family units and community ties, youth of the 1990s are often without such familial and communal support.

Fifth, young people today are exposed to a wide variety of experiences that are health- and life-threatening. Among these are drugs, smoking, sex, and violence.[14]

There are many definitions of "adolescence." The American Psychiatric Association's definition offers the best framework for appreciating the adolescent's experience. According to the Association, adolescence is

> a chronological period beginning with the physical and emotional processes leading to sexual and psychosocial maturity and ending at an ill-defined time when the individual achieves independence and social productivity. This period is associated with rapid physical, psychological, and social changes.[15]

The above definition emphasizes several helpful points. Adolescent change involves the total person; physical, psychological, and social features are all vital ingredients in defining the adolescent. Second, one of the most frustrating points in defining adolescence is determining: "When does it end?" (Parents may ask this question with a little more urgency than academic writers!) Studies are now indicating that after graduation college students often return home for a time. Reasons for this include the high cost of living on one's own, but often include various family-related issues as well. Can we consider these live-in children adults? Are they still adolescents? Psychologists refer to college undergraduates as "young adults" (young adulthood is seen as the period from twenty until forty), a transition from adolescence to adulthood. A growing consensus among developmental researchers is that college undergraduates (young adults) are, from an emotional standpoint, still very much emotionally tied to their parents. Developing a mature, interdependent relationship with parents and being able to view them as fully distinct individuals with strengths and limits does not usually take place until the late twenties.[16] Thus, the definition's phrase "ill-defined time" is quite appropriate.

There exists no one type of adolescent; there are many groups of youth today, for example, urban, rural, and suburban youth. There are several ethnic distinctions: white, Hispanic, Asian-American, African-American, and Native American. Youth can be homeless or reside in poor, middle- or, upper-class neighborhoods. I mention this point to highlight the numerous factors that shape youth's experience; every youth's acquisition of identity will in some ways be influenced by such ethnic and socioeconomic factors. Furthermore,

> as the number of young people in our aging society has been declining, the relative number of minority children has increased and they constitute larger and larger proportions of those entering the adolescent years. The number of black adolescents is declining but not as rapidly as the number of whites, and so they are becoming a proportionately higher percentage of the adolescent population. There have been similar increases in the proportion of Hispanic and Asian-American youth, but this is in part due to actual increases in number as a result of immigration. The effects of this increasing proportion

of minority group youngsters in the adolescent cohorts of the last two decades of the century are dramatic, and ruling out any unlikely changes in immigration or mortality rates, will continue to be so. Given the relationship between ethnicity and socioeconomic status which still prevails in America, more and more adolescents will experience the social ills resulting from minority group membership, such as lower levels of educational attainment, higher unemployment and arrest rates, poverty, and higher fertility.[17]

As a consequence, schools will more and more reflect these population shifts. For example, in 1982 nearly three-quarters of the school-age population was white. By the year 2020 this figure will drop to little over half the student-age population. The largest increase will be among Hispanic youth, who will make up a quarter of the student-age population by 2020.[18]

Stages of Adolescence

Though we have offered a general definition of adolescence, it is also helpful to delineate various stages of adolescence. These are usually defined as early (twelve to fifteen years of age), middle (fifteen to eighteen), and late (eighteen to twenty-one).

Early Adolescence   This period is considered the most tumultuous for the adolescent. Behavior is most apt to be inconsistent or erratic during the early adolescent phase. There are of course some obvious reasons for such behavior. The early adolescent experiences pubertal changes that may be threatening. Yet changes occur beyond the physiological level. Adolescents also advance cognitively. The adolescent might become self-absorbed in thought, to the exclusion of other important issues, or blurt out impulsively questions containing the rudiments of more sophisticated thinking. (For example, "Why are we alive?") In addition, early adolescents are often confused about their very selfhood. Early adolescence is best viewed as the *initial* phase of leaving childhood and encountering a yet-to-be future that is unknown.

Given this clouded and unknown future, early adolescents are prone as never before to be distracted, frustrated, and perplexed. A natural consequence of their uncertainty is the lack of consistency in their everyday behaviors. This period best explains the adolescent who one minute is visibly upset and feels the world going "to pieces" and within the hour appears perfectly calm as if "nothing happened." Adults can often hear themselves asking: "Is this the same person?"

As the young adolescent proceeds through this difficult period, a strong ally is found in the peer group. Unsure of themselves and often unable to "hear" what adults are saying, young people seek solace in the peer group, whose purpose is to assuage personal doubts and questions while furnishing a sturdy shelter for dealing with their own insecurities. The peer group becomes, in effect, the substitute identity the adolescent needs. This influence can in turn lead to the "tyranny of the peer group" wherein peers exert undue and at times harmful influence on the adolescent. More frightening, "by age fifteen, about a quarter of all young adolescents are engaged in behaviors that are harmful or dangerous to themselves and others."[19]

The behavioral changes observed in adolescence are not just a result of puberty. We must be also sensitive to the *context* that early adolescents experience. A primary feature of this context is the evolving school setting. It has now been documented that early adolescents experience several changes in their school environments (shifting from primary to junior high and secondary school) that have the potential for disruption. Some of the changes early adolescents must adapt to include the following. First, the high school classroom is perceived as one where there exists more teacher control and discipline. Second, teacher-student relationships are reported as less positive than teacher-student relationships in the elementary school years. Third, while elementary school instruction involves small groups and more individualized instruction, the high school environment is noted for whole-class learning and competition. Fourth, junior high teachers feel they are less effective as teachers. Fifth, the cognitive skills that early adolescents employ are often not challenged when they begin junior high. Finally, high school teachers employ higher standards of evaluation than their colleagues in primary school. All in all, these changes in school environment can prove disconcerting if not disruptive to many children as they enter early adolescence.[20]

Psychologist Robert Hendern notes that each phase of adolescence has distinguishing characteristics:[21] For the early adolescent these include:

- struggle with sense of identity
- moodiness
- improved expression through speech
- tendency to express feelings by actions rather than words
- increased importance of close friendships
- less affection shown to parents; occasional rudeness
- realization that parents are not perfect; identification of their faults
- search for new people to love besides parents

- tendency to return to childish behavior, fought off by excessive activity
- peer group influence on interests and clothing styles
- girls ahead of boys
- same-sex friends and group activities
- shyness, blushing, and modesty
- greater interest in privacy
- experimentation with body (masturbation)
- worries about being normal
- rule and limit testing
- occasional experimentation with cigarettes, marijuana, and alcohol
- capacity for abstract thought

Middle Adolescence   The middle adolescent period is associated with the secondary school years. The central developmental task for the adolescent resides in defining more concretely who he or she is; the adolescent more decisively provides answers to the question: "Who Am I?" One way the adolescent answers this question is through the various roles that he or she experiments with. Thus, the adolescent might attempt to balance being a son/daughter, friend, student, athlete, club member, worker. The pulls and demands of these various roles often lead to tensions and conflicts, yet they provide the necessary grist that enables the adolescent to explore commitment, decision-making, and ethical reflection. The independence struggles of early adolescence continue and at times are dramatic. During this period peer group influence, though still significant, evolves into more personalized relationships with both sexes. Behavior becomes less erratic and, on average, one can expect more behavioral consistency with middle adolescents. The adolescent continues the process of separation by questioning adult norms and behaviors and, as a result of cognitive transformations, offers opinions on a wide variety of topics that at times differ substantially from prevailing adult standards. These statements demonstrate the adolescent's need to construct a personally intelligible framework for interpreting the wider world.

Late Adolescence   The college years provide the environment for more serious reflection. The young adult now constructs an initial life philosophy that guides decision-making and personal behaviors. The identity quest continues but coexists along with the increasing need for intimacy. The late adolescent's interests and time are

8

increasingly future-oriented. A career, the possibility of future commitment, and future roles all take center stage for the young adult. Even so, the college student remains in many ways an adolescent. That is, developmental issues and early negative life experience continue to influence the adolescent's thinking and behavior. Even though the college student will often like to be accorded the status of "young adult," there is no denying the continual intrusion of painful and unresolved issues within the adolescent's psyche. For example, the adolescent whose family experience was marked by divorce, family conflict, or chemical addiction will more likely experience difficulty in negotiating the demands of emotional maturity and stable adult commitments. Many late adolescents carry considerable "baggage" throughout their young adult years.

Some Guidelines for Adults

Though our discussion centers for the most part on youth, we would be negligent if we did not consider the adult's role. The roles themselves vary considerably: teacher, youth worker, mentor, campus minister, counselor, adult advisor, religious educator. Failure to consider the adult's attitudes and assumptions can lead to unnecessary frustration as well as some serious pastoral quandaries. In my travels and workshops over the years I have talked to thousands of adults who work with youth. Drawing upon these encounters, I offer adults the following guidelines when ministering to high school and college age youth.

1. *Reflect on what it means to be a "healthy adult."*

One of the adult's obligations is to model for youth the meaning of "happy, healthy, and whole." (Not that this guideline is always easy to fulfill!) Many adults who work with youth have themselves experienced difficult and problematic backgrounds. Perhaps this is one of the reasons the adult has chosen to work with youth. Adults might profitably discuss in a group context the meaning of "healthy adulthood." In one survey mental health professionals included the following as essential attributes of mental health: self-competence, adequate interpersonal functioning, capacity for commitment, and a developed philosophy of life.[22] With the above in mind, ask yourself: To what extent do I possess these and other valued characteristics? What are my needs and what are the "adult ways" I use for getting my needs met?

2. *Ask yourself to what extent you have been able to forgive your own parents.*

No parent is perfect. We all know this, but far too often we suffer the consequences of the tacit assumption that our parents must be perfect and we hold them to such standards! A general rule here consists in being able to accept the positive features of our parents' lives while trying to improve on the areas where they were limited or deficient. This is an especially important point given the current popular trends that utilize terms such as "toxic parents" and "dysfunctional family." Though many self-help movements provide welcome and at times needed insights, a downside to them is that in some instances they foster parent-blaming. A helpful technique is to spend a few moments imaging each of your parents. Then think of the words "grateful" or "thank you" and associate them with each parent. What thoughts and feelings come to mind? I find it important to begin this exercise on a positive note. Ask yourself how you reflect your parents' positive features and in turn share these attributes with others. Then image your parents and ask yourself in what ways they were limited and what experiences with them were nongrowthful or even painful? Note these and reflect on how your own life response is different and how it is similar. Other important questions are: "What feelings do I associate with my own parents' shortcomings?" "Does my work with youth evoke some personal characteristics that mirror my parents' behavior?"

3. *Ask yourself how you deal with "loss."*

The popular writer Judith Viorst notes that "losses are a part of life — universal, unavoidable, inexorable. And these losses are necessary because we grow by losing and leaving and letting go.... It is only through our losses that we become fully developed human beings."[23] Her comment resonates with my own experience as well as with that of therapy clients I have worked with. In other words, to grow means to let go. The theme of "loss" is especially significant for adolescents whose experience of loss is acutely felt. They are shedding the innocence of childhood and increasingly are expected to act responsibly in a soon-to-be adult world. Yet for adolescents the world is not "safe" as they attempt to negotiate the push of society's demands with the pull of their own felt uncertainties. Adults who are comfortable with developmental issues in their own lives and who are aware of their own experiences of loss and growth offer a presence that provides the adolescent tremendous security. No doubt this theme of loss pervades the adolescent years. One might think that it is an issue with early adolescents more than older youth. Though early adolescents experience loss very directly through bodily changes and growing awareness of societal pressures, loss also is part and parcel of the late adolescent's life. I can recall numerous conversations I have had with college students reflecting with them on themes of loss (e.g., leaving college, family changes). Adolescents need adult models who can speak openly about such life experiences and how "letting go" is integral for becoming loving and caring human beings.

4. *Have healthy relationships.*

Any adult who works with youth knows that questions about relationships are central. What does it mean to be loving to someone? What is friendship? We need to model in our own relationships the relational experiences we desire young people to have. One question pivotal for every adult is to reflect on the meaning of friendship, more specifically, "What is my theology of friendship?" That is, how do I speak to young people about friendship and how do my friendships reflect my faith commitment? Adults need to be able to speak openly about and share with the adolescent the characteristics that they value in friendship.

5. *Find time for solitude.*

My impression is that adults who find moments of solitude difficult also experience their relationships and work as problematic. In order to engage others in meaningful ways, we require time alone with ourselves. In a culture that overvalues relationships, solitude is undervalued. Yet solitude performs a critical role in healthy functioning. In times of stress, solitude can be a welcome respite. It also serves a healing function when we confront loss. Moreover, solitude is vital for the nourishment of our imaginative capacities and creative endeavors.[24] As a clinician I reflect with clients on themes like "How are you creative?" "Do you have a hobby or interests that energize you?" Because ministry with adolescents can be exhausting, all adults need time and space to nourish themselves and their creative capacities. Solitude requires effort and the development of healthy boundaries between us, our work, and our social encounter. I suspect that solitude is subject to a developmental process; it takes on greater meaning with age. As a twenty-two-year-old Jesuit novice, at times I found solitude difficult. However, now in my mid-forties, I find I have come to relish more and more the solitary time so necessary for personal reflection and creation.

With the above in mind, some interesting questions emerge for self-reflection: "What do I do when I am alone?" and "How do I experience myself when I am alone?" "What feelings and reactions does my solitude elicit?"

6. *Maintain adequate boundaries.*

One phenomenon commonplace for many adults who work with youth is their difficulty in establishing boundaries. Quite frankly, not maintaining boundaries or "always" being available represents a serious error in judgment on any adult's part. Adults who are unable to separate from their work or from the adolescents they are ministering to are in danger of becoming "compulsive caregivers." Compulsive caregivers are always there but never take time for themselves. In some ways, these adults need adolescents more than adolescents need them! In a more serious manifestation of this tendency, adults try to "fill up" the emotionally barren part of their lives through their work with youth. Often this emotional void arises from earlier deprivation in the adult's life. Ask yourself: "How much do I need these adolescents?" "How much do I feel I *have* to be with them?" "What need might I be satisfying in my own life by working with adolescents?"

7. *Realize and accept the fact that you can't save every adolescent.*

Adults who minister to youth are usually conscientious and very giving people. A subtle tendency for some adults is to feel the obligation to help *every* adolescent they encounter. Though they know they can't help every young person, this thought, nonetheless, is a tacit assumption that guides the adult's behavior. Evidence of this phenomenon arises when the adult uses words like "I should be available" or "I have to be at this youth function." Obviously such thinking eventually proves frustrating. Adults need to realize their limits and be at peace with them. Pose this statement to yourself: "I can't save every student." Now ask yourself: "What are my reactions to this statement?" Do I feel uncomfortable? troubled? guilty? In this regard, I think the Jesus of the Gospels presents an appealing role model. The Lord found time to pray and play; he didn't cure everyone nor did he feel he had to be everywhere at once! Why do we insist on asking more of ourselves humanly than Jesus appeared to ask of himself? He had boundaries and priorities for his life, and he certainly knew how to enjoy himself through friendship and social gatherings.

8. *Focus on the experiences of gratitude and cultivate a sense of being grateful.*

When we experience gratitude we come to know ourselves as valued and accepted. Experiences of gratitude provide substance for the fundamental orientation of the Christian that is contained in the inescapable fact of God's love (1 John 4:10). God's love for me is the pervasive and foundational life theme that orients, sustains, and nourishes my life. Moments of gratitude make the reality of God's love a *conscious* experience that in turn beckons me to service and discipleship.

Gratitude serves as a powerful antidote to feelings of bitterness, cynicism, and self-pity. I am continually fascinated by how clients in therapy can reframe their thinking and thereby alter their emotions by focusing on other features of their lives (focusing, for example, on gratitude rather than their hurt and pain). I continually observe that when one feels grateful one is more inclined to offer oneself in service to others.[25] Try the following exercise. Ask yourself: "What am I grateful for?" Spend a few moments every day with this question. Also consider the question: "What actions do these feelings of gratefulness lead me to?" After completing this short exercise, spend a few moments becoming aware of what you are feeling. In most instances, feeling "grateful" leads to moments of peace and serenity. These positive feelings often, in turn, beckon us to service toward others; that is, we wish to give back in service as a result of the gratitude we feel.

Adolescents and young adults are often blind to how much their negative feelings distort and bias their own perceptions. Most certainly we want to aid adolescents in acknowledging their pain and hurt and be with them as they confront such negative feelings. At the same time, we must challenge them to be aware of experiences and situations that bring a healthy sense of joy and contentment. Because of their developmental stage, adolescents can all too easily be locked into a "negative set" whereby they come to focus only on the negative aspects of their lives. Acknowledging pain and difficulty is not wrong, yet in virtually every case it remains an *incomplete* account of the adolescent's experience. We must become an "intrusive presence" that invites adolescents to reflect on positive dimensions of their lives. Otherwise, many adolescents will develop narrowing blinders, focusing excessively on lingering hurts that, in some instances, might eventuate in bitterness and self-pity. The basic rule of thumb here is be a ready listener who "hears" the adolescent's struggle and offers him or her adequate time to converse about the experience. Then gently lead the adolescent to consider the *wider* picture. For example, after discussing *adequately* with the adolescent a particular issue or problem, I will ask a very general question such as, "José, we have talked about this situation, and I am now wondering what else might be going on in your life. For instance, what good things are happening in your life?" I leave the question a general one. Often, just allowing the adolescent to verbalize some positive experiences is very helpful. Such discussion brings positive experiences to consciousness and offers a felt sense of hope to the adolescent.

9. *Remember that ministering to youth does not mean you are expected to do everything right.*

One common mistake that many adults make is believing there can be no shortcomings in their work with youth. In other words, "I can't fail" or "This is so important I can't make any mistakes" are the unacknowledged premises that guide the adult's work. Such distorted thinking is understandable. After all, caring adults want to be involved in young people's lives. If the adult is a product of a difficult home environment, then his or her focus might be swayed even more toward some type of perfectionism in ministry. In ministry with youth, as in all ministerial endeavors, we must acknowledge that at times we will make mistakes or fail. The questions we asked or the activity we planned will sometimes miss the mark. We must continually remind ourselves that this is "okay" and reframe such thoughts in terms of "what I learned" from this experience.

10. Maintain a sense of integrity.

For each of us there will come moments when we are faced with a difficult decision. Whether in our personal lives or in activities involving colleagues or adolescents there are times when a complex situation surfaces or demands a response that is difficult or "costs" us in some way. At such moments adults must ask themselves, simply, "What does my integrity call me to do?" Once we lose our integrity we, in a sense, lose everything. The adult needs to take time to reflect on the question of personal integrity and how it is nurtured and sustained in everyday life.

The Contexts for Pastoral Care

In addition to the "helpful hints" discussed above, the adults need to pay particular attention to the contexts of their lives. By "context" I am referring to the perspective or framework that the adult utilizes when ministering to the adolescent. There are several contexts we need to mention.

Personal Context   This refers to the adult's personal situation. In other words, the adult who works with youth comes out of a particular life history. For example, the adult who is an adult child of an alcoholic might be prone to respond in certain ways to young people who abuse drugs (e.g., rescue them, become overly involved with them, lose boundaries). As noted above, when working with youth we need to be aware of our own life histories.

Interpersonal Context   Another context is the interpersonal relationship that exists between the adolescent and adult. This relationship is the summation of the thoughts, perceptions, and feelings of each person as well as the expectations each has for the relationship. Moreover, it includes the role each plays in the other's life. For example, is the adolescent looking for a parent figure in the adult? On the other hand, does the adult have the desire to be a "friend" to the adolescent? A helpful hint here is for adults to list and reflect on the roles they play in the adolescent's life. Some of these might be teacher, friend, coach, pastor, minister, mentor, authority figure.

Theological Context   This context refers to the adult's pastoral theology. What is the adult's understanding of how the Lord works in his or her life? How does the adult understand human growth?

sin? grace? A major feature of this "theological context" is the adult's view of the role of human freedom and dysfunction. For example, how might severe trauma such as child abuse influence the adolescent's capacity to make moral choices? Another aspect of this context is the fact that adults are representatives of the church. As such, the adults need to reflect on their personal attitudes toward church tradition and teaching. For those ministering to youth, one area in need of particular exploration is the adult's "theology of sexuality." Adults need to reflect on the ideals and moral teachings of the faith community to which they belong and how these are set forth in their pastoral approach with youth. Two questions to reflect on here are "How do I describe my relationship with the church?" and "How is this relationship reflected in my pastoral work with youth?"

Pastoral Context   This context refers to the adult's comfort with what I term the twin themes of pastoral ministry: loving care and compassionate challenge. Pastoral ministry entails accepting people where they are and being able at the same time to gently challenge them to future growth so that their behavior might more reflect Gospel values. At times we might be called simply to be with someone in that person's pain or loss (e.g., death of a loved one). In such instances we reach out to others and support and journey with them in their sorrow. An adolescent who becomes teary over the breakup of her relationship with her boyfriend will probably lead us to listen gently and understand the pain she is going through. On the other hand, pastoral encounters call us also to help the person to realize more fully the Gospel's vision of discipleship. The Jesus of the Gospels most certainly reflected care, but he also challenged. He reached out compassionately to others, yet was quite capable of confronting others' statements and behaviors. Most often, the "challenge" aspect of the pastoral context is accomplished through gentle questioning. Through our questions, we hope to aid young people to look more discerningly at their behavior and discover the reasons behind their actions in order that they may more freely understand and respond to the Lord's call. Sometimes one's challenge of adolescents has the goal of helping them to be more open or understand more fully their behavior. At other times, the challenge is more direct and centers on providing feedback about behaviors and even comments by the adult regarding specific behaviors. The goal for one's relationship with the adolescent is to realize more fully a pastoral vision; this vision is best described as growing self-acceptance of who one is humanly and greater interior understanding of the Lord's working in one's life. At the same time this vision entails the presence of humility as expressed in recognizing the ways one still needs to grow spiritually and morally and the openness to explore more fully one's thoughts, feelings, and behavior to realize a more mature sense of Christian adulthood. As a consequence, every adult needs to reflect seriously on the "pastoral vision" he or she hopes youth to grow into. This clarity of vision fosters in pastoral practice both acceptance of young people as well as a commitment to aid them in their search for Christian adulthood.

The Nature of Pastoral Counseling

How might we delineate between pastoral counseling and traditional counseling or psychotherapy? Psychiatrist Jerome Frank offers, I think, the best definition of psychotherapy. He says that "psychotherapy is a planned, emotionally charged, confiding interaction between a trained socially sanctioned healer and a sufferer."[26] Crucial to Frank's definition is his advocacy of the "demoralization hypothesis" as a significant variable in the therapy process. This hypothesis is defined as follows:

> Demoralization occurs when, because of lack of certain skills or confusion of goals, an individual becomes persistently unable to master situations which both the individual and others expect him or her to handle or when the individual experiences continued distress which he or she cannot adequately explain or alleviate. Demoralization may be summed up as a feeling of subjective incompetence, coupled with distress.[27]

There are many aspects to Frank's insights relevant for understanding pastoral counseling. First of all, however, let's note some distinctions. The "socially sanctioned healer" that Frank speaks of is usually a licensed mental health worker (psychologist, psychiatrist, social worker). Most adults who work with youth in pastoral settings are not licensed professionals. Second, the nature of "confiding interaction" also needs some comment. State laws (though they vary) normally protect licensed health care professionals such as psychologists from divulging information unless the client grants explicit permission through the waiving of confidentiality. The issue of confidentiality is one that more than a few pastoral workers have had to confront. Normally, civil laws do not recognize confidentiality outside of set religious ritual and practice (e.g., in the Catholic tradition, the Sacrament of Reconciliation). Thus adults who work with youth must seriously consider their obligations and commitments, particularly when the adolescent's or young adult's self-revelation is manipulative or might lead to harming self or others. Of course, even licensed professionals are ethically bound to "break" confidentiality when, in their professional judgment, they discern a person probably will inflict self-injury or cause injury to others. My point is that the adult who works with youth must realize that confidentiality is somewhat elusive in the pastoral counseling context.[28]

One final point needing comment is the use of the term "counseling." Because of the large amount of litigation occurring throughout the country, I have found many religious workers — both clergy and lay — reticent about designating their work as "counseling." The source for this demurral is the fear of being sued. I think this concern is well-founded. Given these circumstances, then, a better term for our work with youth might be "pastoral care." Under this umbrella term exist various areas for working with youth, including liturgical service ministry, youth group activities, various service ministries, teaching, and what might be termed helping ministries. Under this last group is the adult-adolescent relationship out of which, through a dialogical encounter, the young person develops in a healthy manner humanly, spiritually, and morally. It is in these contexts of dialogue that we use the term "pastoral counseling." However, some adults might be more comfortable with the term "pastoral care."

One of the most significant benefits that religious education and youth ministry offer youth is the opportunity to relate with an adult mentor. Young adults and adults continually comment upon the fond memories they have of a helping adult who modeled mature Christian faith for them, experiences that became sturdy allies as they progressed through their adolescent and young adult years. We cannot afford to allow fears of litigation to lead us to jettison this valued service to the young. In sum, adults must offer youth "wise counsel" and help them with the normal struggles of growing up and at the same time be aware of our *limits*, knowing when to refer to a professional.

Let us again look at Frank's definition. Pastoral counseling includes an identified "healer": a caring adult occupying an acknowledged role in the faith community who, on the basis of his or her own faith commitment, offers time and energy in service to youth. The time together is for the most part of a "confiding" nature and the content of the discussion includes problems in living that at times can be quite "emotionally charged" (e.g., parent-child problems). Though many dialogues with youth might not be as emotionally charged, the content of such discussion often includes problems in living that are threaded with emotional overtones that youth often experience as difficult and painful.

More tellingly, the "demoralization" spoken of above is very pertinent to the adolescent experience. "Demoralization" refers to confusion of goals, feelings of inadequacy, and subjective distress; the underlying theme for such experiences is "subjective incompetence." People often seek help when they are experiencing problems in living, when they cannot accomplish their goals, or when they feel inadequate. Perhaps at one time or another, every adolescent has difficulty feeling (1) significant, (2) competent, and (3) powerful.

> Significance refers to the belief that people are liked by, and important to, someone who is important to them. Competence is defined as being successful at some task that has value and is reinforced within the environment. Power or potency refers to people's ability to control important parts of their environment.[29]

A good rule of thumb here is for the adult to think of "significance," "competence," and "power," in terms of the letters SCP; I label this the "SCP method." In virtually any general counseling situation with students the adult can spend profitable time reflecting with the adolescent over the issues of significance, competence, and power. Adolescents need to be able to voice in their own words who is significant, how they feel competent, and how they experience themselves in control of their lives (power). The adult might simply start up a conversation with questions such as:

Significance: "Who is important to you?" (Have them then reflect why the people they named are significant.)

Competence: "What do you enjoy doing?" (Have them focus on what they do well and why they like doing it.)

Power: "What are some of the decisions you make in your life?" (Discuss the decisions they make and what is important about these decisions to them. Also, note in what areas of their lives they do have some "power" to make decisions and in what areas they do not.)

If the adolescents are unable to talk about significance, competence, and power, reflect with them on whom they might like to be significant for, in what areas they would like to feel competent, and in what areas they would like to make decisions.

Adolescent demoralization (subjective distress) often arises because of difficulties centering on these three dimensions. Relationship problems often make them wonder if they truly are important. Developmental changes and lack of opportunity often make them question their competency or ability to function, while they are often not allowed to participate or give significant input for decisions that affect their lives (feelings of being powerless). Effective ministry with adolescents requires that we pay particular attention to how the adolescent feels significant, competent, and powerful.

Before offering a definition of pastoral counseling with adolescents and young adults I wish to address an issue of great concern to those whose work integrates the dimensions of both psychology and theology. This issue is the "psychologizing" of pastoral counseling.

In discussions with people who do pastoral counseling I am increasingly struck at how often they wish to wrap themselves under the mantle of psychology. I suspect the reason we overemphasize psychology's role is because we live today in a "psychological" society. The ruling paradigm in today's modern world is psychology; increasingly, people evaluate their well-being and interpret their lives in terms of psychological understandings. As a consequence, many pastoral personnel believe that to have credibility they must focus specifically on the psychological dimension of their work. The question I am often left with, however, is: What is "pastoral" about their counseling? or, How does their work differ from the secular counselor or psychologist? "The field of pastoral counseling has come to rely too heavily upon the discipline of psychology as its base of operation and evaluation and, as a result, has become merged with other mental health professions that share a similar, one-pointed base."[30] Psychiatrist Robert Coles has also addressed this issue:

> Especially sad and disedifying is the preoccupation of all too many clergy with the dubious blandishments of contemporary psychology and psychiatry. I do not mean to say there is no value in understanding what psychoanalytic studies, and others done in this century by medical and psychological investigators, have to offer any of us who spend time with our fellow human beings — in the home, in school, at work, and certainly, in the various places visited by ministers and priests. The issue is the further step not a few of today's clergy have taken — whereby "pastoral counseling," for instance, becomes their major ideological absorption and the use of the language of psychology their major source of self-satisfaction. Surely we are in danger of losing our religious faith when the chief satisfaction of our lives consists of an endless attribution of psychological nomenclature to all who happen to come our way.[31]

We need to point out that part of pastoral counseling is "pastoral" — the belief that values are central to human experience and that some core values provide a frame of reference for making choices and interpreting one's life experience; further, that some central values possess a self-transcending dimension — for example, love, forgiveness, humility, sacrifice; and that these values speak to the essence of our humanness: creatures made in God's image and co-creators with God to bring God's reign more fully to this world.

I now offer a definition of pastoral counseling for adolescents and young adults: *Pastoral counseling can be defined as an encounter wherein the adult and adolescent/young adult collaborate to reflect upon personal experiences, issues, and attitudes in the young person's life. The fruits of this dialogue in turn lead the young person to gain deepening self-insight into*

19

his or her response to the Lord, ongoing awareness of significant values, and a growing capacity to make healthy moral choices.

Several points in this definition need to be addressed. First, there is teamwork involved; the adult and the young person are partners collaborating to examine the young person's life. Emphasizing this collaboration addresses the need to help the adolescent feel significant without abandoning the obligation to offer guidance and wise counsel. Most important, this definition addresses what I view as the *three goals* of the pastoral counseling process.

The first goal is fostering *self-insight.* If we are to be open to the Lord's self-communicating presence, then we are obligated to become self-aware. Our thoughts and feelings sustain or hinder our growth toward healthy human living and growing Christian maturity. Simply stated, grace must work through who we are at this *concrete moment of our existence.* During the adolescent years, thoughts can be distorted and feelings acutely felt, thus eclipsing self-insight or awareness of the Lord's working. Often before questions of value can surface with young people, the priority must be to attend to their personal feelings and concerns. Questions we need to help adolescents work through include: Who are they? Who are they becoming? Whom do they love? What do they desire? and What influences (e.g., their feelings) have shaped their lives?

The second goal of pastoral counseling is fostering *value awareness.* A basic tenet of most psychotherapy schools is that "the essence of being human is the right and the capacity for self-determination, guided by purposes, values, and options. Out of our free will we can give our lives meaning even in the face of inevitable death."[32]

Values represent core beliefs that often take on an evaluative focus. These beliefs are threaded with affection and are vital for our self-definition. Some of our beliefs are best defined as opinions, for instance, we like cherry pie or the Chicago Bears. Yet these opinions, though loosely called values, are often not intensely held and certainly do not define us. On the other hand, core values are intensely held and exert significant influence on both our actual and idealized self-definition (the latter consisting of what I term "idealizations"). Let us examine more closely the meaning of idealization. If I asked you what could hurt you more than anything, your response might center on statements about you that question the cherished roles you deem vital for your self-definition. For example, "You are a terrible mother," or "You are a lousy friend," or "You are an awful teacher" are statements that could wound deeply. Most people become intensely upset at such accusations. Why? Such statements threaten our very core — what is most central to our self-definition. In other words, these roles reflect what we most value and desire to be: "good parents," "good friends," or "good teachers" (our core idealizations). These roles reflect our aspirations and deepest desires. They are the prisms through which we view our sense of moral adequacy. They are "moral reference points" according to which we evaluate ourselves in relationship to the Lord, the community, and all the experiences of our lives. As is so often the case, when we are feeling frustrated, angry, or guilty, it is often because we have used these roles, albeit on a tacit level, to judge our hopes, intentions, or actual behaviors and found them wanting. And our subjective distress leads us to conclude that we have not lived up to these idealized roles. A fundamental goal of pastoral counseling is to aid young people in discovering within the concrete experiences of their everyday lives what they desire to become, what values are associated with such desires, how such expectations guide their lives now, and how their current behavior helps or hinders realization of their idealized self-definitions.

Conscience formation, helping youth to make maturing and healthy moral decisions ("healthy moral choices"), is pastoral counseling's third goal. If there is one thing we desire young people to achieve, it is the well-developed capacity to make moral decisions. Such decisions are the building blocks for adult Christian faith. In *Morality and the Adolescent,* I presented a theory of conscience formation; I refer the reader to this work for understanding the adolescent/young adult conscience.[33] Conscience can best be defined as the "ought-ness" we bring to our decisions; it is making decisions in accord with other-centered values. Such a notion of conscience explicitly endorses an essential altruism that reflects care for others. From a human perspective, the foundational soil for healthy conscience formation is the development of one's capacity for empathy.[34] From a spiritual perspective, the consequences of healthy conscience are increasing evidence of the "fruits" of the Spirit.

One of the problems in addressing issues of conscience resides in the fact that for too long we have viewed conscience formation as simply a cognitive experience. Conscience was restricted to dos and don'ts. Such a view of conscience is both narrow and negative; it encourages viewing moral discussion solely in terms of rules and regulations.

I have often heard religious educators speak about the breakdown of moral pedagogy occurring after Vatican II. Throughout the late 1960s and 1970s, moral instruction appeared aimless. The jettisoning of the old catechetical approach left a vacuum that only recently seems replenished. A more interesting question, though, is *why* students so easily (at times almost effortlessly!) abandoned rules and regulations and embraced attitudes and behaviors previously viewed as unacceptable or taboo. To be sure, numerous factors must be considered — the breakdown of the family, the lures of culture, increasing individualism as the ethos for life. However, I think there is a more fundamental reason. Moral instruction never tapped the total human experience of youth. Moral pedagogy was too focused on rules and regulations and paid little attention to human experience and developmental tasks.

Though rules and regulations are important, they do not constitute the whole of conscience. A more enlightened view of conscience incorporates the various dimensions of human experience. Consequently, when I speak of conscience I understand it as incorporating three features: intrapsychic, affective, and cognitive. I think a primary reason students rejected the rules and regulations of the late 1960s and early 1970s was, simply, that moral pedagogy spoke only to the cognitive aspect of conscience (moral principles, rules — the "dos and don'ts"), with little time given to the internal (intrapsychic) and emotional (affective) features of conscience. My own seven-dimensional view of conscience attempts to offer an approach for incorporating a more holistic view of human personhood.[35] By attending to the multifaceted nature of conscience we can more effectively invite youth to both healthy humility and ethical commitment. Below are listed the seven dimensions of my conscience model with a brief explanation for each. My thesis is that healthy conscience in adolescence and young adulthood requires the effective functioning of these seven dimensions.

1. Psychic Energy   Psychic energy represents the psychological fuel for adaptive, healthy functioning. Our emotions, dreams, fantasies, and thoughts are all products of the psyche's expenditure of energy. The adolescent utilizes psychic energy in a distinctive approach to life; this is best expressed as the capacity to attend and focus. By examining the adolescent's focus of attention we are provided revelation regarding the adolescent's maturity level and potential for growth. Psychic energy has two features. First, the way the adolescent focuses and attends (what he or she is attracted to and invests time in) goes a long way in determining future growth and life accomplishments. Second, this energy is limited. Positive use of attention enhances the forming of a developed conscience. A realistic focus on career goals, maturing and positive attachments with both sexes, and honestly facing the struggles of moral questions and choices are all worthy recipients of the adolescent's attention. Adolescents who expend their psychic energies without attending to these necessary aspects of development (e.g., drug usage, excessive television viewing, unhealthy relationships) find difficulty in achieving the self-reflection and maturity necessary for adequate moral decision-making. Ask yourself: How does this adolescent use her time? What does this adolescent invest in? How does the adolescent profit from her experience? Reflect with the adolescent on her use of time.

2. *Defense Mechanisms*   Defense mechanisms are unconscious psychological responses we use to lessen anxiety and enhance self-esteem. Psychologists note there is natural desire in every person to maintain a felt sense of being moral. Thus, even criminals are apt to live by an ethical code. The stresses and insecurities of adolescence lead youth to employ a wide variety of defenses to shore up all too fragile feelings of self-worth. Defenses can be classified as either mature or immature. The adolescent's use of immature defenses is apt to have several undesirable results: distorting reality, avoiding self-examination, and limiting emotional maturation and moral growth. In sum, reliance on unhealthy defenses inhibits not only maturing developmental growth but moral decision-making as well. The next chapter offers a detailed discussion of various defenses that adolescents employ in their everyday lives. We will speak more about defense mechanisms in chapter 2. At this point, we simply need to point out their vital role in conscience functioning.

3. *Guilt*   The emotion of guilt is integral for well-functioning conscience. To be sure, unhealthy aspects of guilt are crippling. They include weakened self-esteem, depression, a sense of personal devaluation, and compensating behavior that often take on a compulsive quality. Still, guilt is vital for moral growth. Admittedly, the experience of guilt is one of the most difficult tightropes to walk. That is, if guilt is experienced too intensely its effects can be degrading. On the other hand, to deny the experience of guilt deprives one of a naturally occurring psychic experience whose function nourishes sensitivity and altruistic responses. Maintaining a proper balance concerning guilt is difficult at any age, and all the more difficult during adolescence. The young person may deny guilt because it looms as overwhelmingly threatening or may surrender to guilt because of inadequate self-esteem, thus leading to even more self-denigration. I have found that the most adequate pastoral response to adolescent guilt reactions is to support adolescents in acknowledging and taking responsibility for personal transgressions while focusing not on what has happened but on what the future can become, on how their future lives might be different, on what they can do for others in light of their current failings, and on how added self-knowledge gained from their present experience will aid them in responding more appropriately in the future.

4. *Idealization*   A crucially important aspect of conscience is the idealizations expressed in our dreams, hopes, and deepest desires. In

other words, conscience includes not only the discernment of "right and wrong" but what might be termed metaquestions — those inquiries that frame our lives and hopes: What do I dream for? What am I becoming? In what should I invest my life? What projects do I wish to take on? A crucial task we adults have is to help youth sort out their hopes and dreams. In this way, we nurture a positive morality. Though dos and don'ts are essential for the adolescent to learn, if relied upon exclusively they are prone to foster only a negative morality. A more instructive path is to help youth understand their ideals and what they desire to be. The mature conscience develops, in part, by nurturing these aspirations. Awareness of healthy ideals is a vital feature for moral maturity. The cherished roles we spoke of earlier in this chapter are a vital part of idealization. Focus with the adolescent on what it means to be a "good" son/daughter, student, athlete, friend, etc. What are the characteristics the adolescent associates with the "good" when discussing each of these roles.

5. *Empathy*   We might view empathy as the emotional foundation for conscience. Empathy provides the human capacity needed for responding to another and the human sensitivity for bonding. Empathy is especially critical for adolescents since their experience is so interpersonally grounded. The most developed form of empathy arrives during the adolescent years when the young person is capable of empathizing not only with individuals (friends, peers) but with groups of people (the poor, the homeless). In fact, well-developed commitment to social justice requires sophisticated empathic responding. I believe that the success of secondary school and undergraduate social service projects is directly tied to the adolescent's capacity for empathizing with those he or she serves. Emotional arousal at experiencing another's situation or plight often proves a catalyst for rethinking previously accepted ideas and thoughts about politics and culture. Explore with adolescents what stimulates their sensitivity. At the same time, discuss whether they are able to have adequate boundaries in relationships; some adolescents become too involved in their relationships or projects. There is need, at times, for a healthy distance.

6. *Self-esteem*   When we refer to feelings about ourselves, we are speaking of self-esteem. Adequate self-esteem means having a sense of inner pride or a sense of self-appreciation. Ultimately, it reflects the self as valued, not only for what it does, but for what it *is*. Sufficient self-esteem depends upon adequate parental care. The numerous changes adolescents undergo and the challenges they face often render self-esteem fragile. Adolescents unable to achieve success and adequate mastery of developmental tasks are subject to feelings of self-denigration and self-doubt. Moreover, some adoles-

cents can develop a profound sense of personal inadequacy, which leads to a precarious tentativeness regarding their own commitments. Burdened by inner doubt, some adolescents find themselves seeking solace within the peer group or yielding their own decisions to the advice of not-so-well-intentioned friends. Ask yourself: How does the adolescent appreciate himself or herself? What behaviors show this appreciation?

7. *Teleology (Moral Principles)* Underlying our moral choice is the "sake for which" we do something. The telic dimension of conscience challenges us to think "why" we do what we do. It points to the personal responsibility we must take for our actions and the responsible use of our freedom. All of us must examine the fundamental value orientation that guides our life. It is through this process of self-examination that we take personal responsibility for our lives. This self-exploring focus is vital for the development of the adolescent's moral self. Adolescents must face directly the intentional nature of their lives and develop guidelines for a maturing consistency regarding behavior. Increasingly, adolescents are expected to provide reasons for their behavior and be able at the same time to express the values that guide their lives. From a Christian perspective, reference points for adolescents when they give reasons and take responsibility for their behavior include: the Decalogue, the Beatitudes, Gospel teachings, the writings of Paul, and the informed tradition of the faith community to which they belong. Moreover, implied in such moral principles is a *vision* one has of the future. What does the adolescent desire for the future? Who is he or she becoming? Adults need to aid adolescents in developing a "vision" for their lives. Further, explore with them how their actions even now are allowing this vision to come about. Reflect with adolescents on what moral principles they use to make moral decisions. Another helpful point for discussion is what criteria the adolescent uses to determine that something is even "moral." As we proceed through our discussion of adolescent pastoral counseling, we will incorporate various dimensions of our conscience model.

As adolescents make moral decisions we desire these decisions increasingly to be made out of a growing maturity that reflects a healthy sense of self, a growing sensitivity toward others, and well-grounded moral principles. The seven dimensions of conscience discussed above further the moral growth we desire young people to have. In the pages ahead I incorporate various features of my conscience model in order to help students make decisions that are both healthy and moral.

Conscience is central for Christian living because it is the guiding light for behavior (Rom. 13:5, 14:23); nonetheless, it remains quite fragile. The frailty of conscience results from its intimate tie to the self. That is, conscience is not an ethereal concept. Conscience remains the moral source for personhood, residing in the person *as person*. As such, conscience is wedded to the human limitations and personal shortcomings that accompany all growth and development. The developmental struggles that adolescents undergo (separation issues, identity struggles, etc.), therefore, influence conscience's functioning and can and do lead to behaviors that are unhealthy, not growthful, or morally at odds with Gospel values.

In sum, pastoral counseling with youth includes three essential elements: helping young people develop growing self-insight, deepening value awareness, and maturing moral decisions.

The Adult as Questioner

Before concluding this chapter we need to shift our focus back to the adult. One area needing examination is the adult's capacity to listen effectively to the adolescent while still maintaining a reflective questioning stance. One way to foster this effective listening is to keep in mind four levels of questions when working with the adolescent or young adult.

Let us say that Joan comes to you and discusses a difficult situation she is having with her mother. As you listen to Joan share her experience of her conflict with her mom, the following four questions should be kept in mind:

1. Problem Focus　　Ask yourself: What is the problem? It is important that the adult and adolescent agree on the specific problem needing attention. In this case, the problem is most likely one of conflict with authority. I would reflect this back to Joan: "It sounds, Joan, like you and your mom are not getting along very well. I'm wondering if you can pinpoint what the major issues are that you have conflicts over?" or "Joan, I'm hearing you speak about your problem with your mom, and I'm wondering how it is affecting your feelings and home life?" Stating and agreeing upon the problem is a vital component of effective pastoral care with the adolescent. Nonetheless, my own experience is that effective pastoral counseling goes *beyond* discussing a specific problem. That is, "effective" pastoral counseling also "hears" the developmental struggle the adolescent is undergoing.

2. Developmental Issue　　As you listen to Joan, besides reflecting on what the problem is, ask yourself: "What is the developmental issue that Joan is experiencing?" The most effective care of the adolescent comes about when the adult can refocus the question on the underlying issue of developmental growth. In Joan's case, the conflict with her mom probably points to separation struggles and Joan's attempt to establish more firmly her own identity. The conflict with her mother can be viewed in this light; that is, adolescents often "test" their parents as a way of discovering "who they are." The parents' reaction provides data for them to incorporate into their growing sense of self-identity, thereby augmenting their self-understanding and fostering their sense of limits. In Joan's case, then, I would listen intently to her story and reflect with her on what the problem is, how it has come about, and what distress it provokes within her. Then I would move to a discussion of identity. I might ask Joan to reflect on other authority figures she might be having conflicts with. I would say something like, "Joan, it sounds to me like you are struggling with how to be a good daughter and how to be Joan — who you are." The advantage of reflecting back this statement is that it touches upon Joan as daughter, her conflict, and who she wants to be (the idealization of a "good daughter"). After getting her response I would ask her to talk about what she is learning about herself, what being a daughter means to her, and what this conflict is saying to her about herself. The object here of course is to have Joan address issues of self-identity and self-understanding (the developmental focus). From this discussion inevitably flows self-insight, which becomes another building block for her identity. Such reflection will enable Joan to understand better her reactions, thereby increasing her self-confidence and sense of control. From this discussion Joan will probably feel more "whole"; this feeling reflects her developing sense of felt identity. Finally, I would also reflect with Joan how she might handle such situations in the future.

3. *Value Focus*   Both the problem and developmental focus could be provided by any "caregiver." Recall above the need for the "pastoral" in counseling. Hence the third question that needs asking by the adult working with Joan is: What are the values at stake here? I like to refocus the question in terms of the roles the adolescent experiences. In Joan's case she is a daughter, and I would reflect with her on what it means in her eyes to be a "good" daughter — someone who cares about her mother, other family members, and herself. By focusing on the role of "good daughter" we are utilizing an idealization that is central to Joan's sense of self. Notwithstanding their conflicts, adolescents virtually always have affection for their parents and siblings. (This is one of the reasons they are distressed about their conflict even though at times they would have a hard time admitting this point.) I would then relate their care with the current conflict by asking an open-ended question such as: "It must be difficult to really care for your mom and yet to have this conflict?" I

would follow up with a question such as: "I wonder if there are ways you can think of that will allow you to show care and concern for your mom and still find a way to be yourself?" These questions acknowledge the reality of the situation yet allow for a vital shift in focus; they bring to the forefront the question of *value* and how Joan lives her life in a loving and caring manner.

4. *Mental Health Focus*   The final question the adult needs to attend to is this: Is the adolescent's problem such that there is need to enlist professional help? Again, adults working with youth need to know their limits. Being a professional means having boundaries. In chapter 3, I offer some questions that will aid the adult who needs to address issues of mental health concerns and referral.

In sum, adults need to view their work with adolescents in a questioning stance. This requires attention to: (*a*) the nature of the adolescent's problem, (*b*) the adolescent's developmental level, (*c*) the Christian values reflected in the adolescent's situation, and (*d*) the severity of the problem (the mental health focus). By keeping these four questions in the forefront, adults can provide the optimal level of pastoral care to youth.

Conclusion

As we conclude this opening chapter, it will be helpful to summarize some of the major points. First, the role of the adult is crucial to any pastoral counseling relationship with the adolescent. Second, the pastoral counseling relationship has specific goals for the adolescent to accomplish: acquiring self-insight, fostering value awareness, and enhancing moral decision-making. The premise on which we are operating is that the adolescent is engaged in a process of deepening self-discovery. The adult, by his or her presence, questioning, and feedback in the adolescent's life, helps the young person utilize his or her freedom to discern more clearly and experience more fully Jesus' call to discipleship. More concretely, the role of the pastoral counselor is not counseling as counseling. Rather, the adult's role is encouraging in the young person those behaviors, thoughts, and attitudes that reflect a grace-filled, authentic response to the Gospel. In order to foster these responses we must first explore more fully the nature of adolescent functioning and the issues centering on adolescent dysfunction.

CHAPTER TWO

Adolescent Development and Dysfunction

In this chapter we examine a theoretical basis for adolescent dysfunction. Effective working with youth requires some conceptual understanding of adolescent behavior problems. Indeed, conceptual understanding is a requirement for professional competence. Though adults who work with youth in pastoral settings may not be trained mental health professionals, they should be able to demonstrate at least a general understanding of why a particular youth experiences difficulty. But before turning to a discussion of why the young have emotional problems, we need to explore some basic developmental features of adolescence. In *Adolescent Spirituality* I provided an extensive overview of adolescent development and how this development relates to youth's spiritual growth. I refer the reader to this work to gain a more complete understanding of adolescent development.[1] In this chapter I address two significant developmental aspects of adolescent growth that help regulate emotional health: *cognitive maturation* and *identity consolidation*. Both these dimensions of adolescent development have notable influence on youth's self-understanding and behavior.

Cognitive Development

Around the age of twelve children begin to flex their cognitive muscles; this newly developed reasoning ability is called formal thinking. Psychologist Jean Piaget has offered the most thorough understanding of how we come to know and understand our world. From birth until two the child experiences the world through senses and actions. The ages two until seven represent what is called pre-operational thinking. At this stage, the child acquires a growing ability for using words and images yet lacks the ability to reason logically. Logical thought emerges at around the age of seven. A child at this stage thinks logically, but the logic is tied to concrete experiences familiar to the child. Thus the child can reason how her parents spend their day (because she has concrete experiences of them), but she reasons neither accurately nor realistically about where each parent works nor the business's overall relationship with its employees or issues in the economy such as the Gross National Product (GNP) that might affect her parents' livelihood. Such thinking is too abstract and not wedded to the child's concrete experience.

With adolescence, however, the child is now capable of abstract reasoning not tied to concrete realities. Several features are associated with formal thinking.

• Adolescent thinking becomes more *introspective*. Adolescents spend more time thinking about topics and personal issues in more intense ways. Sometimes they become overly absorbed in their own thinking, and such reflections might take on a brooding quality.

• Adolescent thinking becomes more *logical*. Adolescents more readily understand relationships among various variables and situations. They more readily see "what makes sense" (though of course they don't always act appropriately on such information).

• *Abstraction* is another quality of adolescent thinking. Adolescents can discuss more abstract concepts such as "justice," "rights," "equality." If the question "What is justice?" is asked of young children, they probably would give an example (this reflects the concrete nature of their thinking) whereas an adolescent (particularly middle and late adolescents) could discuss various definitions of justice and attend to more abstract features of the definition.

• Adolescent thinking is often *future*-directed. By the adolescent years, youth have the capacity to look more at the consequences of their behavior as well as to plan for the future. Relationships, college plans, career goals are a few of the issues that begin to preoccupy the young person's time. Unfortunately, though this capacity exists, moods often consign the adolescent to focus on the present without reference to long-term goals.

• Formal thinking includes a *critical* dimension. Adolescents can become very critical of people, situations, or ideas. They use their newly found logical powers to discern that adults do not always live up to what they preach. They can view adults, particularly parents, as hypocrites. Unfortunately, like adults, they refuse to acknowledge their own shortcomings and engage quite liberally in what is termed "adolescent hypocrisy" (freely criticizing others but failing to examine critically their own behaviors and the extent to which they might be at fault).

• A very important feature of adolescent growth that parallels development in thinking is the young person's ability to have *affection* for his or her thoughts. Adolescents can fall in love with their own ideas. One can often see this in young people's tendency to get involved with a social issue, candidate, or personal pursuit. The high school or college student can become impassioned about selected causes, and much time and energy are invested in whatever the adolescent deems important. At times, young people become too focused on their own ideas and ignore other pursuits or legitimate developmental tasks requiring attention.

We can easily discern the consequences of the above features of adolescent thinking on youth's emotional development. Because of formal thought adolescents periodically become self-absorbed; self-consciousness pervades many young people's thinking. Moreover, evaluations of self and others become more distilled and focused. When adolescents are exposed to stressful and traumatic experiences, these tendencies might unduly complicate the adolescent's emotional state. On the other hand, such thinking also allows the adolescent to evaluate the self and others in ways that can lead to self-improvement and autonomous functioning. Further, formal thinking provides the adolescent with the capacity for planning ahead and achieving constructively valued goals.

Developmental psychologist Jerome Kagan has observed that Jean Piaget probably will be most remembered for his insights regarding the adolescent's attainment of formal thinking. Consider the following excerpt that reflects the power of formal thought over the adolescent's life.

> But Piaget's suggestion that a major cognitive restructuring occurs at adolescence is, in my opinion, original and of immense importance for understanding this period of development. If, as Piaget claims, the 14-year-old is disposed to examine the logical consistency of his existing beliefs, we should expect a special tension that is not solely the product of emerging sexuality. The adolescent must deal with the temptations of sex, new evaluations of his parents, and, in America, incessant demands for independence. These perceptions and associated experiences rub up against old beliefs, and the resulting incompatibility is usually resolved by delegitimizing the earlier assumptions. As a result of the cognitive competences that accompany formal operational thought, the adolescent begins to question old ideas and search for new premises. Piagetian ideas lead us to expect that the adolescent will be in a state of uncertainty and provoked to resolve the state. As a result of the mental work, older premises will be changed. The ideational rebellion that is definitional of adolescence in the modern West does not primarily serve hostility to the parents but rather the more pressing need to persuade the self that its mosaic of wishes, values, and behaviors derives from a personally constructed ideology. This conception of the psychological state of the adolescent flows directly from Piagetian theory.[2]

Kagan's observations are insightful and point to the notable role formal thinking serves in aiding adolescent development. The power of newly found thinking (formal thought) propels the adolescent to negotiate between newly felt urges/needs and previously unquestioned assumptions (childhood beliefs). The logical rigor of this analysis usually yields both to some jettisoning of prior beliefs and to the birth of an initial yet tentative value system that is gradually modified and "owned" by the adolescent. Such experiences are vital for healthy autonomy. Without doubt, such "owning" of one's beliefs and behaviors has consequences for the adolescent's moral and emotional development.

Psychologist David Elkind has identified several characteristics that emerge during the adolescent period. Elkind calls the first the adolescent's construction of an "imaginary audience."[3] Adolescent formal thinking allows the adolescent to think about the other's thinking; in this way, the young person develops more sophisticated and accurate interpretations of others' feeling and thoughts. But there is a pitfall. Adolescents falsely attribute their high degree of preoccupation to other people. That is, their thinking follows more or less the following pattern: I'm interested in me so others must be interested in me (and thinking about me) too! Adolescents, in other words, construct an imaginary world in which they assume that everyone else is as focused on them as they are focused on themselves. This construction can take on a narcissistic flavor and lead to attention-seeking behaviors ("Hey, notice me!") that at times can prove irritating to adults as well as peers.

Another characteristic that emerges with formal thinking is the "personal fable." Because adolescents believe that others are watching them and observing what they do, then they must be special! Young persons construct a personal mystique in which they can do nothing wrong or are exempted from the typical consequences of such behavior (e.g., personal injury or hurt). In other words, adolescents develop a felt sense of being invulnerable. Good examples include reckless driving, elevator shaft riding, subway car jumping, and drug use ("Others might have an accident or overdose on drugs but not me").

Another area where the personal fable might be operative is that of adolescent sexual activity ("Others might get AIDS or become pregnant, but I won't have any problem"). As the above examples indicate, such thinking promotes high-risk behaviors. Naturally, there exist multiple causes for any behavior, but we need to be aware of the possibility that these behaviors might to some degree be influenced by the adolescent's cognitive growth. In general, the "imaginary audience" and "personal fable" are more commonly seen in early adolescents, yet my own clinical experience says that senior high and even college students at times might experience their lingering influences. From a counseling perspective, the best way to counteract "at-risk" behaviors arising from the "personal fable" is to point out gently but firmly as well as consistently to the young persons the consequences of such behaviors. Hopefully, with enough examples and input from adults and wiser peers, they will begin to realize that they can be adversely affected by such behaviors.

On the other hand, not all research agrees that adolescents display a sense of invulnerability. Studies indicate that adolescents can perceive risks more or less as well as adults.[4] My own clinical impression is that adolescents are capable of perceiving risk. However, given the emotional turmoil that some adolescents experience, an emotionally aroused adolescent in a particular situation might well resort to specific at-risk behaviors. For example, a hurting sixteen-year-old boy who is unable to share his feelings in his family might overly rely upon and erroneously overestimate his own talents because of statements made by peers, thereby leading to risk-taking. Such an adolescent might think of himself as special and conclude that his thoughts are "the" reality.

Identity Consolidation

In order to discuss the nature of identity, we need to provide more rigorous definitions for several terms. There are many definitions for various psychological terms and no universal agreement on their meaning. Nonetheless, we are in the mainstream of psychological theorizing if we adopt the following definitions.[5]

Self-concept: One's self-concept refers to beliefs one has about one's self. Thus the adolescent might believe she is attractive or intellectually bright or athletic. Of course, one might endorse negative ideas about the self. Unfortunately, many adolescents are burdened with negative self-evaluations. We speak of the adolescent, for example, who thinks she is unlovable, and thereby displays a poor self-concept (negative beliefs about the self).

Self-esteem: Self-esteem reflects the feelings one has for one's self. Self-esteem results, in part, from ongoing evaluations of self-worth. High self-esteem results from positive evaluations whereas evaluations we make that leave us feeling self-denigrated or subjectively distressed result in low self-esteem.

Ego: Though no universally accepted definition of "ego" exists, we use the term here to mean an internal construct that fosters psychological functioning as well as adaptation to the environment, in other words, the inner mechanism that attempts to negotiate internal needs with the outside world. The ego is both conscious and unconscious. The former is evident in the ongoing capacity to perceive reality and successfully adapt to the demands of everyday life whereas the latter is reflected in behaviors such as lack of awareness of true motivation for certain actions or continual misinterpretations regarding events or the motives of others. A good example of the latter consists in the employment of defense mechanisms that protect the ego from anxiety and unwelcome impulses.

Self: No term is more widely used in psychology today than "self." We can view the self as both subject ("I" do something) and object (I focus on "me"). In a sense the self is everything about me — my very existence and all that defines me (e.g., attitudes, opinions, feelings, values). Yet many psychologists say we do not have a "self" but many "selves"; thus we consist, for example, of a "moral self," a "physical self," a "thinking self." Of course we will not arrive in these pages at a totally satisfactory definition of self. For the sake of clarity, though, we refer to "self" to mean one's sense of oneself as either subject or object and as an all-encompassing term that accounts for who one is. In other words, as social psychologist Roy F. Baumeister notes, the self is viewed as "a physical entity overlaid with meaning."[6]

With the above offered as general guidelines, let us now examine more closely the concept of "identity." Erik Erikson proposed youth's identity quest as one of the defining features of adolescence. Indeed, consolidating a sense of identity is for him the primary developmental task of the adolescent years.[7] In addition, the solidification of identity is vital for favorably completing the next developmental task: establishing intimacy. Successfully negotiating identity and intimacy preoccupies the adolescent and later the young adult; moreover, the two tasks are inseparably linked. Psychologist James Marcia describes the interplay of identity and intimacy when he writes, "It is the paradox of intimacy that it is a strength that can be acquired only through vulnerability; and vulnerability is possible only with the internal assurance of a firm identity."[8]

For Erikson, identity takes on multiple meanings. Identity, in his view, allows the adolescent to set forth a self-definition. This self-definition is characterized by a sense of inner cohesiveness, an experience of growing self-continuity. This inner sameness joins one's past self-history with the demands of the present as well as an increasingly distilled sense of the future; the adolescent experiences the self as not only connected with a past but more and more purposefully oriented toward events yet to come.

The accompanying figures offer a helpful way to view identity. As you look at the three figures it becomes obvious that they are various stages of a completed triangle. The triangle represents the adolescent's consolidated sense of his or her identity. Now look only

Identity Development in Adolescence

Early Adolescence
12–15 years

Middle Adolescence
15–18 years

*Late Adolescence (young
adulthood)*
18–mid-twenties

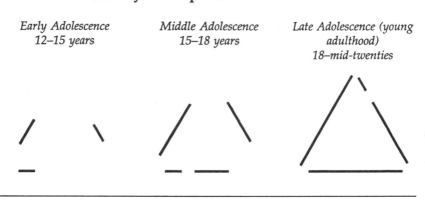

at the first triangle, the most undefined of the three. In fact, if the second and third figures were absent, would you be able to conclude that figure one is even a triangle? Probably not. This figure is an apt image for understanding early adolescent identity. Early adolescents feel the most vulnerable and confused; consequently, their behavior is often erratic. As one colleague of mine remarked, "They are all over the place." They have left the security of childhood but are as yet unable to enjoy the safety that comes with a well-defined identity state; their behaviors and actions appear at times scatter-shot and diffuse, with few perceived goals. One other word comes to mind when viewing the first figure. This triangle is "fragile." Besides being undefined, it cannot stand on its own. Clearly something else must be added to provide support. Early adolescents find this "addition" to their identity through their peer group, that is, their own identity is often encased within their peer group, which serves as a substitute identity; the peer group provides the protective shell needed to bolster the adolescent's fragile sense of self. The power of the peer group is seen when a parent asks the early adolescent to do something that is contrary to the attitudes and behaviors of peers. Often adolescents will protest such requests because to accede to parental demands separates them from the felt security the peer group provides. The influence of peers continues through the middle adolescent years, but often without the intense affective pull that so characterizes the early adolescent's experience. Middle adolescents, though often relying heavily on the peer group, on average show more autonomy and focus more on one-on-one relationships. By late adolescence, the pull of the peer group has subsided considerably. Several exceptions to this developmental trend occur with the "deviant" form of peer group expression that can be seen in gangs and cults. In these situations the gang or cult can become the dominant identity structure for the adolescent.

Another feature of early adolescents is their difficulty with solitude. One need not be a professional working with youth to know that, on average, high school seniors or college students can handle quiet time better than junior high adolescents. Imagine the following scenario: You are working on a retreat with junior high students. You gather the thirty thirteen-year-olds together and you say, "Okay, now I want all of you to go to your rooms and spend the next two hours alone quietly praying and reflecting." How long do you think it would take before the adolescents would find one another and gather in groups? Perhaps fifteen minutes? However, if you gave the same instructions to a group of mature high school seniors or interested college students, your instructions would probably be carried out. Early adolescents find solitude difficult because alone, experiencing a more diffuse sense of self, they fear being overwhelmed by their impulses (again, recall the fragile nature of the first triangle). A ready antidote is turning to a group of peers for solace.

Identity struggles (separation from parents, making decisions, working out roles) continue through the middle and late adolescent stages. Gradually the young person develops a more coherent sense of self that is guided toward purposeful action and sustained goals. In addition to identity consolidation, in these latter two stages there arises the developmental task of intimacy; the question of "Who am I?" is complemented by the question of "Whom do I love?" Obviously there exists mutuality between these tasks. To have a healthy, mature relationship, one must have a sense of identity separate from the other; on the other hand, experiencing intimacy allows one more and more to define the self, thereby fostering a more differentiated and coherent sense of self-identity.

Psychologist Richard Logan has pointed out that many adolescents enter an identity-diffuse state that engenders a series of behaviors that enable them to deal with the drift and confusion they experience.[9] For one, says Logan, the adolescent can engage in "temporary escape." There are numerous examples of this diffuse state; they involve a preoccupation with an activity such as intellectual or physical pursuits, partying, drug taking, or even excessive television watching. This escapism counterbalances the sense of drift that permeates the adolescent's life.

Second, some adolescents find "substitutes" for their diffuse identity state. They can find gratification in a specific role, such as athlete, leader, or excellent student. This limiting role provides a respite from identity confusion. A variation of this substitution finds the adolescent overidentifying with a particular cause. In my own pastoral work I have found such substitution in the college student who uncritically embraces a fundamentalist religious outlook toward life. This time-consuming devotion to dogma and Scripture offers adolescents a socially acceptable substitute for the identity they are lacking. Another way for adolescents to substitute for their lack of mature identity is through obsession with material goods. Thus, purchasing clothes or an automobile or taking a trip provides something to have and possess, in effect, a fleeting stand-in for a weak identity structure.

A third approach to solve the confused and meaningless drift of role diffusion is to engage in expressions that reinforce the present state of confusion. Fast driving, taking drugs, and sexual acting-out, for example, can all be immediate palliatives that enhance one's mistaken sense of well-being. A variation on this third approach occurs when the adolescent attempts to compete with peers scholastically, athletically, or in other ways. The experience of competition gives adolescents the sense of being someone, thus mitigating their confused, drifting state. A further variation is for adolescents to enhance a secure sense of self by exhibiting prejudicial attitudes toward others. Their personal attacks on others seem to augment their own sense of personal well-being. Thus, degrading others becomes the vehicle for enhancing one's own self.

A fourth way for the adolescent to counter diffusion is to engage in a variety of meaningless activities such as fads, games, and ridiculous behaviors. When adolescents invest psychic energy in these meaningless activities, they unconsciously assert that the present state of meaninglessness is in fact legitimate. Thus, ironically, their own meaninglessness is legitimated by meaningless behavior.

I believe it will be helpful if we offer a definition of identity that is functional, that is, one that incorporates the actual experiences that adolescents undergo and that adults are likely to observe in their pastoral work with youth. With this goal in mind, I define identity as the adolescent's growing awareness of an increasingly articulated life history that more and more interweaves a past (awareness of how one has evolved and what events significantly contributed to who one is currently), a present (growing understanding of who one is at one's current life juncture), and a future (maturing vision of who one desires to become). From a relational perspective, the adolescent's identity unfolds within the context of adapting to multiple roles (e.g., son/daughter, student, friend, etc.) that are in turn forged from internal needs, family dynamics, and cultural influences.

An example of culture's impact on identity is the growing part-time employment of adolescents during their high school and college years. Working several hours a week is likely to be helpful for the adolescent's identity development. On the other hand more and more adolescents are working longer hours in part-time jobs. The effects of this employment can be detrimental. The adolescent is exhausted trying to balance work, school, and other activities. Further, some adolescents find themselves with large amounts of money that they spend imprudently. With such purchasing power, "wants" soon become "needs" and youth become confused regarding priorities and goals. Having such cash readily available can also alter the adolescent's relationship with his or her parents. Power is shifted from the parent to the adolescent, who is now able to make purchasing decisions independent of parental desires or input. An adolescent's identity is bound to be influenced by society's growing acceptance of working youth.

As we have already noted, adolescence is a more or less "ill-defined time" that lasts at least ten years. During this period the adolescent must successfully complete a wide array of developmental tasks. Defining these tasks helps us to specify the construct of identity in terms helpful to the pastoral minister. On the basis of my clinical and pastoral work I list below some defining identity characteristics that might aid adults in determining to what degree healthy identity formation is taking place in the adolescent. Acquiring these characteristics should be viewed in the context of a developmental time frame. Late adolescents, generally speaking, are expected to exhibit more of these characteristics than early adolescents. More specifically, identity acquisition is a *process*. The adult should not expect the adolescent to all of a sudden "have" a particular characteristic; rather, each of these features is slowly acquired. The adult's reflective stance and well-placed questions stimulate the adolescent to reflect on meaningful developmental issues while at the same time the adult's inquiries encourage behaviors that foster identity growth.

1. Growing Time Perspective   Through this decade of development, we hope to see in adolescents the assimilation of past, present, and future life histories. Thus, late adolescents should be able to discuss, for example, how their view of God changed between the ages of ten and twenty. Moreover, adolescents should be able to utilize this perspective with a number of issues, e.g., friendship, church activity, personal behaviors. Growth in this dimension also enables the adolescent to generate future projects and goals and to recognize how they have arisen at least in part from current and previous life situations. The adolescent increasingly formulates future life goals and directions while at the same time recognizes how past life experience (e.g., a family situation) and current undertakings (e.g., school performance) shape and influence future projects.

- Take an issue such as "friendship" or "God" and invite the adolescent to explore how the meaning of this issue has changed over time (provide the adolescent a particular time frame: "when you were twelve and now"). Also, reflect with the adolescent on what about herself or her situation she believes is responsible for this change.

- Is the adolescent more able to reflect on her future and relate it to her present and past life history? Given her past and present history, where does she see her life going? Is she growing in the capacity to view past experiences in perspective and gain insight into how they have influenced her current thinking and behavior?

2. Finding Time for Solitude   The maturing adolescent is increasingly capable of profitably utilizing time alone. The adolescent finds benefit from periodic solitude (as noted above, appreciating solitude is most problematic for the early adolescent). An excellent example of this phenomenon is the adolescent who is able to make a private retreat in late senior high or the college years. Other healthy markers are time for prayer, a hobby, and insights derived from solitude. Some questions to keep in mind when reflecting with the adolescent are:

- What is the quality of this youth's experience of solitude? Is it satisfying? anxiety-provoking? Does the adolescent seek too much solitude? too little?

- Is the adolescent growing more comfortable in his ability to spend some time alone?

- Does the adolescent profit from reflection? When the adolescent "thinks about" an issue, does he usually derive helpful insights regarding his behavior? Another way to ask this question is: Does the adolescent "learn" from his experience?

3. Inner Complexity   With a growing sense of identity, the adolescent is prepared to grapple with issues in new ways. The young person views the various sides to issues and comprehends their complexity. Simple answers are no longer so easily forthcoming and the adolescent accepts this reality. In a similar fashion, the adolescent thinks more deeply. Questions of meaning become more salient. "Who is God?" And "Why is there evil?" are two that come readily to mind for most adolescents. Expanding complexity might be experienced when a tragedy intrudes into the adolescent's life. For example, if a close friend is killed in a car accident, the adolescent, besides attempting to cope with the emotional hurt, will often discover that the tragedy stimulates basic life questions such as:

39

"Why would a 'good' God allow such a thing to happen?" "What is the meaning of friendship?" "How do I take responsibility for my life now?"

However, this "inner complexity" resides in more than the cognitive realm; it touches affective life as well. Adolescents come to view their relationships as more complex. They understand others to have, like themselves, unique life histories that are interesting, multilayered, and to some degree inscrutable. Further, with time, during the adolescent life phase there comes an increasing capacity to handle ambivalence. Ambivalence is best defined as being-in-relationship that pulls on both positive and negative emotions. Handling ambivalence successfully requires significant psychological resources (such as "healthy identity"). Ultimately, a person is able to say she is committed to another; at a practical level this means she accepts the positive features of the other while being aware of limitations and drawbacks. Accepting her ambivalence toward the other, she remains in the relationship and contributes to it, rejoicing in the positive features and accepting the other's limitations. At the same time, she tolerates in an appropriate fashion her own disappointment and negative feelings when they surface. Individuals have ambivalence toward those most significant to them. In the adolescent's case this is most seen in her relationships with parents and other significant adults; it also manifests itself in relationships with peers.

The final dimension of this identity characteristic is growing self-knowledge. Think back to a time when you came to an insight about yourself. Perhaps it was regarding a family matter or a relationship problem — something troubling you now made sense or you were able to understand a parent or friend's behavior in a new light. Now think back about how you felt. Chances are you felt more complex; in other words, another piece of your life puzzle fell into place. More than anything, by gentle yet relevant questioning we seek to further young people's feelings of complexity as they acquire self-knowledge.

- Is the adolescent increasingly able to reflect on an "inner narrative" that allows her to realize the complexity and depth that makes up her own as well as others' lives?

- Over time can the adolescent provide more insight and complex reasoning into the "why" of his behaviors?

- Does the adolescent tend to view others as "all good" or "all bad?" Is she too uncritical or overcritical? Is the adolescent capable of ambivalence?

- How comfortable is the adolescent with viewing the "positive" and "negative" features of his relationships?

4. Growing Boundaries   One very telling sign of healthy identity growth is the adolescent's capacity to experience appropriate boundaries. An apt image for the adolescent's boundary-making is a magnet. The adolescent experiences considerable affective pull to become overly involved in situations and relationships (e.g., outbursts, overreactions, withdrawal). It is as if the adolescent cannot be in the situation or with this particular person without responding inappropriately. The two areas where such boundary problems are most apt to surface are family situations (relationships with parents and siblings) and more intense friendships, particularly those laced with romance. As might be expected, boundary issues are likely to be most troubling during the early and middle adolescent years. Even so, I can recall numerous times when I lived as a residence counselor in a college dormitory that undergraduate and graduate students returned from home visits worn and troubled over problems with family. It is safe to say that boundary issues with family members often preoccupy us throughout the twenties (and beyond!). Further, it might be unrealistic for any of us to think that our boundaries will always be perfect and set. How many adults can gather with family members over a holiday and avoid all tension and arguments? We are emotionally involved with our families no matter what the age or geographic distance. This reality merely points out that we *never* totally resolve all identity issues, no matter what our age.

Boundary issues also surface in the adolescent's interpersonal relationships. Often the newly discovered feelings evoked by finding a friend or romantic partner lead the adolescent to become overly absorbed in the other. In an extreme case a psychic symbiosis takes place. An example can be seen in the tragic case of one adolescent who commits suicide and another in response does likewise. How does such a tragic incident arise? The two adolescents had become psychically fused, unable to differentiate a sense of self as separate. Consequently, given this psychic fusion, when one adolescent died, in a sense (psychically) so did the other.[10] The suicide proclaims this psychic reality.

A final area where boundaries surface is that of peer group interactions. The early adolescent uses the peer group to considerable degree as a substitute identity. Consequently, as noted above, the adolescent at times might be unduly influenced by the peer group and find difficultly refraining from the behaviors the peer group adopts. With time, the adolescent is more able to resist unacceptable peer group demands and stand back from the peer group and criticize it when necessary.

- Is the adolescent growing in her sense of self as separate and distinct from others?
- Can the adolescent step back and analyze the relationship he is involved in?
- Discuss with the adolescent how she is "different" from the other.
- What is the affective pull within the family for this adolescent? Are some of these "pulls" leading to unhealthy behaviors (e.g., emotional outbursts, arguments or fighting with siblings or peers)? Discuss with the adolescent strategies that enable him to deal effectively with such "pulls."
- Is the adolescent unduly influenced by the peer group? Inquire from the adolescent in what ways she is similar to her peer group and in what ways dissimilar.
- How does he characterize the values of the peer group? His own values? What are the similarities? the differences?

5. Developing Healthy Relationships   Perhaps the best definition of a healthy relationship in adolescence is one in which the adolescent is encouraged to do "healthy" things. Do the relationships that the adolescent experiences support the adolescent's attention to developmental tasks? (See chapter 9 for a discussion of healthy relationships during the adolescent years.) Experiences to reflect upon with the adolescent include those dealing with trust, self-disclosure, honesty, fidelity, and value awareness.

- Does this relationship aid the adolescent's growth in trust?
- How are values recognized by both adolescents?
- Does this relationship foster healthy developmental growth?
- How is identity acquisition (discussed earlier) being fostered by this relationship?

6. Growing Self-acceptance   One of the first tasks early adolescents must confront is becoming comfortable with bodily changes and accepting their physical selves. For some adolescents this is a struggle, and a particular concern for those youth who do not view themselves as attractive. Other problems in this regard are seen in adolescents who feel they have few if any talents and, the opposite extreme, in those who possess an inflated view of their own abilities. Another feature of growing self-acceptance (occurring more in middle and late adolescence) is the ability to discuss strengths and weaknesses in a realistic fashion.

- Does the adolescent enjoy some successes?
- Utilize the "SCP method" discussed in chapter 1.
- Is the adolescent growing in her ability to discuss strengths and weaknesses?
- How do you characterize this adolescent's self-image?

7. *Knowledge of Roles*   As noted previously, one of the most significant ways that adolescents "feel" their identity is the way they understand, balance, and negotiate their various roles. Adolescents can easily identify with the words "son," "daughter," "student," "athlete," etc.

- Have the adolescent list all the roles that he plays in his life. Inquire about his feelings toward each of these roles. Reflect with him on what he most values about each; then reflect with him on what he finds uncomfortable and difficult in the everyday living out of these roles. What would he alter in the situations surrounding each role?
- Discuss any conflicts occurring between roles. (Often role conflict is an excellent way for the adolescent to discover the need for priorities and responsibility, e.g., in the use of time.)
- For middle and late adolescents a good strategy is to reflect with them about what they "desire" in each of their roles. What do they really want to be in each role? This strategy is an excellent way to incorporate values into the discussion; questions about desire and about who one wants to be can generate discussion of values.

8. *Developing a Philosophy of Life*   As we have already noted, throughout the adolescent years there is a growing ability to think reflectively and abstractly. The end result of this cognitive advancement is the development of an intelligently articulated approach to various political, religious, and ethical issues. Several questions may prove helpful:

- Simply discuss an issue with the adolescent. Is she able to present a well-thought out view of the issue? Is she able to "hear" other sides to an issue? Is she "open" to information that might challenge her own views?
- To what degree do her opinions and beliefs reflect Gospel values? Does she recognize a "moral" dimension that needs consideration when she discusses her views?
- What values guide the adolescent's belief system?

9. Competency Functioning   Another sign of maturing identity is a growing sense of competence across various life domains. The adolescent "feels" he is better able to handle life tasks and obligations. There is a growing sense of mastery.

- Ask the adolescent what he feels most comfortable doing.
- Inquire about the areas he feels he is or is becoming an adult.
- What criteria does he use to make the judgment that he is succeeding in these areas? (This is an excellent way to reflect on how values are part of his criteria for success).
- What values does he find most fundamental to his belief system?

10. Appropriate Display of Emotions   Growing awareness and growing intensity of feelings are part of every adolescent's life. Adolescents can feel intense joy, disappointment, anger, and passion. Being aware of such feelings, controlling them, and expressing them appropriately is the final characteristic of healthy identity acquisition. Such awareness, control, and expression demonstrate the adolescent's capacity to engage the world with a growing maturity of purpose.

- What are the primary emotions the adolescent displays? Are they displayed appropriately?
- How aware is she of her feelings?
- Is she coming to understand better what events and people trigger specific emotional reactions?
- Do emotional reactions at times blind her from understanding or realistically evaluating an event, situation, or person?

Having reviewed the "psychological" characteristics that make up healthy adolescent identity, adults need to reflect on what might be added to the above in order to forge Christian identity. I suggest five characteristics that make up a healthy Christian identity:

1. Ongoing development of a personal relationship with Jesus Christ that becomes the model for other friendships.
2. A growing commitment to Gospel values and the ability to articulate, reflect on, and live these values in everyday life.
3. An openness to new experience. Recall that the triangle displayed earlier to symbolize identity growth is not totally sealed. This lack of closure points to the need for adolescents to maintain some flexibility in identity. Later, as adults, they will come up against numerous crises and events that will call for ongoing

reflection (e.g., death of parents, breakup in relationships) and that in turn will shape identity.

4. A growing purposeful direction for one's life.

5. A growing sense of autonomy that includes personal responsibility for one's actions.

6. An increasing realization of the need for connection to a faith community.

Sex Differences in Identity

One of the most exciting (and controversial) discussions taking place in psychology today is the extent to which sex differences exist in various areas of personality functioning. One area that has received significant attention is that of sex differences in ability testing. Researchers have concluded that there are brain differences based on hormonal factors that lead to small divergences in specific intellectual abilities between the sexes.[11] At the same time, it should be noted that similarities in intellectual functioning far outweigh differences.

Another issue receiving wide attention is moral development. Is there a distinction in the ways women and men come to view and reason about morality? Initial focus on this issue centered on Nancy Chodorow's provocative work, *The Reproduction of Mothering: Psychoanalysis and the Sociology of Gender*. Though the argument advanced by Chodorow is complex, a basic understanding includes the following. The mother is both the caregiver and love object for her children. For the boy, there is the need to separate from this intense attachment and form an identification with the father in order to achieve a masculine identity. Hence there is value in separating, achieving, and becoming oneself. The girl, on the other hand, faces different obstacles. Though needing to be separate from her mother she is still intensely attached to her because she is the locus for developing her own feminine identity. Hence there develops a more intense pull toward the mother characterized by an internalized sense of attachment and relationship.

Psychologist Carol Gilligan carries this argument forward in what has become one of the most influential and provocative psychological works of the last quarter century, *In a Different Voice: Psychological Theory and Women's Development*. Gilligan's research has led her to claim that there exists a tendency for women to favor a "care orientation" as opposed to the more "rule-oriented" morality favored by men. Borrowing upon recent revisions in psychoanalytic thinking, Gilligan weaves together a perspective of feminine morality that values connectedness, interpersonal relationships, and a caring stance toward the needs of others (hence "a different voice" from men). By contrast, she notes that the male view tends to favor separation, to emphasize rights and duties, and to need to resolve competing interests in a just fashion. Gilligan's ideas have created controversy in psychological circles and have spawned a wide range of research.

The question of whether men and women differ in moral orientation is vigorously debated in academic circles today. Recent research seriously questions Gilligan's claim that women speak with "a different voice." The social psychologist Carol Tavris has written that "on the contrary, research in recent years casts considerable doubt on the notion that men and women differ appreciably in their moral reasoning, or that women have a permanently different voice because of their closeness to their mothers."[12] Psychologist Sidney Callahan writes that "in the end, there is no automatic moral developmental process that can unfold magically because of gender, specific female experiences, or early experience with a nurturing female."[13] Even though there might not be distinct "voices" for men and women, Gilligan's contribution is both helpful and admirable, for it challenges scholars to look beyond the "justice" orientation and incorporate the themes of relationship and care as vital ingredients for any meaningful morality. Thus the most substantive understanding of morality incorporates both justice and duty as well as care and relationship, albeit in any particular moral situation one dimension might be more significant and beneficial.

Spurred by at times heated and controversial exchanges focusing on intellectual ability and moral development, the issue of adolescent identity development has also received scrutiny. The central question posed by researchers is the following: Does women's identity development differ in significant ways from men's? As we have seen, a number of theorists have commented that men are socialized in our culture to achieve, to separate, and to produce whereas women are encouraged along the road of caring, relating, and bonding. Recall that Erikson believed that consolidating identity preceded the tasks and challenges of intimacy. Erikson's theory, however, was a theory about men and for men and has only "more or less" been able to be applied to women.[14] Still, Erikson noted that biological differences oriented the woman to proceed in identity development through nurturing attachments as mothers and spouses whereas the male's biological makeup predisposed him to be focused outwardly through work and career.[15] Given the relational focus that some theorists have maintained are primary for women, could it be that for women, intimacy development precedes identity development or that identity and intimacy are contemporaneous occurrences?

Utilizing Erikson's framework, psychologist James Marcia has generated very fruitful research on identity development. Marcia conceptualized the late adolescent period (college years) as a time of crisis and commitment. During the adolescent experience of crisis, young people come to reevaluate their present views and behaviors, explore various life options, and make numerous choices concerning various life issues in religion, occupational choice, and politics. Commitment is defined as the adolescent's personal investment toward one of these life issues (e.g., taking on a political ideology, a commitment to a field of study or occupational choice). As a result of his research, Marcia was able to place most undergraduate adolescents in one of four categories:

- *Identity achievement:* young adults who have achieved identity have experienced a crisis and now appear to have found some sense of commitment in their lives.

- *Identity moratorium:* young adults in the moratorium category are presently in a state of crisis and are attempting to resolve the crisis by examining various life options.

- *Identity foreclosure:* these young adults are committed to a certain set of beliefs, often as a result of parental influences, and are not open to examining or questioning their present beliefs.

- *Identity diffusion:* young adults in this category lack personal commitment and at the same time appear not to be making any effort to find commitment for their lives (or at least not in some areas of their lives). The various "temporary escapes" and "substitutes" that Logan described (cited previously in this chapter) represent the adolescent's attempt to contain the sense of drift and aimlessness that can characterize his or her life.

Marcia's research was originally carried out with a male sample, and he admits that "arguably" the identity construct was more likely to describe male than female identity development.[16] Sharing Marcia's concern, a number of researchers began to add "interpersonal" themes to the research on identity as a way to better capture women's concerns. Commenting on the data at hand, Marcia and his colleagues noted:

> The task of identity formation appears to begin in adolescence for women as it does for men. For some women (notably those who will follow nontraditional lifestyles of continuous employment), late adolescence is expected to be the optimal time of life for resolution of the identity versus identity confusion task. For other women, the task

of defining a personal sense of identity may wait, not, as Erikson supposed, for the arrival of a mate and children, but for the partial departure of children, which allows the time for these women to identify and pursue identity commitments of their own choosing.[17]

Marcia and his colleagues now conclude that interpersonal themes are crucial for women's identity and that an "interpersonal" piece needs be added to the identity struggle and acquisition that characterizes adolescent development. In other words, just as the adolescent male might experience crisis and commitment in life "domains" such as occupation, the adolescent female might center her identity struggles on the areas of relationship. In a related manner, one aspect of future research is to assess how relationships function in configuring male identity development.

Some work in this area has already begun; as the identity construct has increasingly been researched, the range of domains studied has expanded. To the more traditional domains of study, such as religion, politics, and occupation, that were applied solely to men, there have been added the domains of friendship, sex roles, parenting, and values, as well as several others.[18] Feminist psychologist Sally Archer has found that males and females show some but not many gender differences across their identity domains, though each sex might give priority and focus to some domains over others. Other studies for the most part have confirmed her findings. A common pattern appears to develop in which identity-achieving males and females appear to value both trust/relationship as well as mastery/accomplishment in their undertakings.[19] In a related study, psychologists Patricia Dyk and Gerald Adams used complex statistical procedures to map the developmental progression of identity and intimacy. Their findings led them to conclude that identity precedes intimacy for both males and females but that when focus is given to factors such as sex-role orientation (self-descriptions based on masculine or feminine characteristics) and empathy, a group of females labeled feminine demonstrated more fusion of identity and intimacy. The data suggest that there may exist a type of female whose personality development occurs through the mutual interplay of identity and intimacy rather than through a hierarchical progression from identity to intimacy.[20]

Though this distinction/fusion of identity and intimacy might well exist, we must ask if they have to be conceptualized as separate entities. Sally Archer has raised this issue of "dichotomizing" in our understanding of identity and intimacy. This simple division, says Archer, has led "to the assumption that if one is not an individual with a distinct sense of identity, then one is intimate, connected, communal, caring, and probably female." This dichotomy of identity-intimacy leads males to be identified with the former (separate, distinct, and committed) whereas females are viewed as intimate (connected, communal, and relational). As a consequence, "exclusivity of sex has thus been conveyed."[21]

I think Archer has offered a valuable insight inasmuch as stereotyping in academic research is all too common. At the same time, I see the need for self-definition as well as connectedness to be so much a part of human experience that there is merit in studying them as separate constructs, albeit with the caution to avoid gender exclusivity. In maintaining this point, I fall back on my own clinical experience. I believe strongly in Freud's dictum that the sign of a healthy personality is, simply, *lieben und arbeiten* (to love and to work) and these tasks are best lived out through self-definition (identity) and faithful commitment (intimacy). There is an interplay, obviously, between these two constructs. One needs a healthy self-definition in order to connect with others, while at the same time interpersonal connection leads to a deepening sense of identity.

Before leaving this topic it is important to mention the research carried out by psychologist Ruthellen Josselson, who studied a group of late adolescent females (college seniors) and did a follow-up study of these women in their mid-thirties. Josselson emphasized that relationship takes on particular significance for women. She defines identity as

> the stable, consistent, and reliable sense of who one is and what one stands for in the world. It integrates one's meaning to oneself and one's meaning to others; it provides a match between what one regards as central to oneself and how one is viewed by significant others in one's life. Identity is also a way of preserving the continuity of the self, linking the past and present.[22]

Josselson believes that identity development in men is straightforward, whereas for women developing an identity framework is a more complicated undertaking.

> Men are wont to define themselves by occupation or by their distinctiveness from others, which makes their identity easy to name. Women, by contrast, orient themselves in more complicated ways, balancing many involvements and aspirations, with connections to others paramount; their identities are thus compounded and more difficult to articulate.[23]

What are we to make of these findings? Essentially, optimal personality development for both male and female adolescents is most apt to occur when they make their way in the world through the development of healthy relationships and commitments to projects outside the self. These relationships and projects take many forms, and the number of relationships or activities that the adolescent/ young adult undertakes depends on particular background and needs. Psychologist James Marcia notes that identity might take longer for women than men because of the numerous social expectations (balancing family role with career), whereas intimacy takes longer for men than women because of male socialization that provides less stress on relationships. The key point for adults working with youth is to keep in mind the need for each adolescent to develop an increasingly sophisticated sense of self that incorporates both relationships and project commitments. This developmental progression is best expressed in the adolescent who forges an active inquiry of the world through healthy experimentation and questioning that leads to self-knowledge. Again, adolescents obtain this self-knowledge through focus on different domains, or areas of interest. Psychologist Nancy J. Cobb says it best:

> Taken together, the research on gender differences reveals that the *process* of identity formation is comparable for adolescents of either sex. Adolescents who allow themselves to question, explore, and experience the uncertainty of not knowing — to experience a period of crisis — mature in the process. The particular content that adolescents address in finding their own way can still differ for either gender. Thus similarities in process do not rule out other gender differences.[24]

In sum, for healthy personality development to take place *all* adolescents need to question, explore, and make choices. As they go through this process adolescents choose distinctive domains for their identity growth. For the adult working with youth several lines of inquiry are evident. For one, reflection needs to take place on how adolescents are investing their energies that lead to a healthy self-knowledge. What does the adolescent invest in? How does the adolescent spend his time? Ask what questions he has about life. The following also might prove helpful:

- I sometimes ask adolescents to write down or talk about their self-definition, and I reflect with them on the definition they describe. Another fruitful avenue is to have adolescents imagine that others are writing a definition of them. Ask them to imagine what others would say and reflect with them on these responses.

- Use a time perspective. Ask adolescents to write or talk about how they would have defined themselves five years ago as compared to now, five years from now, and ten years from now. Discuss common themes of these definitions as well as the changes. How do they account for these changes?

50

- Go over recent decisions they have made in their lives. Ask what values are part of these decisions.

Cultural Differences in Adolescent Identity

Besides gender issues, another area needing discussion when exploring adolescent identity development is that of multiculturalism. Do adolescents from minority groups experience their identity development differently from white adolescents? When we speak of minority groups we are focusing on African-American, Asian-American, Hispanic, and Native American cultures. As pointed out previously, minority youth make up an increasing proportion of the adolescent and young adult population. Minority youth must answer the question of identity (who am I?) in the context of a culture distinct from the dominant white culture. Often they must also deal with discrimination and prejudice in their own life histories.

Because of their growing reflective capacity, minority adolescents have the opportunity to address their self-definition in the context of their racial and cultural backgrounds. In their identity development, minority youth need not directly address questions of ethnic identity, yet those adolescents who do consider the consequences of their minority membership appear to achieve a more advanced level of life satisfaction. For these adolescents, this developmental process proceeds through a consideration of their minority background to a realization and valuing of their ethnic identity. In contrast to minority adolescents, whites appear not to question their ethnic identity. They are more apt to see themselves simply as "American," with little consideration given to being white.[25]

Psychologist Jean Phinney has provided some of the most extensive research in the area of adolescent ethnic identity. The issue itself is quite complex, and she notes that "ethnic identity" incorporates numerous dimensions. Along with colleague Doreen Rosenthal she offers the following summary of the situation minority youth must negotiate:

> In spite of differences among groups, it is clear that the family, community, and societal contexts in which adolescents develop pose a number of conflicts that minority youth must resolve in establishing an ethnic identity. These issues and conflicts do not necessarily result in psychological problems for minority youth, who are no more likely than other adolescents to suffer from low self-esteem. Rather, minority youth, like all adolescents, face a specific range of identity questions, depending on their own particular life experiences and the resources they bring to deal with these questions. As with many issues faced by

51

adolescents, questions about ethnicity are likely to involve competing, often ambivalent feelings.[26]

When working with minority youth I have found it helpful at some point to reflect with them on their cultural, racial, or ethnic origins, to pose questions about how these associations have made them "who they are" and what they are grateful for in their background and current life situation. It is often necessary to let them speak about their struggles within a dominant culture. It can be profitable to consider the feelings they have about their ethnic identity. I have also inquired about how their ethnic identity has spoken to them of God's love.

Because culture is a vital factor affecting attitudes and behavior, I want to sketch here some salient issues affecting adolescents in major minority groups.[27]

African-Americans   Many African-Americans suffer the scars of racism and feel a sense of powerlessness as they attempt to function in white culture. African-Americans tend to find support in broad forms of kinship such as the extended family, as well as churches and other informal support groups. The family is often headed by a female and itself often draws upon an extended family to provide support (e.g., grandparents). There is a significant gap between the educational achievements of African-Americans and whites, and this gap appears to be increasing. Unemployment and illiteracy are significant problems facing African-American youth. Despite such serious problems, it needs also to be pointed out that 50 percent of African-Americans qualify for middle- or upper-class economic status.

Native Americans   Though Native Americans constitute the smallest major ethnic group, they also constitute the most diverse, with hundreds of distinct tribal groups, each with its own culture and customs. Alcohol and drug abuse have reached "epidemic" proportions among the Native American population. Poverty and unemployment are very serious problems. Native Americans prize focusing on the moment, sharing and cooperation, and being at one with nature rather than attempting to control it. These values are at stark variance with the white culture's emphasis on individualism, competition, and mastery of the environment. Because of such differences, Native Americans often find difficulty in relating to the majority white culture.

Hispanics   There are distinct differences among those whose ancestral roots are south of the United States border; terms such as "Latinos" and "Mexican-Americans" are often used to describe these groups. Demographic indicators forecast that Hispanics will surpass

African-Americans as the largest minority group sometime early in the next century. The average age of Hispanics in the United States is considerably younger than the white population. For many Hispanics Spanish is their first or only language and English is poorly understood. "Hispanic students have a very high drop out rate, which rises with age. Nearly half drop out before completing high school."[28] Hispanics are strongly family-oriented and demonstrate a strong respect for authority.

Asian-Americans   The Asian-American population includes Koreans, Chinese, and Vietnamese, among many others. This ethnic minority is increasing quite rapidly and is expected to double by 2010. A significant number of Asian-Americans have been quite successful; educational achievement is highly valued by this ethnic group, and the family as a whole supports each family member's educational goals. Mental health concepts are often foreign to Asian-Americans, and showing emotional distress can be perceived as a failure on the part of the individual. The popular stereotype that Asian-Americans are the "model" minority who exhibit little emotional turmoil, however, is false. Many Asian-Americans suffer from homesickness, low self-esteem, prejudice, and poverty.

The Extent of Emotional Problems among Youth

The exact number of young people needing professional mental health services is open to debate; nonetheless, the number is large and the inadequacy of treatment is scandalous.

> Children have been referred to as one of the most neglected groups in mental health. Although it is difficult to get accurate estimates, the latest epidemiological data available indicate that from 15 percent (9.5 million) to 19 percent of the nation's approximately 63 million children and youth suffer from emotional or other problems that warrant mental health treatment....Children's mental health problems exist along a continuum — from transient conditions in the child's environment to diagnosable mental illness.[29]

At the same time, a growing body of research is altering our understanding of what adolescent mental health means. Increasingly, definitions of adolescent mental health are "based on the description of a wide variety of patterns of adaptation to the biological, psychological, and social challenges of adolescence."[30] Research shows that the "storm and stress" label so often applied to adolescents is false. "The majority of this research of the past 20 years clearly refutes the notion that most adolescents undergo severe emotional stress during this period of life.... The current consensus is that adolescence is not ordinarily a time of great psychological turmoil."[31] The number of emotionally impaired youth, which perhaps approaches 20 percent, is close to the rate of psychopathology in the adult population.[32] Nonetheless, this figure represents millions of children and adolescents. Furthermore, less than half of children and adolescents receive the treatment they need, and "treatment resources" allocated for mental health are disproportionately spent on the most severe cases.[33]

Emotional illness is also a growing concern on college campuses. In one survey of counseling center directors "results indicated that 85 percent of the center directors saw an increase in the overall level of psychopathology being treated at their counseling centers."[34] Another study comparing college freshmen with freshmen of a decade earlier found "college students seem to be more troubled today than they were 10 years ago. There seems to be an increase in reported distress by college students in every aspect of their lives."[35]

However, the important question remains: in the future will the decline in the emotional functioning of adolescents continue? Though we cannot predict with accuracy what the emotional climate will look like ten years from now, a prudent speculation is that the emotional health of youth will decline.

One reason is that family fragmentation is a significant factor in many young people's lives. Another factor (already noted) is the rising number of minority group adolescents and young adults. "For many youths, minority status is also associated with low socioeconomic status, higher incidence of clinical dysfunction, and poor access to health and mental health services."[36] Finally, youth themselves are increasingly engaging in behaviors that are considered harmful:

> By age fifteen, about a quarter of all young adolescents are engaged in behaviors that are harmful or dangerous to themselves and others. Of 28 million adolescents between the ages of ten and eighteen, approximately 7 million are at serious risk of being harmed by health- and even life-threatening activity, as well as by school failure. Another 7 million are at moderate risk. Only half of the youngsters in this age group, or about 14 million, appear to be growing up basically healthy. But even these young people are not immune to risk since most of them at the very least lack sufficient problem-solving skills.[37]

The Biopsychosocial Model

One of the most important points for the reader to grasp is the *complexity* of emotional dysfunction. Contemporary models of mental health stress the unity of biological, psychological, and social variables in order to understand the etiology of mental illness and promote psychological health. This perspective is termed a *biopsychosocial* approach. The following is a brief sketch of this model as applied to the adolescent's life.

Temperament is the most significant *biological* factor we need to address.[38] Temperament refers to emotionality, specifically, one's proneness toward reactivity and the intensity of one's feeling states. For example, when encountering an unfamiliar situation, "some children consistently become quiet, vigilant, and restrained while they assess the situation and their resources before acting. Others act with spontaneity, as though the distinctions between familial and novel situations were of minimal psychological consequence."[39] Thus a young boy might be very shy and withdraw from novel situations and exhibit a significant degree of timidity. Such tendencies might well influence the competency of his interpersonal skills as well as feelings of self-esteem.

Psychological factors come into play when we explore the adolescent's learning history and unique life experiences. An adolescent girl, for example, who has suffered a childhood loss (e.g., death of a parent or parental divorce) might well find trusting others difficult, which in turn influences the quality of peer relationships. Psychological factors exercise a large role in the young person's ongoing relationships.

Social factors are best represented by the environment in which the young person lives. Unemployment, poverty, and community situations that foster sexual/racial stereotyping all shape emotional health in adverse ways or become obstacles to health.

To be more specific, on the day I typed these words on my computer I noted the following headline in a page one article in the *New York Times:* "Teen-Age Gunslinging Is on Rise, in Search of Protection and Profit." The article goes on to note that "throughout New York City these days, there are teen-agers toting guns, armed from the arsenal of tens of thousands of pistols and revolvers, sawed-off shotguns and submachine guns.... "[40] A nationwide survey of over twenty-five hundred sixth to twelfth graders "painted a bleak portrait of violence and fear among American school children."[41] Of the young people polled in this survey, 9 percent had fired a gun at someone, 11 percent had been fired upon, almost 40 percent stated they knew someone who had been fired upon or experienced a gunshot wound, and 15 percent said they had walked around with a gun within thirty days of the survey.[42] Confirming this trend, studies now indicate that gunshot wounds constitute the second leading cause of death among high-school-age youth and is increasing faster than any other cause for this age group.[43] The questions must be

asked: How can emotional, physical, moral, or spiritual health flourish in such an atmosphere? What are the cumulative psychological
consequences for youth who must face such violence on a daily basis?

One vital ingredient needs to be added to our discussion of social
factors that influence the emotional and moral health of youth: the
role of culture. Adolescents today are decidedly immersed in their
culture and their cultural experiences often overwhelm the devoted
commitments and intentions of adults to foster moral reflection and
emotional health. I term the insidious influence of culture on healthy
adolescent development "cultural impairment."[44] Let us explore this
issue further.

The social critic Alan Durning quotes one analyst's vision at the
close of World War II.

> Our enormously productive economy ... demands that we make con-
> sumption our way of life, that we convert the buying and use of goods
> into rituals, that we seek our *spiritual* satisfaction [emphasis added],
> our *ego* satisfaction [emphasis added], in consumption.... We need
> things consumed, burned up, worn out, replaced, and discarded at
> an ever increasing rate.[45]

Ongoing consumer purchases lead to an experience of fleeting
value and parallels the sense of impermanence that so characterizes the adolescent's psyche. From a developmental perspective,
adolescents and young adults must negotiate a significant amount
of impermanence. During their undergraduate years they often
make some initial, if tentative, commitments. A love relationship,
the excitement over finding a close friend, or the discovery of a
career possibility that "fits," all enable the student to acquire self-
knowledge. Unfortunately, this road of initial psychic investments is
fraught with negative experiences as well. Fondness for another is
often transient, and the end of a relationship is an all too real possibility in the young person's life. Friends sometimes go their separate
ways or have misunderstandings. Vocational interests wax and wane.
The vicissitudes of changing desires and the sometimes painful realization of limited talents are added factors. Even the support of family
can be eclipsed by the sometimes urgent need to distance oneself
from family in order to meet identity needs. I am struck at how many
youth assuage their uncertainties through consumer purchases and
distract themselves by obsessing over ever-changing styles. Indeed,
our consumerist culture is often the *source of identity* for adolescent
and young adult self-definition, with education, the family, and the
church community exercising far less influence.

Yet this incessant purchasing bears directly on the very meaning
of "the good life." In his important work *All Consuming Images*, so-

ciologist Stuart Ewen describes the triumph of style over substance and the emergence of transient image-making as perfected by today's advertising and technology:

> The danger is this: as the world encourages us to accept the autonomy of images, "the given facts that appear" imply that substance is unimportant, not worth pursuing. Our own experiences are of little consequence, unless they are substantiated and validated by the world of style. In the midst of such charades, the chasm between surface and reality widens; we experience a growing sense of disorientation.[46]

As noted above, a relentless feature of consumerist "style" is its impermanence; fleeting changes of style invite continual purchase. In such an atmosphere, the stark reality for many young adults is that "being good" is equated not with "doing something" but with "buying something." Tragically, in our culture, youth's exposure to advertising teaches them that "the good life" is not lived but "bought." When one is reared in such a culture, ethical reflection falters in the onslaught of glitz and illusion. A student's manipulated consciousness — one that construes altruism and commitment as unrealistic if not unobtainable — might well have difficulty forming enduring values. We must face the sobering fact that our consumerist culture complicates and even undermines attempts to engage students in substantive ethical reflection.

This consumerist mind-set is supported by suppositions undergirding our culture. Alasdair MacIntyre has characterized the current state of moral thinking as one of disarray; he notes that the contemporary state of moral discourse is one "of grave disorder."[47] Robert Bellah reframes this "disorder" in terms of sociological insight:

> Now if selves are defined by their preferences, but those preferences are arbitrary, then each self constitutes its own moral universe, and there is finally no way to reconcile conflicting claims about what is good in itself.... In the absence of any objectifiable criteria of right and wrong, good or evil, the self and its feelings become our only moral guide. What kind of world is inhabited by this self, perpetually in progress, yet without any fixed moral end?[48]

The ethos of individualism, says Bellah, has sundered persons from their historically felt rooting in community. The result has been the illusion that well-being for oneself and others arises from individualistic pursuits culminating in material gratification. We live under the "treacherous notion that we can create a good life simply by striving for individual comfort and security, and that by so doing we are indirectly enriching the lives of those around us."[49]

I suspect this individualism has heavily influenced many young adults today. I am struck at how many students speak of their desires merely in terms of a "good job" or being "successful." I suspect too that current economic insecurities exacerbate self-preoccupation and the drive for success. In an individualistic world, one is evaluated by material success and any threat to or forestalling of this success tempts many to retreat to a defensive posture that enshrines the self and its pursuits. Moreover, in such a cultural climate the personal values of compassion and care find difficulty taking root with many young people, but equally threatened is any type of moral sense of community and social bonding. Preoccupied with private pursuits and individualistic concerns, adolescents, like their elders, are more inclined to think in terms of "private" rather than "public" well-being.

Two areas where the cultural climate directly influences adolescent and young adult health are the effects of the media industry on antisocial behavior and advertising influences on the self-image of women.

A growing consensus exists in psychological circles that media influences contribute to violent behavior. Through the end of middle adolescence (high school graduation) most youth spend more time watching television than they do in school. During the "impressionable" years of childhood and junior high (early adolescence) young people view thirteen thousand murders and over a hundred thousand acts of violence.[50] "It seems fair to say that the majority of researchers in the area are now convinced that excessive violence in the media increases the likelihood that at least some viewers will behave more violently."[51] This tendency is probably more pronounced among disadvantaged, intellectually limited, and less popular youth. "These less popular, less intellectually able children watch more television violence, identify more with television characters, and believe the violence they observe on television reflects real life."[52] Tragically, a vicious cycle ensues. "The violence they see on television may reassure them that their own behavior is appropriate or may teach them new coercive techniques, which they then attempt to use in their interactions with others. Thus, they behave more aggressively, which in turn makes them even less popular and drives them back to television."[53]

Another area where the media's influence has proven problematic for youth is mass communication's creation of a distorted view of body image. Psychologist Jean Kilbourne, through her examination of advertising images, has shown how advertising has both distorted the self-image of women and has linked such advertising with violence toward women. One of the most disturbing aspects of advertising's message is its power to "normalize" our perceptions and attitudes; thus advertising images become the "norm." Those who do not measure up to the impossible standards portrayed in advertising images feel inadequate (e.g., women who compare themselves to the models that saturate TV commercials and newspaper ads). The ads and commercials become the self-reference point for evaluation. Advertising especially distorts the self-image of women, as we shall see later when we discuss eating disorders.[54] Kilbourne has remarked that the stringent criteria that advertisers demand today would rule out Marilyn Monroe, who would be judged too heavy! As psychiatrist David Herzog notes, "If Marilyn Monroe were a young woman today, she'd probably feel very uncomfortable with her body."[55] What does such a statement say about the tacit cultural norms youth use to measure their happiness and success?

Obviously, the exact intricacies of relationships among biological, psychological, and social variables as well as their specific influence vary with each adolescent. The point at issue is the need for the adult to realize the complexity of any discussion regarding adolescent mental health and to take seriously the numerous variables that influence the adolescent's emotional functioning.

Conceptualizing Adolescent Mental Health and Dysfunction

How do we best come to understand the development of mental health problems during the adolescent years? Many theorists have argued that the presence or absence of an attachment bond looms large in the emergence of emotional difficulties. We will examine the development of emotional problems utilizing an attachment model. In a sense, attachment is the psychological soil in which healthy human development is able to flourish.[56]

Psychiatrist John Bowlby and psychologist Mary Ainsworth working independently and in collaboration are the major proponents of attachment theory. In his early training, Bowlby became dissatisfied with the Freudian emphasis on children's fantasy and internal psychic processes as the basis for assessing mental health and focused instead on real relationships in the child's life, specifically, the mother-child bond; as a consequence, he hoped (and to a large degree succeeded) in redirecting clinical work to focus on the child's actual experience. With his theorizing and Ainsworth's groundbreaking empirical studies they set forth the basic tenets of attachment theory, which has achieved increased acceptance in clinical and developmental circles.

Attachment is defined as the emotional bond developed between child and caretaker that provides security and trust, thereby allowing the child to venture outward and experience in a healthy manner other relationships; in the long run, healthy adult functioning is premised on a stable early attachment bond. "Attachment theory regards the propensity to make intimate emotional bonds to particular individuals as a basic component of human nature, already present in germinal form in the neonate and continuing through adult life into old age."[57] Attachment has survival value, and the infant is naturally disposed to seek attachment and proximity with the caretaker (usually the mother). "Attachment behavior is any form of behavior that results in a person attaining or maintaining proximity to some other clearly identified individual who is conceived as better able to cope with the world. It is most obvious whenever the person is frightened, fatigued, or sick, and is assuaged by comforting and caregiving."[58] Through her study of the infant-mother attachment Ainsworth concluded that infants are either securely or insecurely attached and that their attachment state is related to the parenting styles of their mothers. "Ainsworth's central premise was that the responsive mother provides a secure base. The infant needs to know that his primary caregiver is steady, dependable, there for him.... Fortified with the knowledge of his mother's availability, the child is able to go forth and explore the world. Lacking it, he is insecure, and his exploratory behavior is stunted."[59]

Attachment theorists believe that although the infant has a dependence on the mother, it is this very dependence that allows for increasing independence and later autonomy. In other words, having experienced such a "secure base," the infant uses such security for mastering later developmental tasks.

> This brings me to a central feature of my concept of parenting — the provision by both parents of a secure base from which a child or an adolescent can make sorties into the outside world and to which he can return knowing for sure that he will be welcomed when he gets there, nourished physically and emotionally, comforted if distressed, reassured if frightened. In essence this role is one of being available, ready to respond when called upon to encourage and perhaps assist, but to intervene actively only when clearly necessary.[60]

But how does the attachment that infants experience in their early months continue to affect them? Bowlby notes this continued influence results from the child's incorporating within the self a "working model" of his or her experience. In a sense, then, this attachment experience becomes part of the child:

> The working models a child builds of his mother and her ways of communicating and behaving towards him, and a comparable model of his father, together with the complementary models of himself in interaction with each, are being built by a child during the first few years of his life and, it is postulated, soon become established as influential cognitive structures.... The forms they take, the evidence reviewed strongly suggests, are based on the child's real-life experience of day-to-day interactions with his parents.[61]

As development proceeds, these "models" function unconsciously and guide one's actions and interpretations of later relational experiences; in other words, these "working models" aid or hinder later relationship-building. According to Bowlby, the child who is securely attached utilizes a working model that forms accurate perceptions of later relationships, deals effectively with changes and growth in relational encounters, and possesses insight and maturing adaptive capacities to deal with life experiences as they arise. The insecure child, on the other hand, possesses impaired working models that frustrate or impede proper developmental growth. These will be later manifested in distorted interpretations in others' actions and motives, lack of self-insight, and inappropriate responding in interpersonal situations. Needless to say, for such a child adequate and healthy peer relationships become more problematic.

Among adolescents, healthy attachment to parents is associated with life satisfaction, healthy family life, and better functioning. "Adolescents with strong attachment relationships with parents present a better profile of adjustment than do insecurely attached adolescents."[62] Moreover, a study of college students demonstrated that those undergraduates judged to be securely attached were "rated as more ego-resilient, less anxious, and less hostile by peers and reported little distress and high levels of social support."[63]

Secure attachment produces several highly valued features. First, children who are securely attached develop adequate self-esteem. A second feature of such children is healthy conscience functioning. Third, young people with secure attachments tend to be self-reliant and take initiative. Fourth, such children are better able to contain and deal with their emotions and, likewise, are able to tolerate frustration and negative feelings. None of these characteristics is surprising. Children who have a felt sense of security are more able than their less securely attached peers to venture outward, take initiative, tolerate disappointment, and accept rules. For such children the world is a reliable place and relationships are satisfying and nurturing. For such young people an optimism develops with regard to discovering relationships and new experiences.

Though we have given considerable attention to the attachment

61

construct, we must avoid the mistake of viewing future emotional health and happiness as residing solely in early attachment bonding. Some theorists have argued that the attachment school fails to give adequate consideration to more genetic-based understandings of behavior such as temperament.[64] The more extreme one's temperamental disposition, in other words, the more temperament might exercise a significant role in one's later attachment functioning. Other studies have shown that a large number of factors influence future health and happiness (e.g., talents, personality, intelligence).[65] A realistic view holds that secure attachment is beneficial to the child and that disrupted attachment patterns in early childhood experience can affect adversely the child's later emotional functioning. At the same time, we must be open to the effects of other factors that might promote or hinder the child's relational and emotional functioning.

The powerful role of early attachment as well as its limits can be seen in studies of resilient children. Resilient children are youth who surmount extreme adversity in the family of origin (e.g., poverty, a schizophrenic parent, abuse, family alcoholism) and grow up to live relatively mature and stable lives. These children are "resilient" to the numerous traumas that befall them in their early years. What must be stated of course is that the vast majority of children from such backgrounds are significantly impaired by such early adversities; hence we see the influence of early attachment bonding and what such disruption does to a child. Nonetheless, a small number of youth apparently are able to weather such emotional hardship and appear to function adequately. What allows for these successes? Various studies have found several features associated with resiliency in the face of such early childhood difficulty. For one, resilient children often have some asset they can draw upon such as a personality disposition (a pleasing smile, physical attractiveness, or friendly demeanor) or personal talent that serves them well (e.g., success in school). These assets are buffers to stress and invite others (peers and adults) to provide the child with attention and support. Second, those found to be resilient speak fondly of having in their childhood or adolescence some adult who believed in them. Such adults (a grandparent, teacher, aunt, neighbor) provided these youth with support and a sense of hope.[66]

Thus attachment remains vitally important, but other factors must also be considered when predicting a child's future emotional health. Moreover, the adult's own relationship with the adolescent can offer a sense of security and hope as the young person attempts to sort through the questions and struggles that lead to self-understanding, maturing value choices, and a developing philosophy of life. Psychologist Carol Gilligan perhaps says it best when she writes that "psychological development in adolescence may well hinge on the adolescent's belief that her or his psyche is worth developing, and this belief in turn may hinge on the presence in a teenager's life of an adult who knows and cares about the teenager psyche."[67]

Adolescent Defense Mechanisms

Defense mechanisms can be viewed as unconscious processes utilized by the ego to ward off threat and danger. The adolescent ego must negotiate and resolve ongoing conflicts between and among internal needs and urges, the realities of the world, significant people, and cultural expectations and prohibitions. For example, the high school student might wish to marry yet knows that parental expectations and personal wishes make it necessary to postpone marriage until the completion of college. (The adolescent is here employing the healthy defense of suppression.)

Defenses, whether healthy or unhealthy, serve the following needs.

1. They protect the fragile nature of adolescent self-esteem. Given the numerous changes and often powerless state that many adolescents experience, they often show significant insecurities and doubts as well as self-questioning regarding their own adequacy. Defenses shield these doubts and enable adolescents "to feel good" about who they are.

2. Defenses serve to keep mood states within appropriate limits. Adolescence is a time in which the mix and variety of emotions are constant. Such emotional expression is often intense, erratic, and of various duration. At some point, if only for a short period, most adolescents are described as "moody" and "irritable." The adolescent's ability to control mood swings and emotional expressions remains, to various degrees, ineffectual. As adolescence proceeds the young person establishes better control over impulses and greater consistency over emotional expressions. A large body of research has found that with adulthood there exists more control over emotions and more stability in moods.[68]

3. Another purpose for defense mechanisms is to buffer the adolescent ego from the problems associated with unresolved conflicts. Separation from parents and dependency issues can create turmoil for adolescents, often requiring the employment of defenses.

4. A final purpose of defense mechanisms resides in their ability to defend against and resolve the feelings of self-denigration associated with guilt.

Naturally, when healthy defenses are employed, the adolescent is able to progress, to complete developmental tasks adequately, and to achieve emotional maturity. On the other hand, if unhealthy or immature defenses are utilized, healthy development is compromised and corresponding behaviors prove inadequate in resolving conflicts and meeting growing societal expectations. With time, such defenses lead to increasing behavioral dysfunction. Such immature defenses create difficult roadblocks to the adolescent's quest for well-functioning adulthood.

Adolescents use defenses in ways different from adults. Social worker Helen Rabichow and psychiatrist Morris Sklansky note the following differences between adolescent and adult use of defenses.

1. The adolescent uses defenses more intensely than the adult does, because the greater intensity of adolescent life is manifested in all ego functioning.

2. Defenses are more transient in adolescents, more persistent in adults.

3. The adolescent tends to use a wider variety of defenses than the adult does.

4. The adolescent is more flexible in the use of defenses, because the use is not yet totally integrated. The adult's defenses are part of a total and more consistent character structure.

5. Adolescent defenses are influenced by parents and other adults, peers, and partners in beginning sexual relationships, while for an adult, inner motivations are the primary determining factors.

6. Adolescents have a need to identify with their peer group and are so anxious not to be different that they may be motivated to alter their defenses, while adults do not feel this motivation and develop defenses primarily out of inner needs.

7. In adolescents, the realization that time is passing is a less significant pressure for change than in adults, who feel it as a strong need to modify defenses or adapt differently.

8. In the adolescent, the concept that reality can easily be changed to suit oneself (wishful thinking) is strong, but an adult better realizes the nature and limitations of reality.

9. The great store of hope in adolescents makes it possible for them to postpone any alteration of maladaptive defenses, while an adult is more realistic and knows that efforts must be made to change in order to adapt.[69]

From the above points we can characterize the adolescent as one who employs a wide variety of defenses that, at times, might be intense and erratic. There exists, then, an inconsistency in the adolescent's use of defenses. Many are experienced in order to see what "fits," though, of course, every adolescent develops a distinctive pool that he or she draws upon. With time, particularly by the college years, defenses are more in place, though inconsistency is still observed.

Let us now examine various mechanisms used by the adolescent and young adult. First, we explore the use of what might be termed maturing or healthy defenses.[70] As a clinician I look for the following defenses as healthy signs the adolescent is progressing on the road to emotional maturity.[71]

Anticipation   This defense is utilized when the adolescent realistically plans ahead and evaluates the wise use of time, talent, and energies. For example, a term paper due on Monday might mean the college student arranges her schedule the week before in a way that allows the paper to be completed.

Suppression   When the adolescent is able to postpone gratification of conscious or unconscious impulses or conflicts, then we have the use of suppression. Naturally, this defense exercises a critical role in adolescent development. A continuing challenge for the adolescent is the mastery of impulse (which includes the belief that impulses can be controlled). Adolescents unable to employ this defense often relate to others impulsively, thereby precluding maturing experiences and healthy relationships. In an age of drug usage and sexually transmitted diseases, insufficient use of this defense poses a particularly dangerous situation.

Sense of Humor   Having a good sense of humor provides the young person, particularly the early and middle adolescent, a way to diffuse naturally occurring sexual and aggressive urges. A healthy sense of humor fosters likeability and positive feedback from both peers and adults. A distinction must be made, however, between "healthy" and "unhealthy" uses of humor. Humor is healthy when it provides joy to self and others or "builds others up." Often adolescents or young adults use humor in self-denigrating or passive-aggressive ways with peers. It is important to reflect with adolescents on the goal of their humorous comments. A question I often ask is: "How do you think your humorous comment affected ___[name])___?" or "How do you think he/she felt when you told that joke?" or "How do you think your joke made _____ feel?"

Sublimation   One sublimates when creative energies are expended in mature and socially accepted ways. Healthy uses of sublimation are hobbies and personal interests that foster creativity. Artistic, literary, and musical endeavors are often signs of the adolescent's attempts to channel sexual feelings in socially constructive ways. Questions I reflect on with young people are "Do you have a hobby?" "How do you spend your free time?" or "Do you have a way to be creative?" Then I discuss this activity or help the adolescent come up with such an activity.

Altruism   Caring behaviors are a natural way to promote healthy relationships. They sustain the Christian vocation to love while promoting healthy emotional and moral development. Such caring stances, in turn, go a long way in insuring positive feedback from both peers and adults. One caution here is the adolescent who is the "compulsive caregiver" — the youth who "has to" do for others and will not allows others to reciprocate. Such behavior is compensatory rather than maturing.

Fantasy   Everyone has dreams and desires, perhaps no one more than the adolescent. Adolescents and young adults often have rich fantasy lives. A helpful technique is simply to reflect with the young person on his or her goals and desires. I sometimes ask young people, "What do you dream about becoming or doing?" Then I reflect with them on the values contained in such responses. If used properly, fantasy is a healthy defense. However, if used to excess, fantasy undermines adolescent growth.

Let us picture an adolescent who has incorporated the above defenses. For example, Theresa plans ahead and has a healthy sense of control over her impulses. Her sense of humor is pleasing and makes her liked by her peers. She has several creative projects she invests in, and one of the first things her friends mention about her is how "caring" she is. When you talk to her you discover that she is able to share her hopes and dreams for the future. You reflect how her goals appear both realistic and growthful. Theresa is popular with her peers. Adults in turn give her positive feedback. In sum, both peers and adults value her company and respond positively to her. This brief sketch of Theresa enables us to see the maturing power and benefits of defenses.

Unfortunately, many adolescents employ defenses that are less adequate and, in some cases, decidedly nongrowthful. The long-term consequences of such defenses are developmental immaturity and adult dysfunctional behavioral patterns.

Adults working with youth need to be aware of immature and dysfunctional adolescent behavioral patterns. At the same time we must recall that defense mechanisms are more or less unconscious and at times quite intricately embedded within the adolescent's psyche. This being the case, adults, often lacking professional or formal training in counseling, cannot for the most part be expected to discern such defenses nor interpret accurately such behavioral expressions. Nonetheless, an insightful adult working with youth can often detect instances where these defenses are employed. Over the years I have observed a good number of campus ministers, youth ministers, or teachers correctly recognize these defenses. A prudent position is the following: Acknowledge that behavior is complex and multicausal and not limited merely to defense mechanisms. At the same time, if you have a "hunch" that an adolescent is utilizing particular defenses, look for concrete behavioral evidence, but always acknowledge to yourself its complexity and the fact that there might be more to the behavior than you think.

Below are some less healthy and adaptable defense mechanisms that adolescents employ in their everyday behaviors. Some of these defenses in themselves and others when overused lead to lingering emotional problems and frustrate productive adaptation to the environment.

Intellectualization   This defense is activated when the adolescent needs to avoid the painful emotional significance of an event. For example, instead of talking about parental divorce, the adolescent recites extensive statistics about divorce and talks about its effects. The adult should be sensitive to what is painful in the adolescent's life and the extent to which the adolescent can acknowledge this hurt. A good strategy here is not to point out the intellectualizing but challenge it indirectly through questioning in order to get at the emotional content. For example, with the divorce episode above you might inquire: "I know when people divorce it is often hard and difficult for the children involved. I wonder how it is with you?"

Inhibition   When an adolescent holds back from taking initiatives, the defense of inhibition might be suspected. Ask yourself: "In what areas does this young person find difficulty in taking initiative?"

Minimization   When utilizing this very common and immature defense, the adolescent minimizes his or her behaviors. Common examples include: "Cheating on the test wasn't that bad" or "What I said didn't hurt his feelings." The best way to respond to such statements is first to address the reality: "Cheating is wrong" or "Hurtful statements do hurt others." Then repeat the statement in a personal way and make reference to the adolescent. For example: "I think cheating is a serious moral issue and I also think *you* are minimizing the real issue, which *is* a real issue. Could you respond to what I said, John?"

Externalization   When we blame others and refuse to take responsibility, we employ the defense of externalization. Adolescents often use this defense. "It's the teacher's fault." "They made me do it." "The other guys on the dorm floor caused it." Adolescents are like players in a basketball game. They want the ball and want to play with it, but when times get "tough" they are all too willing to throw the ball back to you. The adult's task is gently but firmly to throw the ball back so that the adolescent takes responsibility for his or her life. When working with the adolescent keep this image in mind. Is the adolescent trying to "throw the ball" back to you? The best way to work with externalization is to determine whether the adolescent is playing with the ball or trying to throw it away and have you or someone else take responsibility. If you believe it is the latter, after describing the situation you and the adolescent are discussing, ask: "Tell me, Sue, is there any responsibility you have to take in this situation?" Ask the question in a neutral way and simply reflect with the adolescent on the ability to accept responsibility for at least some of the issues at hand. After all, responsibility for a situation is rarely totally one-sided.

Totalism   Totalism arises when the adolescent becomes totally absorbed in a project or goal. The advantage of this defense is it establishes an identity for the adolescent and wards off facing other more threatening behaviors or thoughts. This defense is best handled by reflecting with the adolescent "factually" on the amount of time and energy invested in a certain activity (e.g., athletics, school job, dorm resident assistant, club president, etc.) and inquiring into attention being given to other developmental tasks and obligations.

Acting Out   When conflicts remain unresolved or are intensely felt, then some adolescents act them out. Their behavior becomes oppositional, and conduct in school settings is often inappropriate. Moreover, this defense is very common in delinquent adolescents and can at times take on overtly aggressive behavior. Acting-out adolescents need understanding, but they also need limit-setting, not only to protect others but often to protect themselves from their own impulses. This defense is more common in early adolescents and lessens through the middle and late adolescent phases. Continual acting out through these later stages can be indicative of significant psychological conflict. Data indicate that this defense is primarily employed by males. That is, males tend to act out whereas females are prone to internalize conflicts. Even so, there have been significant increases in female adolescent acting-out behaviors (e.g., fights at school).

Rationalization   Making excuses best highlights the meaning of rationalization. This defense is one of the most commonly employed. We all makes excuses at one time or another (perhaps almost daily!). When you think an adolescent is making an excuse, an open-ended, nonthreatening question is the best strategy. For example,

Maria offers a clearly inadequate excuse for her incomplete homework. A helpful response is to summarize the reason she has offered and then inquire: "Often, Maria, there are many reasons why we do things. Do you think there might be any other reasons you can give why your homework wasn't done?" Such open-ended questions do not threaten adolescents but rather invite them to reflect more deeply on their behaviors.

Compartmentalizing This defense comes to life when adolescents isolate an area of life from examination. Thus they might talk about various issues quite self-critically, but in the area of sexuality they will not look at their behaviors or explore them in terms of commitment, fidelity, and honesty. A technique to open discussion is to have them list all areas of their life that are important and meaningful. Then you can mention those areas that they fail to bring up or do not speak about. Another way to foster insight is to speak about "maturity" and have them apply the word "mature" to various areas of their life. I might also reflect with them on the meaning of "maturity," which requires that attention be given to *all* aspects of life.

Stereotyping Stereotyping others is a way to deal with fears and that which is unknown. Stereotyping others (a group, class, dorm floor) also gives the adolescent a sense of "control." Stereotyping is especially common in early adolescents and somewhat in middle adolescents because of their need for control in the midst of so many developmental changes. A good way to handle this defense is, after a stereotypical statement, to inquire gently about the "evidence" the adolescent has for her judgment.

Provocation The adolescent who is attempting to provoke others utilizes this defense. "This dynamic is common among adolescents who tease or provoke parents and others, particularly with actions that in themselves do not seem serious or hostile. Not hearing when spoken to, persistent humming, tapping fingers or kicking feet, and grimacing are examples of ordinary kinds of provocation that adolescents frequently use."[72]

Compensation Everyone needs to feel adequate. When there exists a felt sense of inadequacy, then we often seek other avenues to build ourselves up. In other words, we compensate by finding other roads toward success. Compensation is not necessarily harmful unless taken to excess, yet it often aids adolescents to discuss whether they view themselves as adequate or inadequate in some specific area and what behaviors result from these feelings.

Displacement Often feeling powerless, adolescents vent their negative feelings onto others. For example, an adolescent who is treated unfairly by her parent might direct her anger toward a

69

younger sibling; in effect, she displaces the anger from the parent toward the younger child. A helpful technique here is to provide feedback, explaining that the attitude or behavior appears excessive, inappropriate, or unfair in light of the person to whom her reaction is directed.

Projection   This more primitive defense mechanism is employed when one attributes unconscious negative feelings to another. For example, an adolescent might not like his teacher. Instead of acknowledging such feelings (which might be a blow to his ego) he projects them on to the teacher and accuses the teacher of not liking him. Significant use of this defense mechanism in early adolescence and most certainly its common use in middle and late adolescence might well be a sign of emotional disturbance requiring professional intervention.

Passive-aggressive Behavior   Since adolescents cannot usually act out their negative feelings, they redirect them in passive ways. A college student angry at her boyfriend might conveniently "forget" their prearranged meeting time. The adolescent upset with his parents might not put back the keys to the car in the designated key area. Recall the adolescent's need to feel powerful. Often adolescents feel they are allowed little input into decisions affecting their lives. It is important to ask yourself how adolescents have healthy opportunities to feel powerful or significant in the eyes of peers and adults.

Denial   This defense is employed when adolescents refuse to admit painful experiences, actual realities, or negative feelings. Denying such occurrences allows them to avoid anxiety and other painful feelings. Because we deny for a reason, if the adult chooses to bring something to a young person's attention, it should be done gently; it is best posed at least initially in the form of a nonthreatening question rather than a direct statement that the adolescent is denying something.

Fantasy   Though fantasy can be helpful, it also has the potential for being counterproductive in the adolescent's growth process. Some adolescents spend an inordinate amount of time in fantasy as a way to avoid the painful realities of life. Adolescents also employ fantasy in a grandiose way that allows the shoring up of their self-esteem through unrealistic aspirations or triumphs.

Identification   This defense is commonly employed during the adolescent years. Adolescents will identify with older peers and adults who are significant in their lives. They might also associate closely with a cause or organization. By utilizing this defense, adolescents are able to sustain their own identity search. Reflecting with the adolescent about who are influential in their lives and who they would like to be like is helpful. Identification poses problems when it leads to diminished maturity. A good question is simply whether the adolescent's identification with a group, cause, or person is leading to the accomplishment of developmental tasks and healthier behaviors.

The healthier and more significant our relationships, the more apt we are to be less defensive and to employ healthy defenses. It must be emphasized that even in the healthiest intimate relationships, no one appears totally psychologically naked to another. This is why we employ defenses. Even in the most intense and deepest relationships trust is not perfect, and we defend ourselves against the other's perception and knowledge of us. From a psychological perspective, this is perhaps what awaits us in heaven — where in the Lord's loving gaze we experience ourselves as totally understood and loved without condition and with absolute vulnerability (defense-less).

The fact of the matter is that we all (whether adolescents or adults) employ some combination of healthy and unhealthy defenses. However, adolescents, on average, because of reasons already cited, are prone to utilize unhealthy defenses to a greater degree. Most of the time our challenge of their defenses must be gentle and inviting of growth. Correspondingly, we must be able to provide them with insight and constructive feedback in order that they have an alternative set of behaviors and defenses to replace their more immature ways of perceiving and relating. Gentle questioning and reflection that respects youth's experience should be the norm. In short, we should never attempt to strip away the adolescent's defenses without offering or encouraging healthier defenses or behaviors.

Affective Equilibrium

One final topic needs attention as we end the discussion of adolescent development and dysfunction. Consider the following question. What is the end result for an individual with secure attachment, positive identity growth, and healthy defenses? The constellation of these experiences leads to what I term "affective equilibrium." Affective equilibrium can be defined as *emotional functioning — whether in a child, adolescent, or adult — that sustains and promotes the completing of developmental tasks and fosters in one's current life situation adaptive functioning, psychological growth, and ethical commitment.* More broadly, when a person's emotional functioning is healthy, then that individual possesses the emotional resources to negotiate successfully dilemmas, obstacles, and challenges as well as to work through the potentially disruptive and inevitable conflicts and stressors that go with daily living.

71

An adequate affective equilibrium also figures prominently in spiritual and moral growth. With adequate emotional resources and functioning, one can find the time to discern and reflect on life choices and actions. Likewise, hurt and frustration can be more easily tolerated and understood. Unfortunately, for many youth (and the number seems to be increasing), emotional functioning is experienced not as a state of affective equilibrium but in terms of degrees of affective disequilibrium.

Consider the following examples: John feels the rejection of his father who has abandoned the family and divorced his mother; Eileen struggles with the sexual abuse that continues to haunt her; Victor feels tremendous hurt over the breakup of his relationship with his girlfriend; Sarah grapples with her emotions as she continues to work out ambivalent feelings surrounding her relationship with her mother. All of us can think of many adolescents and young adults who are hurting, feel rejected, or are attempting to cope with anger toward family members or significant others. The distress arising from their emotional disequilibrium impairs their decision-making and freedom. Such adolescents are prone to respond inappropriately, to act impulsively, to withdraw, or to fail to consider viable options.

For such adolescents how can the Lord's grace be felt or the emotional resources obtained for adequate living of a healthy moral and spiritual life? In the pastoral care of adolescents, the burden of affective disequilibrium looms as an imposing and difficult challenge. Adults ministering to adolescents and young adults must consider the level of affective disequilibrium when undertaking pastoral care.

CHAPTER THREE

Counseling: Some Issues and Approaches

Adults ministering to adolescents often have a wide variety of concerns about what questions or approaches are most beneficial. In this chapter we explore some of the basic issues needing discussion when working with this age group.

Initial Contact and Overview

Pastoral counseling with adolescents is usually much more informal in terms of issues and setting than many other situations of counseling and psychotherapy. For example, the setting, the length of the discussion, and the number of times the adult and adolescent meet vary tremendously, depending upon the adolescent and the issue. Nonetheless, even when counseling extends over only several meetings, it is helpful to obtain an overview of the adolescent's situation.[1] The following categories can be helpful in understanding the adolescent's overall functioning.

Relationships   Who are the adolescent's friends? What are the quality of these friendships? Who does the adolescent find most significant in his life? Does he appear to have the quality of relational bonds that are typical for his age? Can he talk about why specific individuals are important in his life? What is it about these individuals that make them significant? Is the adolescent romantically involved?

Time Allocation   How does this adolescent spend her time? Have the adolescent go through her day (I call this doing an "Inventory"). What are the high points? low points? Does the adolescent appear bored? Is there a sense that goals are part of her life? How does she invest her time? How does she handle solitude? What does she like to do for fun? Does she have any hobbies? Is she resourceful and productive in her use of free time? Does she have healthy ways to enjoy life?

Family Life   What is this adolescent's family situation: two parents? one parent? stepparents? foster parents? How many siblings? What feelings does discussion of family life elicit from him? Whom is he closest to in the family? Whom does he have problems with?

What is meal time like? Does the family find time to be together? What is the level of support in the family?

Adolescent Concerns   What concerns does this adolescent have? Does she recognize problem behaviors in her life? Are there serious issues in her life, e.g., truancy, failing grades, behavior problems, drug use, sexual acting out? Is she aware of her moods and the effect of her emotional reactions on others. How does she cope with stress? How adaptable is she?

Health Concerns   Does the adolescent have any health concerns that worry him? Is he taking any medication and does it have side effects on his behavior? Is he engaging in any behaviors that would be classified as "high risk," such as reckless driving or drug use?

School Life   How is the adolescent doing in school? What are her favorite subjects? Least-liked subjects? Who are her favorite teachers? What are her vocational and career goals? Why is she attracted to a particular occupation? If she is an undergraduate, inquire about college major and future plans.

Spiritual Life   What is the adolescent's prayer life like? What is his image of God? How has his relationship with God changed over the years? What is the quality of his relationship with God? What is his level of religious practice? Does he have some type of connection to a faith community?

Moral Life   Is the adolescent acquiring a personal philosophy of life? Is she growing in the capacity to articulate values? Does her behavior reflect the values she holds? How much discrepancy exists between behavior and values? Does she inquire about other points of view? How open is she to others' opinions on issues? Does she have a healthy sense of guilt? What defenses does she use to avoid taking responsibility in her life?

Confidentiality

Few issues are more perplexing to the adult than that of confidentiality. The question is important for several reasons. For one, there are ethical issues involved (e.g., respect of the person). Second, the pastoral counselor is often in an ill-defined role. The adult may be employed by an institution, and this fact might "compete" with the loyalty she believes she owes the adolescent (e.g., if the adolescent discloses that she has engaged in a serious violation of a dormitory or school rule). Third, respect for confidentiality sustains trust and professionalism.

The issue is complicated by the fact that there is no explicit set of rules regarding confidentiality. Some professions (e.g., law, psychology, medicine) have formal ethical standards; nevertheless there

is often debate about appropriate behavior for the professional —
not to mention the laxity with which some principles and standards
are applied. But what about the teacher, religious educator, or campus minister? What ethical code do they refer to regarding issues of
confidentiality?

The Context   The question of confidentiality involves several
factors:

1. The adult, who often occupies one or more roles, e.g., coach,
   teacher, moderator, youth minister.
2. The adolescent, who has specific developmental needs.
3. The nature of the information. That is, how personal and private is this information? Is it what could be called benign
   ("what is your class schedule?") or very personal (a family
   problem that no one has knowledge of). Clarifying what is personal is crucial; in other words, what the adult and what the
   adolescent thinks are confidential matters might be different.
4. The consequences of sharing the information: Whom does it go
   to? How far does it go? What are the consequences of sharing?
5. The reason for sharing the information with another: Is it a
   legitimate request?
6. The obligation the adult has to the school, parish, or religious
   institution. He or she is not there solely to be an advocate for
   adolescents.

General Principle   In general, information obtained from an
adolescent through verbal exchange, whether in a counseling center
or in any other setting (e.g., on a dorm floor, at a parish outing), that
touches on a personal issue in the adolescent's life is not to be communicated to another person without the adolescent's permission.
The two major exceptions to this principle are adolescent behaviors
that (*a*) harm the young person or someone else or (*b*) involve illegal
activities that violate laws or institutional policies.

Adolescents, because of their developmental state, are often in
need of a sympathetic ear. Sometimes they need an adult figure
who can just listen in an empathic way about personal, academic,
or family concerns. Obviously, the adult needs a sense of what the
adolescent views as important as well as an understanding of what
she is going through. Concern must be expressed for the difficult experiences of many adolescents who turn to the adult for guidance
and support. To feel they can "trust" an adult is a tremendously
empowering and sustaining experience for adolescents. A reflection
question for the adult is: "How am I *respecting* this adolescent?" or
"How would I want to be treated in a similar situation?"

Besides the empowerment it provides the adolescent, another reason for endorsing the principle of confidentiality is that once information is revealed the adult has no control over it and who else might discover it. The best way to keep information confidential is, simply, not to talk about it.

Dealing with Confidentiality Conflicts   One issue that commonly surfaces for adults ministering to youths is that of sharing information with colleagues. For example, suppose you have several discussions with an adolescent about some personal matters. Then a colleague you respect and know to be genuinely concerned about the adolescent inquires about her. What do you do? On the one hand, you want to respect the student's right to privacy; on the other hand, sharing some information with the adult who also has contact with the adolescent might be very helpful to her. A good strategy here is the following. If the information requested is readily obtainable through everyday observation or the adolescent has openly discussed this information with others, then information can be shared. For example, "In my class it appears...."; "I noticed on the dorm floor..."; "During the club meeting he was talking about...." " It is also helpful to condition statements with words or phrases such as "possibly," "I'm not sure but...."

Normally it is not appropriate to provide information of a personal nature that the adolescent has shared in a pastoral counseling context. Most readers have found themselves in situations where discussing matters with colleagues might prove helpful. In such instances one must consider the trust one has in the colleague as well as the respect one owes the adolescent. Sometimes general statements — such as "Well, you know Megan has had some difficulties," or "It's a complex situation and I'm talking to Jim about it" — can prove helpful. Of course specific information is not shared. The rule of thumb here remains helping the colleague know through some general reference but at the same time respecting the adolescent by not revealing specific information.

Sometimes an adult might be approached by an adolescent's peers who are concerned about the adolescent or who might innocently inquire about their friend. The rule here is to listen to a concerned peer but not to divulge information. When innocent inquiry comes up, an appropriate response is simply to say, "I just don't know." Again, the confidentiality of the adolescent must be maintained.

Generally speaking I do not believe working in a ministry with adolescents or young adults needs to begin with a statement defining the rights and limits of confidentiality. Discussions should be free and open. If, however, a question of confidentiality does come up, then confidentiality issues should be addressed. The two most common issues here are harm to self or others and violation of institutional rules.

The issue of self-injury and suicide will be taken up in a later chapter. At this point, it suffices to say that confidentiality is not absolute and in such cases confidentiality should not be maintained. In a similar vein, when the adult suspects that an adolescent has significant life stresses or mental health problems, a referral should be made to an experienced counselor or mental health professional. Of course an adult might wish to discuss a case with an experienced colleague, counselor, or mental health professional. In such instances, a name need not be divulged. Just the facts of the situation should be presented in order to get the other's input and advice.

We have mentioned several times the obligations the adult has in terms of the parish, organization, or school. If the adult suspects or knows of adolescent behaviors contrary to school rules or the organization's policy, then early on in the dialogue with the adolescent, he or she needs to make clear these other obligations. Adolescents can at times manipulate adults into being their allies, and adults must realize that this possibility exists. It should also be pointed out that many youths are developmentally immature, and because of developmental issues or other problems might not really be aware of the seriousness or consequences of their behavior.

Some Suggestions

1. It is important that the adult have colleagues with whom to share personal feelings and questions regarding confidentiality. Ministry to adolescents takes its toll, and adult support is essential. Also, working with adolescents can evoke regressive tendencies in the adult. At times the temptation might exist to be more a friend or ally to the adolescent when being an adult is what is called for and needed.

2. If the adult is tired or dealing with a considerable amount of confidential information or under considerable stress concerning conflicting interests, it is prudent that he not constantly place himself in situations where more information will lead to more confidentiality conflicts. At times, the adult might prudently abstain from being present in some situations (e.g., meetings, activities).

3. It is helpful for the adult always to keep in mind the question: "How is my behavior *respecting* this adolescent?" I find the word "respect" best captures the spirit of confidentiality.

4. When an adult is tired (end of a day, week, semester), she is more apt to be susceptible to not attending adequately to others, to missing important information, or to saying something that should

not be said. The adult needs to know when she needs a break or is a candidate for burnout.

The above discussion is, obviously, not complete. Confidentiality is a very complex issue with an infinite number of variable situations that do not quite "fit" the situations we have spoken of above. Nonetheless, because confidentiality is so integral to the building of relationships, the fostering of trust, and the promoting of Christian community, it seems wise to offer the above guidelines. In the long run, respect for confidentiality fosters a Christian climate in ministerial endeavors as well as a Christian witness to the youth we seek to serve.

When to Refer

Some adolescents are in need of professional assistance. Any adult who has worked with adolescents and young adults knows people who fit this category. The critical question is: At what point should adults decide that they are in over their head and more professional expertise should be obtained? When I give workshops to adults working with youth, this is one of the most commonly asked questions. The question itself is difficult for two reasons. First, adolescent behavior is complex. It reflects the adolescent need for discovery; it is also a means to test adults and to deal with frustration. Moreover, a behavior can be temporary, triggered by a specific situation, or it can be the sign of deeper underlying issues. Second, there is often a fine line between adolescent behaviors. For example, the adolescent who is curious might try marijuana on an experimental basis or because of peer pressure. When does such behavior indicate serious developmental or psychological problems? There exists a gray area around much adolescent behavior. The accompanying diagram illustrates the range of adolescent issues and behavior problems.

As noted in the accompanying chart, many behaviors can easily be classified as developmental and normal. On the other hand, some behaviors clearly indicate the need for professional intervention. But many behaviors (those next to the question mark) are often difficult to assess.

In the chapters that follow I offer "content" discussion of adolescent problems that should help clarify this question. However, when an actual decision is needed on whether to make a referral, I have found that the best way to respond is to ask oneself a series of questions about the adolescent. Rarely does the response to one of these questions provide an adequate guideline, but when all questions are addressed, they usually provide the necessary perspective that en-

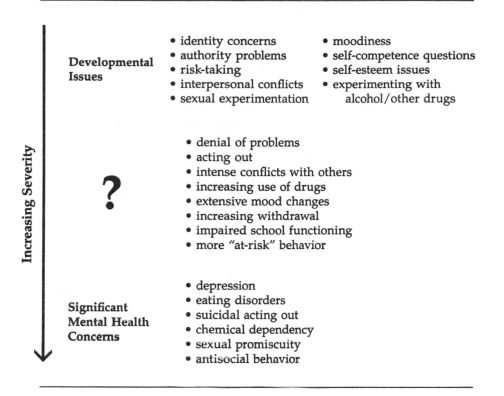

ables one to determine if the adolescent is in need of professional help. These questions are as follows:

1. How much psychological discomfort, hurt, or pain is the adolescent experiencing?

2. Is this discomfort, hurt, or pain getting worse? How so? How do you know this?

3. What are issues expressed by this adolescent that are a cause for concern? Be as *specific* as possible and describe the issues in behavioral terms. In other words, what are the behaviors that I am concerned about?

4. How *serious* are the issues discussed in number 3 above?

5. What supports and resources does this adolescent have? (A rule of thumb here is that supports and resources such as healthy peer relationships or personal talents can buffer to some degree the adolescent's difficulty. Consequently, the adolescent with few supports or resources will have more difficulty dealing with problematic issues).

6. Are the problems getting worse?

7. What will be this adolescent's situation in six months or a year if no professional assistance is sought? (In many instances this is an excellent question to ask the adolescent: "John, what do you think you will be like in six months if you don't talk with someone?")

8. How does this adolescent compare with other adolescents you know who might be experiencing similar difficulties?

9. What do others say?

If there are several adults concerned about the adolescent, then a profitable exercise is for them to discuss some or all of these questions among themselves. If all of these questions are addressed, then a reasonable answer to the question of the necessity of a referral can usually be ascertained.

When a referral is made some adults feel guilty because they believe they have let the adolescent down and that they should have been more able to help the adolescent. This is an all too frequent response of many adults in youth ministry. A way to deal with this feeling is to reflect on the meaning of the word "professional." One characteristic of a professional is to know one's limits. That is, professionals have an adequate grasp of their abilities and do not exceed them. Thus, instead of feeling inadequate or guilty, the adult should think something like the following: "I am a responsible professional, and this means I must act professionally. In this particular situation I have judged it is in the adolescent's best interest that she be referred so that she is provided the care she needs." Adults who have lingering doubts about making a referral need to reflect on boundary questions and what their motives are in working with adolescents (e.g., to be the one who rescues).

Sometimes adolescents will be hesitant or even hostile to a suggestion regarding referral. In such instances, I have found the best approach is to let them know how much you care about them and that it is out of this care that you are suggesting a referral. For example, a statement like, "I really care about you, Cindy, and it seems to me that to be true to the care I feel for you I need to make a referral." Again, emphasize care and allow the adolescent to specify her concerns about talking to a mental health professional or her fears of abandonment. Reassure her that you are still available to talk to her, but let her know that someone else must also be part of her care.

Structure for Counseling

As noted previously, there are many different formats for the pastoral counseling of adolescents. The following are general guidelines.

1. Have knowledge of the adolescent. Use the "initial overview" discussed at the beginning of this chapter as a guide. Ask yourself: "What do I need to know about this young person?" or "How would I describe this adolescent?" "What might be missing in my description?"

2. Have knowledge of the adolescent's problem. Ask yourself the following: "What are the major problems this adolescent is experiencing?" Provide feedback to the adolescent regarding the problem and see if she would describe it the way you do.

3. Utilize the "Adult as Questioner" section in chapter 1 (see above p. 26). Focus on problems, developmental issues, values, and mental health concerns. Remember all four levels are important to assess.

4. Have a stance that is inviting, respectful, and empathic. Communicate to the adolescent that you care about him or her as a person.

5. Try to spend a few moments focusing on the future. Help the adolescent strategize about "what to do" the next time the problem or issue arises.

Helping Adolescents Make Decisions

Adolescents are bombarded with numerous decisions that occupy their time. Unfortunately, and for a variety of reasons, many adolescents find decision-making difficult. The following basic rules may prove helpful.

1. Encourage the adolescent to define the decision as an *issue* that must be addressed. Be as concrete as possible.

2. Reflect with the adolescent on her *goals*. Ask her what she hopes to accomplish with this decision. For example "Okay, Linda, let's say it turns out the way you want it. What would you say you've accomplished?" Reflect with her on the appropriateness of her goals. Are they realistic? healthy? unhealthy? obtainable? idealistic?

3. Frame the decision in terms of *identity-building*. What does the decision or its outcome say about Linda? Reflect with her on the importance of her decision. What is she learning about herself as she makes this decision? Why is it important? How might she be a better Christian because of this decision? Does this decision help her to be who she really desires to be?

4. Reflect with her on various *alternatives*. Go over various options with her. What are the pros and cons or advantages and risks of each option?

5. What are other *factors* that are influencing this decision? For example, is there pressure from the peer group, parents, cultural environment? Are there internal factors such as loneliness that make the decision so important? Adolescents are often unaware of these "hidden" pressures.

6. Reflect with the adolescent on what *other* decisions might have to be made or are influenced by this decision. Many times adolescents fail to discern the chain reaction that one decision creates.

At times adolescents might try to get the adult to make the decision for them. A question adolescents sometimes ask the adult is: "What would you do?" A crucial task for the adolescent is to develop the capacity for mature adult decision-making; making decisions is the basis for healthy identity growth. Answering such a question can cheat the adolescent of an opportunity for growth. When adolescents ask me this question I usually respond with something like, "I appreciate your seeking my opinion, but you know this is a decision you need to make. Nonetheless, I'm happy to help you find a solution." At the same time the adult should be more than a passive sounding board for various options. Adults should not hesitate to guide adolescents with questions that lead them to consider seriously Christian values and sound psychological growth. Further, the adult should not hesitate to point out or express opinions about choices that impair psychological health, are sinful, or compromise Christian values.

Anger

In the developmental quest that adolescents undertake, there are bound to be times when adolescent behavior brings reactions from parents that trigger anger in the young person. Adolescents are attempting to sort out a variety of needs and desires as well as cope with everyday disappointments, frustrations, and conflict. All in all, the interplays of developmental needs, situational demands, and ongoing transitions inevitably provoke reactions that range from periodic upset and brooding to angry outbursts or even physical aggression.[2] Because anger is such a significant emotion in the adolescent's life, it is important to discuss it as well as explore ways to help them deal with it.

Anger is loosely defined as an internal state reflecting a response to being hurt. Usually this "hurt," whether perceived or actual, is caused by someone who is significant in the adolescent's life, a family member, a peer, or an adult in an authority position. Anger, then, is an "interpersonal event." It involves two or more people, and in this interpersonal situation someone feels "wronged." Take a moment and reflect on instances in your life when you have felt angry. Do they not usually revolve around significant people in your life who have in some way hurt you?

Responses to Anger   There is a wide range of responses to the emotion of anger.

1. Yelling back or screaming are typical responses of adolescents when anger is intense. For adolescents with poor impulse control, physical aggression is often a response. From a developmental perspective, this response is most apt to be seen in early adolescents and less frequently in middle adolescents, with late adolescents showing this response least of all.

2. Some adolescents respond by sulking, which often includes chronic complaining.

3. A quite common response is passive-aggressiveness. Forgetting to do something or showing up late are passive ways to show anger. For many adolescents doing poorly in school is a way to "get back" at parents who have high aspirations for their child. Such adolescents know how to provoke their parents and employ behaviors that trigger angry parental responses.

4. Adolescents who are uncomfortable with their anger might evidence chronic tension.

5. Another response is to become a "victim" and take on a feeling of righteousness.

6. Some adolescents obsessively ruminate about their anger and find difficulty in getting rid of such thoughts. In more extreme cases revenge or "getting even" is part of the pattern.

7. For some adolescents who find it difficult to cope with anger, medication becomes the preferred remedy. "Doing drugs" (alcohol or other chemical substances) is a way some adolescents medicate their hurt; in effect, they block out their pain.

8. Illegal activities such as stealing are at times engaged in by youths who do not know how to cope with their anger.

9. At times adolescents might displace their anger onto someone else. For example, anger toward a parent can be taken out on another authority figure, e.g., a youth leader or teacher.

Constructively Dealing with Anger   It is impossible to avoid anger; this emotion is part of everyone's life. The key to managing anger is not to avoid it (though not to look for it either!) but rather to find ways to deal with it. We sometimes have a right to be angry. Further, there are some things we should be angry about (e.g., serious injustice done to ourselves or others). Certainly the Jesus of the Gospels was able to show this emotion, yet was able to maintain a healthy balance that did not allow his feelings to consume him. The key is to acknowledge such feelings without allowing them to embitter us or make us cynical or unable to reach out to others. How do we help adolescents deal with their anger? The following are some suggestions:

1. Always let adolescents have time to talk the situation out. Identify the situation, the people involved, and what was done. Provide feedback to the adolescent that you "hear" what she said. Summarize what she says so she knows that you understand the situation she has described. With early adolescents it is especially important to be very concrete. After the facts have been discussed, I have found it helpful to use what I call a "third-party technique." Let us say that Megan has shared with you what happened between her and Cathy. After discussing the situation I ask, "Megan, I hear what you're saying. Some people really have strong feelings such as anger after being hurt by a friend. I'm wondering what you're feeling because of this problem with Cathy?" The advantage of this approach is that it allows you to address anger in an indirect way. I have communicated to the adolescent that it is okay to feel anger and that some people do indeed have this feeling. This technique works well when you sense that the adolescent is uncomfortable with her angry feelings. If the anger is obvious or I believe that the adolescent is not uncomfortable, then I simply inquire about her feelings, e.g., "What did you feel when this happened?"

2. Sometimes adolescents are hesitant about displaying anger toward parents. Generally speaking, I do not believe it is the mission of the adult to stimulate such reactions in young people. On the other hand, one goal of pastoral counseling is to help youth to be aware of their feelings and how such feelings influence their spiritual and moral growth. In such instances I would use the third-party technique discussed above.

3. Adults will encounter adolescents who are in difficult family situations. Youth in chemically addicted families or families with a history of abuse or neglect are often filled with immensely ambivalent and intense feelings, including anger or even rage. Adults must be aware that they cannot alter the adolescent's family. In most instances, there is little the adult can do to change the situation the adolescent is faced with. In such instances, the adult should exercise a listening and suggestive role. By listening I mean being a forum for the adolescent to share his feelings. At the same time the adult should explore and encourage positive activities and relationships. In such difficult family cases, it is helpful to do an inventory of how the adolescent spends a day or week and to note particularly what positive and healthy activities take place. A good image is a magnet.

In a difficult home environment, an adolescent is often faced with problematic situations and intense feelings. Such occurrences often "pull" the adolescent toward certain negative reactions. By encouraging positive activities and relational encounters, the adult offers an alternative set of experiences that "pull" on positive emotions. In other words, though the adult cannot "fix" the adolescent's home environment, she can suggest an alternative set of time investments that are healing and growthful for the adolescent, or at least a buffer from intensely felt negative experiences.

4. With older adolescents two strategies may prove beneficial. First, note the extent to which the adolescent can understand the point of view of the person she is angry with. Rarely are situations totally one-sided and only one person's fault. Let the adolescent share her side of the story and what is going on. Then ask what the adolescent thinks was going on in the life of the other person. For example, in a situation where a daughter is angry with her mother, I might ask, "I understand your anger, Hillary. I'm wondering what your mom's situation was at the time of the argument?" Through gentle probing of the adolescent's view of the other, we often discover pressures in the other person's life that we can focus on. Or the adolescent may come to realize that some of her anger arises from misinterpretation of the other's motive or situation. Look for the adolescent's capacity to take the perspective of the other as a sign of developmental maturity. Conversely, an adolescent who focuses solely on anger and is unwilling to take another's perspective exhibits immaturity.

A second strategy is to appeal to the idealization we spoke of when discussing conscience in chapter 1. Talk with the adolescent about his anger and acknowledge the feelings he expresses. At an opportune moment shift the discussion to the future. For example, "Bob, I understand your angry feelings. What I'm wondering is what is going to happen in the long run if they simply linger and fester?" We are appealing here to the idealizing desires of the adolescent — to be a "good" son, "good" friend, etc. In other words, help Bob to address the question of whether this is really who, in the long run, he desires to be. It is all right to be angry, but it is not what we desire to be. This appeal to a "deeper desire" helps to counterbalance the anger the adolescent might feel and tends to mitigate the corrosive effects of lingering negativity that all too often are expressed through cynicism and bitterness.

A variation of this strategy is simply to reflect with the adolescent on how his anger affects other areas of his life. How does anger toward one parent influence his relationship with the other parent? How does anger toward this friend affect relationships with other friends? Explore the effects of anger on other significant people and important activities in the adolescent's life.

5. An interesting question arises with adolescents who are dealing with very negative feelings toward a substance-abusing parent. Though forgiveness is certainly the Christian's obligation, sometimes forgiveness *at a particular point in time* is not yet possible. To forgive prematurely can represent a violation of one's integrity and is, in reality, a falsehood. Such premature forgiveness can reflect unresolved developmental issues rather than any authentic forgiveness. In such unfortunate incidents the following might be helpful. Acknowledge the adolescent's anger and hurt. Do not expect what is not yet possible. As noted above, encourage positive activities and relationships and explore how such hurt and anger affect other areas of the adolescent's life. Utilize a developmental time frame and reflect with the adolescent how she has gotten deeper insights or changed her views over time (the first identity characteristic noted in chapter 2; see above p. 38). Suggest that since her experience demonstrates that change does take place, there might come a time when she will experience her parent in a more complex light. However, at the present time continue to *respect* her feelings. Of course adolescents who express intense rage or continual anger and hostility are often in need of professional assistance, and the adult should not fail to suggest such interventions when appropriate.

6. When we began our discussion, we noted that anger is an emotional response that usually results from interpersonal situations. The angry adolescent often feels hurt by some significant other (e.g., parent, friend). After the adolescent has had time to express his feelings, it is sometimes helpful simply to ask, "Dan, how do you hurt?" or "When people are angry they are often hurting. I wonder how _____ has hurt you?" Explore these hurt feelings with the adolescent. Inquire if there are other times he has been hurt or if others besides this person have hurt him. In such instances the emotion of anger is best envisioned as a protective core that insulates the adolescent from more hurt.

Self-esteem Issues

One of the "hottest" topics in therapy and educational circles today is self-esteem. Numerous workshops and seminars focus on how to provide self-esteem to children and adolescents. It is not surprising that self-esteem has emerged as a significant psychological issue for youth. The emotional wear and tear of family dysfunction, marital breakups, and violence no doubt play significant roles in youth's feelings about the self. These feelings are exacerbated by the developmental insecurities of this stage as well as by the powerlessness that many adolescents feel. Self-esteem is best defined as a sense of self-appreciation or felt sense of inner goodness. Self-esteem reflects the legitimate valuing one places on self. Note that this feeling is different from a narcissistic focus on self. Healthy self-esteem reflects feelings that allow one to develop in adaptive and healthy ways. It fuels healthy attachment bonding and productive goal-setting. On the other hand, narcissistic feelings of self-aggrandizement tend to cover up feelings of inadequacy.

For the adolescent, low self-esteem tends to emerge from families in which the parents:

1. expect perfection from the adolescent;
2. neglect to set limits on the adolescent's behavior;
3. fail to provide positive feedback;
4. don't listen;
5. reject their adolescent;
6. provide inadequate or dysfunctional role models;
7. are unable to help the adolescent cope and adapt to cultural changes;
8. force the adolescent into a pattern;
9. allow procrastinating in the adolescent (poor task completion).[3]

Interesting findings have emerged with regard to gender and self-esteem. According to one national survey, there are only small differences between young girls' and young boys' sense of self-worth, but by adolescence "girls experience a significantly larger drop in self-esteem than boys."[4] This change in adolescent girls' self-esteem probably reflects cultural pressures that focus on an abnormally slender body image (and the vast number of girls who simply cannot live up to such unrealistic stereotypes) and the feedback from teachers and other significant adults who tend not to "believe in" girls' ability as much as boys. Thus the message to girls is that "you can't do it," which creates a negative self-image. Girls learn to doubt their own abilities. Adolescent girls, as a consequence, learn to devalue their own feelings and desires. Interestingly, in one study Hispanic females fared the worst in self-esteem when compared to African-American and white adolescent girls. African-American females' self-esteem was more resilient than that of their white counterparts, but they developed more negative attitudes toward schooling.[5]

Though I applaud school efforts to instill self-esteem in youth, I wish to offer two cautionary notes to the "self-esteem movement."

First, we must not operate under the erroneous assumption that we can always have high self-esteem. Disappointment, frustration, failure, and setbacks are part of everyday living. All individuals have self-esteem problems — simply because we are *human*. None of us does everything well nor are we always accepted and attended to by people we deem significant. In other words, we are bound to be disappointed; it is a natural experience in everyday living. The question that should be asked is this: When does low self-esteem begin to impede the adolescent's healthy functioning? It is to this issue that our efforts at building self-esteem should be directed.

Second, heaping lavish praise or compliments on every adolescent's efforts is misguided. It is not that praising youth is wrong, but if it is done indiscriminately and excessively it becomes hollow. A vital ingredient for adolescent self-esteem is the capacity to cope with frustration and disappointment and to achieve self-mastery and goal-setting skills. Thus the adolescent who can problem-solve, assess situations realistically, master tasks, and cope with disappointment and failure is apt to sustain a healthy self-image. Such adolescents are most likely to show the self-confidence needed to persevere and achieve their goals.

1. One way to assess the level of self-esteem is to ask the adolescent to complete the following sentence, "I like myself because...." Psychiatrist Jim Gill notes that responses to this question generally reveal one of four attitudes that people have about themselves: (*a*) what they are, (*b*) what they do, (*c*) what they make, (*d*) what they have.[6] Answers to this question often reflect external sources of support. Adolescents often find their self-image not in who they are but in what they have or do. One way to help adolescents to deal with a self-esteem issue is to bring up important life situations, such as experiences in the family, experiences with friends, or personal experiences that provide a sense of enhancement. Adults should help adolescents consciously articulate these enhancing moments in their lives. Adults can also share their positive acceptance of the adolescent, thus contributing to the adolescent's self-enhancement.

Adults can encourage adolescents to probe their own experience of God's love for them. As 1 John 4:10 notes, "Love, then, consists in this; not that we have loved God but that he has loved us." What is uppermost is not our love for God, but God's love for us. We are accepted for who we are; God loves us first for what we are, not for anything that we accomplish.

2. The single best approach to enhancing self-esteem in youth is to foster identity growth. Adolescents who engage in consistent development of their identity are most likely to feel integrated, complex, and responsible. Such adolescents have a sense of self-mastery

and adequate levels of self-knowledge. The adult should be familiar with the characteristics of healthy identity acquisition outlined in chapter 2. When working with an adolescent keep in mind these characteristics and focus on the suggestions in chapter 2 to foster this identity growth.

3. One way to address self-esteem issues is to help the adolescent focus on gifts. St. Paul's theology of gifts (1 Cor. 12:4–11 and Rom. 12:6–8) addresses the Spirit's working in each of us. Reflect with adolescents on the significance of gifts and help them name their gifts. For St. Paul, an essential feature of the gifts we possess is their use. They are not to be used solely for personal benefit, but rather, to build up the Christian community. Explore with adolescents how their gifts are being used.

Distorted Thinking Patterns

In chapter 2 we outlined a basic overview of adolescent dysfunction. Dysfunction in adolescence was linked to impaired attachment patterns. Yet, in addition to this emotional component flowing from attachment and the constellation of defenses the adolescent employs, there also exists a distinct set of thinking patterns. One's life history leads to specific interpretations of the world. Given that no one's life history is without stress or some degree of disappointment, failure, and trauma, within each of us there develop faulty interpretations of the world and distorted thinking patterns. Some theorists of emotional dysfunction stress that thinking patterns are the source of emotional upset. Thus, if one can make the client aware of these cognitions, then emotional upset will be lessened.

One school of psychology maintains that we employ irrational ideas in our everyday functioning and such ideas set us up for great emotional distress. Psychologist Albert Ellis observes that such "irrational" ideas contribute to the fact that no person is mentally healthy at all times. According to Ellis,

> I am still haunted by the reality, however, that humans — and I mean practically all humans — have a strong biological tendency to needlessly and severely disturb themselves and that, to make matters worse, they also are powerfully predisposed to unconsciously and habitually prolong their mental dysfunctioning and to fight like hell against giving it up.[7]

Through our life histories there is a large set of irrational ideas that each of us constructs. Over the years of working with young people in a variety of pastoral and clinical settings, I have found the following to be commonly held irrational beliefs.

1. Everyone has to like me.
2. I should be able to handle this role (e.g., son/daughter, athlete, student) without making mistakes.
3. I need to live in a family that is perfect.
4. Everything about my family is wrong.
5. My friend has to be perfect and concerned about me all the time.
6. No one really understands me.
7. Everyone is aware of what I am feeling and thinking.
8. If it doesn't turn out this way (e.g., a relationship with a certain person, being accepted to a certain college or graduate school) my life will be a disaster.
9. There is a perfect solution to every problem.

Operating on only a few of these irrational premises or similar ones sets the stage for frustration and disappointment. Who could live with such absolutes and be content? Yet it is remarkable how often all of us (adults as well as adolescents) seem to adopt such frustration-inducing ideas.

When working with adolescents, I often point to such underlying premises as a major source for their feelings. A good strategy here is gently to mention one of the irrational ideas you suspect the adolescent might be operating under. For example, if the adolescent is expressing frustration about a relationship with a friend, I might suggest "Do you think your friend *always* has to be interested in you and aware of your feelings?" In posing the question refer to the absolutes contained in the adolescent's premise, e.g., "should," "always," or "have to." Sometimes I will add something like, "You know, no one *always* bats a thousand." It is important to stress how such thinking makes life difficult and even damages the capacity for living a healthy emotional life. In other words, help the adolescent to see the emotional toll such thinking takes. Point to the consequences such thinking has on the adolescent's life. It is also important to frame the discussion in terms of love. That is, how does such thinking hinder the adolescent's capacity to love himself or herself as well as to relate to others in a loving and caring way. After all, disappointment and frustration impede one's desire to respond lovingly to others.

Other theorists in the cognitive school emphasize the role of distorted cognitions (also called "cognitive dysfunctions" or "cognitive errors") in burdening our attempts at healthy emotional living. These "mental traps" can be the source of great emotional upset. A few of the common cognitive distortion are given below.

1. All or Nothing Thinking   Everything has to be one way or the other or something has to be perfect or there is a problem. A characteristic in this approach is the lack of tolerance for ambiguity. Example: The adolescent must get accepted by a particular college or date a particular person or he considers himself a failure. (Note: this is a very common error employed by perfectionistic high school and college students: "I must get an 'A' or I am a failure.")

2. Magnification   We blow something out of proportion. Example: After failing to make the team or doing poorly on a test the adolescent feels she is a failure.

3. Tunnel Vision   We acknowledge only those things that fit our state of mind and ignore other equally important things. Example: A son upset with his mother focuses exclusively on negative traits of his mother and ignores his mother's positive features.

4. Overgeneralization   Something negative becomes the script for everything else. Example: Rejected by one peer group, the adolescent generalizes that no one at the school will like her.

5. Selective Abstraction   Focusing on one incident or statement, we ignore the entire context of the situation or discussion. Example: A college sophomore in the residence hall is sitting around late at night in the dorm with a group of friends. One friend describes to the group the baseball game played earlier in the day that this sophomore played in. The next day the sophomore can think only about one particular statement that he takes as a criticism of him and ignores the rest of the previous night's discussion.

6. Subjective Reasoning   Because we feel something strongly it must be true. Example: An adolescent is very angry with her friend; therefore, every interpretation she makes of her friend must (because of her strong feelings) be true!

Readers might profit from taking a moment to assess to what degree these cognitive errors are commonplace in their own thinking. Simply stated, we are all prone to such cognitive errors. The basic approach here is gently to point out such errors to adolescents. Because it is less threatening, I find it helpful to frame such discussion in a questioning mode. For example, I might say, "Juan, from what you just said, I wonder if you might be doing something that we call 'overgeneralizing'?" I then explain what overgeneralization is and explore the adolescent's reaction to my statement. I then encourage him to monitor his own statements to see if in the future he can "catch" such distorted thinking patterns. The adult should note that helping the adolescent "catch" such errors fosters increasing self-insight. In turn, this insight contributes to identity formation as outlined in chapter 2. Because of this newly acquired insight the adolescent "feels" more complex, one of the characteristics we identified as contributing to healthy identity growth.

Irrational ideas and cognitive errors are part of everyone's life. The adult who helps the adolescent discern the presence of a few of these irrational ideas and cognitive errors in everyday thinking has in place a very effective skill for ministering to adolescents.

An Ethical Code for Adults

Given the multiple complexities that the adult working with youth encounters, I think it wise to offer an ethical code. Three factors have coalesced to spur the need for such an ethical code.

For one, pastoral and educational ministries have undergone increasing degrees of professionalization over the past few decades. Certification, special training, and advanced degree programs are more and more the norm for working within the church, whether on a volunteer or a professional basis. The adult's ministerial endeavors are expected to be appropriately professional and to contribute optimally to the church's mission of service to God's people.

The large number of youth "at risk" of developing crippling levels of dysfunction is a second factor. A significant number of young people today suffer from emotional and behavioral problems. Yet even young people not at serious risk experience a significant loosening of supportive bonds as they progress through the childhood and adolescent years. Guidelines for adults working with youth can maximize the quality of their contact and assist them in directing hurting young people to appropriate channels of support.

Finally, we are all aware of the highly charged atmosphere surrounding allegations of sexual abuse. Such occurrences are spiritually and emotionally crippling for victims and sunder the bond of trust essential for the school or parish to carry out its mission.

The rights of youth, as well as the integrity of religious institutions, are protected by a code of ethics. Any ethical code for adults working with youth needs to address four constituencies: youth, adults, the religious institution, and the wider community. The basic guidelines proposed below respect and respond to the legitimate needs of each group.

An Ethical Code

1. *The adult who works with youth demonstrates an adequate level of ministerial, theological, and professional competence appropriate to his or her level of functioning within the religious setting.*

2. *The adult possesses an adequate knowledge of child/adolescent develop-ment appropriate to his or her level of functioning within the religious institution.*

3. *The adult makes reasonable efforts to increase personal growth and self-understanding through activities that foster healthy development and maturity.*

4. *The primary goal of the adult's relationship with the child/adolescent (as teacher, youth worker, etc.) is to foster the welfare of the child/adolescent.*

5. *The adult's relationship with the young person respects appropriate boundaries and the youth's privacy, while recognizing those instances when the welfare of the young person necessitates limits to the principle of confidentiality.*

6. *The adult is aware of the limits of his or her competence when working with youth and, when necessary, makes appropriate referrals to other professionals.*

7. *The adult understands that his or her relationship with youth is in the context of his or her relationship with the religious institution; accord-ingly, the adult is aware of his or her obligations to the rules, bylaws, and mission of the religious institution.*

8. *Whatever his or her role within the institution, the adult is committed to fostering through his or her behaviors the optimal functioning of the religious institution and of colleagues and co-workers.*

Final Thoughts

To conclude this chapter, I summarize below some approaches I have found helpful as a pastoral counselor.

1. Focus on roles. Explore with adolescents the various roles in their lives. How do they experience these roles? What values do they wish to live in each role.

2. Sometimes it is beneficial not to question the adolescent di-rectly. I will often ask the young person simply to think about something. For example, "Heather, just think about this and maybe we can discuss it in the future at some point." There is a twofold advantage to this approach. First, it shows respect for the adolescent and her freedom. Second, by asking the adolescent to "think about" something we are planting seeds for future reflection and deepening insight. (An apt image of the pastoral counselor is the Gospel image of seed planter.)

3. Help the adolescent to *identify feelings*. In particular, concen-trate on how the adolescent's feelings affect his desires and goals.

93

How are values such as forgiveness, fidelity, love, and commitment enhanced or impaired by various feelings? It is important for the pastoral counselor to reflect with the adolescent on feelings and their relationship to the adolescent value system.

4. Always show respect for the adolescent as a person. Periodically ask the adolescent, "What's your opinion about...?" Often adolescents feel powerless, and sensitivity to their views and judgments serves to enhance self-esteem.

5. Widen the context. When adolescents talk about their feelings, they often downplay or ignore wider situational pressures or environmental constraints that influence interpersonal relationships and personal well-being. Reflect with them on cultural and socioeconomic factors that might be influencing them. Also, if the situation involves an interpersonal conflict, reflect with them on what the other person was feeling and thinking as well as any pressures or constraints that person might have been under. Generally speaking, adolescents who can "step out" and see the wider view are more developmentally advanced than those caught up in the moment and their own feelings.

6. Be sensitive and encourage inquiry. Obviously sensitivity to the adolescent is the norm. An apt image for the pastoral counselor is that of an "inviter," — an adult who invites the adolescent to share feelings and thoughts on personal issues. The adult might periodically reflect on what promotes this invitation. "Why" questions should be discouraged because they can provoke defensiveness. Questions should invite responses. I have found the following inquiries helpful: "Can you help me understand...?" "Can you tell me more about...?"

CHAPTER FOUR

The Adolescent and the Family

No one lives in isolation. Definitions of human personhood invariably must address the relationship between the individual and a social system. One system to which most human beings have some relationship is family. In a sense, the family is the source for our discovery of what is human; that is, it is in the family that we first learn what it means to be human. The family provides the nurturing context for discovering those attributes so necessary for the fully developed humanness that sustains Christian discipleship. Relationship-building, conscience formation, goal planning, and capacity for love develop first within the family environment. But the family landscape is changing.

> Divorce and out-of-wedlock childbirth are transforming the lives of American children. In the postwar generation more than 80 percent of children grew up in a family with two biological parents who were married to each other. By 1980 only 50 percent could expect to spend their entire childhood in an intact family.[1]

People want their families to be healthy, secure, and productive. Individuals from dysfunctional families want the lives of their children to be different, and many parents who in childhood experienced such dysfunction go to great lengths to provide a more supportive and nurturing environment for their own children. Unfortunately, because some adults were adversely affected by such dysfunction in their own upbringing, they become less than adequate parents and pass on dysfunctional styles of relating to their own children.

The significance of the family context for the adolescent's growth cannot be overestimated. "The family plays a special role in child and adolescent development. It is the arena in which young people forge their earliest attachments, first experience separation and loss, discover the worlds of siblings, and begin their lifelong learning of social and physical skills."[2] Because of the significance of the family for the adolescent and because dysfunction is best understood when compared to healthy functioning, we will first explore the characteristics of healthy families.

The Healthy Family

Citing a wide variety of research findings on healthy families, psychologist Michele Thomas has discussed characteristics that typify healthy families.[3]

1. Commitment and Spiritual Wellness   Commitment to the family and its members is a key ingredient for healthy family functioning. Often this commitment is tied to some form of religious belief and practice. A religious outlook provides meaning and a sense of purpose in life, thereby fostering security. Also, religious practice offers ties to other individuals and groups, thus providing social bonding and support.

2. Time   Not surprisingly, healthy families spend time together. Functional families tend to make time for leisure activities and various group tasks. Another helpful support comes from establishing friendships with other families who share similar values. These families provide reinforcement for a family's values and foster the adoption of such values in children.

3. Appreciation   Members of healthy families help each other feel good by encouraging self-esteem. "In strong families, the marital partners tend to build the self-esteem of their mates by mutual love, respect, compliments, and other signs of appreciation."[4]

4. Communication   Talking and listening are vital activities for healthy families. Communication allows for the expression of feelings as well as the resolution of conflicts in healthy, productive ways.

5. Coping Ability   A crisis is an avenue for growth for family members when the family is healthy. When a crisis occurs family members work together and support one another to resolve the crisis. Healthy families are able to arrive at a perspective on a crisis that in turn allows for family and individual growth.

Another approach to healthy family functioning has been expressed by the syndicated columnist and popular writer Dolores Curran. She surveyed over five hundred professionals (educators, church leaders, health officials, family counselors, and volunteer organization leaders) and asked them what traits they perceived as most likely to be found in healthy families. The fifteen most common are listed below.

1. communicates and listens
2. affirms and supports one another
3. teaches respect for others

4. develops a sense of trust
5. has a sense of play and humor
6. exhibits a sense of shared responsibility
7. teaches a sense of right and wrong
8. has a strong sense of family in which rituals and traditions abound
9. has a balance of interaction among members
10. has a shared religious core
11. respects the privacy of one another
12. values service to others
13. fosters family table time and conversation
14. shares leisure time
15. admits to and seeks help with problems[5]

My own clinical and pastoral experience tells me that people desire the above qualities in their own and others' families. One cautionary note is that *no* family at all times manifests all the above traits. External stressors (e.g., job loss) or problems with individual family members (e.g., personal crisis, unrealized goals) can undermine some of these qualities. Like individuals, all families have their bad days. Nonetheless, healthy families, generally speaking, have more potential to exhibit the above traits, and sooner or later they actualize them, fostering the life satisfaction of individual family members as well as the family as a whole.

The Dysfunctional Family

The words "dysfunctional family" have become two of the hottest words in the popular mental health literature. There is no single agreed-upon definition of the term. Today it is used with increasing frequency by talk show hosts and writers who draw attention to the poisonous upbringing that many people undergo ("toxic parents") and the unmet needs that many people experience.

What is a dysfunctional family? From a purely descriptive perspective, the writer Pat Conroy, in his best-selling novel *The Prince of Tides,* has accurately portrayed the horror such a family generates:

> I lived out my childhood thinking my father would one day kill me.
> But I dwelt in a world where nothing was explained to children except the supremacy of the concept of loyalty. I learned from my mother that loyalty was the pretty face one wore when you based your whole life on a series of egregious lies.

> We divided years into the number of times our father hit us.
> Though the beatings were bad enough, it was the irrationality of my
> father's nature that was even worse. We never knew what would set
> him off; we could never predict the sea changes of the soul that would
> set the beast loose in our house. There were no patterns to adhere to,
> no strategies to improvise, and except for our grandmother, no impar-
> tial tribunal to which we could appeal for amnesty. Our childhood
> was spent waiting for him to attack.[6]

I define a dysfunctional family as one that impairs the emotional,
physical, intellectual, or spiritual functioning of family members and
that in turn leads to increasing life dissatisfaction and at-risk behaviors. The key word here is "impairs." Impairment is a matter
of *degree*. One might call it the ravages of original sin or the consequences of the human condition, but everyone is impaired in some
way. There is *no* person who functions perfectly across all domains at
all times. Even the healthiest of us fall short in some situations. Impairment is part of the human condition. And because families are
made of individuals who are dysfunctional, every family, at least to
some degree, is also dysfunctional.

The inability to acknowledge this fact is one of the most serious
problems of popular writing on family dysfunction. As I read much
of this literature, I sense the tacit premise that "if" only one's parents were different, then all would be okay. Wrong! As we pointed
out in chapter 1, no parent is perfect; all parents fail, as do all children. Failure, disappointment, hurt, and frustration are all part of
life. When reading this literature one senses the desire to discover a
frustration-free world. A good case in point is the frequently used
phrase "getting in touch with one's inner child." According to some,
if only this "child" had been allowed to flourish or if I could only
appreciate this child within me, then all would be fine. This idealization of the child is revealing. Most certainly children are loveable,
endearing, and a joy to be around. Yet children can also be selfish,
whining, and mean. The mistake is to idealize the child. All children, all parents, all families are *not* perfect. We all experience and
have within us some degree of dysfunction; such inadequacies are
simply part of being human. In some cases the popular literature has
gone too far, suggesting that we can eliminate such dissatisfaction
from our lives. Healthy living includes the capacity to tolerate a reasonable level of dissatisfaction. Of course what is "reasonable" needs
careful definition.

A good case in point is self-esteem. Everyone has some problem
with self-esteem. Why? Because we have all faced disappointment
from not living up to our own or others' standards, from meeting
the expectations of significant others, from being misunderstood or

misjudged, or from being found inadequate to the task. All of these situations generate self-esteem questions. Such misfortune or lack of success is typical of what it means to be human. There is nothing wrong with having such feelings. The key, again, goes back to the question of *degree.* When such feelings begin to impair our life satisfaction or foster at-risk behavior, then such issues need to be addressed and appropriate interventions made. But we should not expect to find perfect self-esteem!

The question of degree, the point at which a family or person has become significantly impaired or in need of professional help, can be difficult to determine. Certainly some behaviors, e.g., child abuse, are clearly inappropriate, and families or individuals exhibiting them need help. If a family experiences chronic problems, continuous struggle to function, or increasing difficulty in mastering appropriate developmental tasks (e.g., relationship-building, autonomy) then that family should seek professional consultation.

Another misguided popular assumption is that those who grow up in "dysfunctional" families most certainly are significantly impaired and face numerous issues that must be resolved if they are to live healthy and happy lives. Such thinking is especially prevalent in writings that feature Adult Children of Alcoholics. However, the scientific evidence we have challenges this assumption. In chapter 11, which deals with addictions, I explore this issue more fully.

By offering the above criticisms of what might loosely be termed the "dysfunctional movement," I do not wish to downplay its insights. Certainly many families are seriously dysfunctional, and many people have been psychologically scarred if not crippled in such environments. This movement has enabled us to see clearly the pain and suffering so evident, for example, in addicted and violence-prone families. I am merely maintaining that every movement is in need of critical self-assessment.

Characteristics of Dysfunctional Families

Based on my clinical work and study I consider families that manifest any of the following characteristics as dysfunction-prone.

1. Family members' boundaries are violated. Personal space and a right to privacy are infringed upon.

2. Family members' strengths (gifts) are not appreciated or encouraged. Family members have a difficult time feeling special about who they are and are plagued by self-esteem doubts.

3. Family rules are inflexible. Such families have an authoritarian style; that is, rules are arbitrarily made and enforced with no

explanation. In addition, no input into or discussion about rules is allowed the children.

4. Conflict situations are either chronic or unacknowledged. Dysfunctional families are not able to resolve family conflict in a mature manner. In many such families conflict takes the form of hostile exchanges, biting cynicism, or passive-aggressive responses. In other families conflict is never admitted and the family members enable one another through sustaining the facade of healthy functioning to outsiders.

5. There is little communication that is supportive and informative. Such families are characterized by the withdrawal and absence of family members from one another's lives.

6. Because of all the above the members experience more hurt, loneliness, and need than they can adequately handle. Unable to talk about, much less resolve, such feelings, members of dysfunctional families resort to a wide variety of behaviors such as addictions and other distractions (e.g., excessive television watching), dutifulness, self-imposed isolation, or at-risk behaviors.

Again, I wish to emphasize that all families experience some dysfunction for the simple reason that every person is to some degree dysfunctional. The significant point is the *degree* that this dysfunction prevents one from becoming a happy, healthy, and whole human being (with the realization that being consistently a happy, healthy, and whole human being is a goal we approximate but never totally achieve!).

Adolescents and Their Families

There is a myth that adolescents and their families must be engaged in ongoing conflict. The data suggest otherwise. An intriguing question, though, is why so many people believe that families with adolescents must be weathering high conflict. One explanation is that many statements about troubles between parents and their adolescent children are written by clinicians who work day in and day out with troubled youth. Their data thus consist of a biased sample and fail to take into account the large number of well-functioning youth who simply never talk (and have no need to talk) professionally with a mental health worker. Second, there are a significant number (albeit a minority) of youth who are to some degree impaired in their behavioral or emotional functioning. Recall from an earlier chapter that the figure might be as high as 20 percent. No doubt this significant number of youth can bias our perceptions. In turn, the wide publicity such troubled youth receive through the media distorts our understanding of the actual parent-child situation. I suspect that a final reason we tend to view the parent-adolescent situation as conflict is because of the ambivalence we experience toward our own younger years. Even if our own adolescence was relatively trouble-free, the acute feelings we felt during that stage of life, though typical of the adolescent period, render us less than fair in assessing how adolescents and their parents function within the family system.

What do the data tell us? The vast majority of adolescents do not experience their home lives as chronically troubled nor are they at significant odds with their parents over values. Most certainly conflict does exist. But such conflict is more apt to be over personal lifestyle issues or lesser concerns, such as curfew hours or dress codes; further, such conflict is not emotionally crippling nor does it impair the adolescent's everyday functioning. There are several reasons why conflicts do occur in the adolescent years. Adolescents are coming into their own. Their self-understandings are more and more psychologically based.[7] As a consequence, they feel and think more deeply about issues and personal concerns. In addition, these concerns are now experienced within a newfound need for autonomy and self-identity. As a consequence, they prefer to make their own decisions and set their own goals. Finally, the experience of the peer group provides a safe haven to express their desires for autonomy, which inevitably clash with what is perceived as an overly regulated home.[8]

In a fascinating study, psychiatrist Stuart Hauser and his colleagues studied the possibility for maturing ego functioning of adolescents in the context of everyday family dynamics. Their findings offer a well-focused approach to studying how families with adolescents function. By monitoring adolescent conversation with their parents over various issues, Hauser was able to conclude that "there is no single path of adolescent ego development along which progress is simply promoted or retarded. A variety of paths are possible, stretching from the profoundly arrested to the accelerated. Our portraits of family members and accounts of how they speak with one another are organized around four of these developmental trajectories."[9]

The first developmental pathway is what Hauser terms "profoundly arrested ego development." The family environment that fosters this impoverished form of ego development (though no doubt numerous factors contribute to such arrested development) has the following characteristics. Parents are often at odds with one another with irritable and mean-spirited comments exchanged between the spouses. Family members seek to distance themselves from one another by ignoring one another's feelings. There is little discussion and no attempt among the members to get to know the ideas of other family members. Little respect or appreciation is shown member's feelings. There is an explosive quality to these families' discussions; the adolescent is often unable to contain his or her acute feelings. Though Hauser does not say this explicitly, such families show strong similarity to the typical portrayal of dysfunctional families. Certainly, such families do not exhibit the healthy characteristics noted earlier in this chapter.

The second pathway of ego development is termed the "steady conforming ego" type. The family context for these adolescents is one of status quo and conformity. These families exhibit pressure to follow the espoused family line. Members who deviate face rejection from other family members. Ambiguity in these families is viewed as threatening. As Hauser notes, "The important point is that, when challenged by uncertainty and change, the members of these families consistently related in ways intended to restore the previous order: prematurely ending discussions, distracting one another, or abruptly withdrawing from ongoing conversation. These families opposed any apparent differentiation of individual members, whether adolescent or parent, and discouraged exploration, curiosity, or new moves of any kind."[10]

Unlike these first two family environments of arrested ego development, the other two pathways both showed movement toward advanced ego functioning. One group was "progressing," while the last group demonstrated "accelerated" ego development. The family experience for both these growth-oriented groups was markedly distinct from the first two family group experiences.

These families had conversations that encouraged empathic expression and curiosity. There was consistent support for personal expression of views and increasing individuality. These families most certainly had conflicts, but they were conflicts that could be faced openly and worked through rather than avoided or ignored. Members in these families actively listened to one another; this engagement sustained further questions and discussions. Hauser also noted that in these families parents, at appropriate times and for appropriate reasons, engaged in personal self-disclosures. Family discussion generated these self-revelations. Being both timely and appropriate, this sharing enhanced discussion and bonding among family members. Nor was such self-disclosure manipulative; that is, it arose naturally out of the conversation at hand rather than being a veiled attempt by a parent to find pseudo-intimacy with the adolescent or subtly enlist him or her to take sides in the parent's conflict with a spouse.

Hauser's work is helpful in showing the importance of family context for the adolescent's development. From the family the adolescent learns how to perceive, interact with, and interpret the world at hand as well as to envision how the self will negotiate the future. Not unexpectedly, varying family environments foster differing developmental paths.

What does research indicate concerning parent-adolescent conflict? We know that as children go through adolescence they begin to believe that some areas of life, such as choice of friends and styles of dress, fall more under their own domain. On some issues they begin to believe that they, rather then their parents, should be able to call the shots, so to speak. This diminishment in the scope of parental authority can set the stage for parent-adolescent conflict. On the other hand, most adolescents still recognize the right of parents to have moral authority and responsibility for general family rules.[11]

Another study found "adolescent-parent conflicts occur mostly over the everyday, mundane details of family life: doing the chores, getting along with others, regulating activities and interpersonal relationships, appearances and doing homework."[12] It appears that parents tend to view these "details" as under their authority as parents whereas adolescents increasingly see any interference with such details as infringements on their personal right to decide what they wish to do. All in all, conflict in households appears to increase as the child enters adolescence. Such conflict should be interpreted as a normal part of the adolescent's development and reflects developmental changes common to this period of life. Families that experience intense and pervasive conflict, however, generally do not reflect developmental transitions but rather more psychologically troubled states.[13]

In a related manner, psychologists James Youniss and Jacqueline Smollar offer some illuminating findings regarding the relationships that adolescents have with their parents. Daughters generally tend to view their fathers as authority figures. Conversations tend to center on directives, rule-making, obedience, and advice on tasks or future goals; though encouragement is provided, this support lacks emotional investment. Girls tend to view their relationships with mothers as more intimate. They are more willing to confide in their mothers about personal issues. For daughters, relationships with mothers are more complicated than relationships with fathers. The mother-daughter bond centers on issues of authority, conflict, intimacy, and equality. Mothers are authority figures with whom the adolescent can share as well as experience conflict.

Adolescent sons' relationships with their fathers center on activities. Fathers are people sons do things with. There is respect but distance in the father-son relationship. Fathers are viewed as authority figures and offer guidance. Mothers also provide advice but are available for sharing of confidences as well as for emotional support. All in all, the differences in relating to each parent are the same for adolescent sons as they are for adolescent daughters; however, the differences between the way the daughter relates to her mother and to her father are more extreme than between the way the son relates to his mother and to his father.[14]

The Single-Parent Family

One area of increasing worry among mental health professionals and scholars who study American family life is the increasing number of single-parent families. No doubt many single parents strive heroically, and at times under the most adverse conditions, to create a nurturing home environment for their children. Nonetheless, the obstacles for many single-parent families are daunting. In American society today many children spend less time with their parents, and there is an increase in father-absence. Many children have their needs placed second to those of adults, and with many families there are weakening parental bonds that often end in divorce. Furthermore,

> a variety of different kinds of studies — from large statistical analyses to in-depth interviews — have suggested that such changes, in turn, are a central cause of rising individual and social pathology in our society: delinquency and crime (including an alarming juvenile homicide rate), drug and alcohol abuse, suicide, depression, eating disorders, and the growing numbers of children in poverty.[15]

Another problem not unrelated to the precipitous rise of the single-parent family is that of gangs and cults. For some adolescents gangs provide a substitute for the family. Gangs offer a ready identity that provides the adolescent with meaning and purpose. Further, gangs enhance self-esteem and allow the adolescent to feel powerful. As long as social institutions such as families, churches, and cities fail to meet the needs of youth and do not offer secure forms of meaningful attachments and connection, gangs will proliferate and undermine the social fabric of society and the future of youth.

Multicultural Families

With the increasing cultural pluralism that accompanies demographic changes in the adolescent and young adult population, it is important that adults be aware of family cultural differences.[16] Let us look at the major cultural groups in the United States.

African-American Families   The adolescent African-American population approaches 14 percent of the total adolescent population. Though a majority live in two-parent families a sizeable number live in one-parent households. Family roles in African-American families are more flexible than in white families, with parents taking on multiple roles rather than simply the gender-based roles more typical of white families. In addition, the African-American family appears to be more extended than its white counterpart. In African-American families relatives such as grandparents, aunts, and uncles often assume caretaking and parenting roles to a degree not seen in white families. Interestingly, research data indicate that African-American adolescents have self-esteem levels similar to those of whites. It might well be that family structure contributes to this.

Hispanic Families   Roughly 8 percent of American adolescents are of Hispanic origin, though this percentage will increase rapidly in the next decade. Hispanic families are traditionally patriarchal. Fathers tend to be decision-makers while mothers are designated as caretakers for children. The role of mothers and daughters is typically restricted, though employment outside the home provides some freedom and status. Traditionally, males in Hispanic households are allowed more freedom than females. The family structure is also hierarchical with older members (e.g., siblings) taking responsibility for younger members.

Asian-American Families   Only about 1 percent of American adolescents are Asian-American, but their overall number will rise rapidly in future years. The typical Asian-American family is both hierarchical and traditional, with fathers exercising primary authority. Asian-American family members are socialized to place priority on family concerns over individualistic needs and desires. Duty and containment of feelings are valued in Asian-American families. The loyalty to family at times creates difficulty for Asian-American adolescents, who are caught up in a cultural conflict between allegiance to their family and the individualistic emphasis on rights and sharing feelings so commonplace in American society.

Native American Families   Adolescents of Native American origin make up less than 1 percent of the adolescent population. Native Americans often have a widely extended two-family system. They are often poorly assimilated into white culture and receive little help from their parents, who often are also poorly assimilated. Many Native Americans speak languages other than English. Poverty and alcoholism are long-term problems that devastate the family environments of Native Americans.

The above characteristics, of course, are only general descriptions; every family has its own unique history and experiences.

105

The Pastoral Response

1. Working with adolescents can be tremendously regressive. That is, adolescents "pull" us to relive many of our own adolescent experiences. At times we can all too easily align ourselves with the adolescent. For example, Alisha shares with an adult that she is experiencing conflict with her mother. If the adult has had such conflict with her own mother, she might all too easily relive such conflict when she hears Alisha's story and unthinkingly align herself with Alisha. In such a situation the adult might become blind to the realities in Alisha's life and relive her own adolescence through Alisha. To avoid such situations, it is important, simply, to *know* yourself. Think through the issues, secrets, and conflicts in your family of origin so that you can maintain boundaries in conversations with adolescents like Alisha. Adults in ministry whose own families experienced excessive parent-adolescent conflict, abuse, or chemical dysfunction must be particularly wary; otherwise they can lose objectivity and engage in inappropriate rescuing and boundary violations with the adolescent.

2. One of the most frustrating aspects of working with adolescents with family conflicts is knowing what to do. The simple truth is that often there are *limits* to what can be changed within the family. The adult must be concerned about raising undue expectations of what aspects of family life can be altered. It is important that this realism be conveyed to the adolescent. My own approach is to talk with the adolescent about conflicts within the family that are causing him difficulty. It is important to let the adolescent share his story and to show understanding and empathy about his situation. Ultimately, however, I also inquire about what the adolescent can do for himself and what responsibility he can take regarding his own behavior. We cannot change the behavior of others but we can take responsibility for our own behavior. I'll often say something like the following: "Adam, from what you say I realize how home life is not as happy a place as you would like it to be. You can't usually change your parents' behavior, but you can control your own actions. Tell me, what do you do that is helpful in dealing with this situation at home?"

Focus on growthful, maturing behavior whether within or outside the family. Sometimes a justice issue develops; for example, a verbally abusive parent's statements might cause the adolescent much emotional hurt. In such instances, help the adolescent to identify what behavior might be a helpful buffer to cushion the conflict. At the same time, it is important not to expect the adolescent to be able simply to disengage from the hurt or conflict. As adults, we might view the adolescent conflict as manageable and think that the adolescent is capable of drawing boundaries with parents. During the adolescent or young adult years, however, such boundary-drawing is often not possible. Relationships between parents and adolescents are affectively charged and threaded with dependency issues. We might say, "Don't take responsibility for your father" or "Don't try to rescue him," but given the adolescent's developmental stage, such statements might well fall on deaf ears. We must be sensitive to the adolescent who is attempting to work out a relationship with a parent and be aware of how complicated (as well as conflicted) such relationships can be.

3. I have often found it helpful to interject a value focus into the discussion. Besides talking about the emotional wear and tear or feelings experienced in conflicted family situations, I have found it helpful, particularly with late adolescents or mature middle adolescents, to reflect on how the family conflict is influencing values and beliefs. For example, "I wonder, Katie, how these problems you are having with your dad influence how you live your life? Have you thought about how they help or hinder your being a loving person or the person you really want to be?" Help the adolescent discern how conflict affects her being a Christian witness to the Gospel. This can be probed by reflecting with the adolescent on how conflicted feelings spill over and influence her relationships, her attitudes toward others, her investment in other types of activities, etc.

4. Nearly every adolescent goes through at least some period of conflict with parents or other authority figures. As noted above, this conflict is the result of the adolescent's increasing need for autonomy and independence and is part of the everyday process of growing up. It is helpful for the adult working with youth to have some understanding of the dynamics surrounding conflict as well as its management. Psychologist Susan Heitler has noted that when we have conflict with significant others several experiences appear automatically to transpire.[17] (It might be helpful for readers to pause for a moment to reflect on a conflict in their own lives. In this situation did any of the following take place?)

(a) We tend to see things in I-you terms. Few statements arc more defensive than "you told me...." When using "you" we naturally place the other person on the defensive, which simply sets the stage for more argumentation and conflict.

(b) Another characteristic of people in conflict is that they tend to utilize absolute terms. For example, "You *never* let me do what I want," or, "You *always* come home late." Again, such statements elicit defensiveness and prolong disputes.

(c) A third feature of people in conflict situations is that they tend to view events and people simplistically. The complexity of motives and the reality of the situation is lost. Perhaps the parent is under stress about a job situation or worried about the adolescent's grandmother or another family member. Or the adolescent might have had a bad day because of problems at school or at an athletic meet. Both the parent and adolescent are vulnerable to being misunderstood, and as a result might have less patience, leading in turn to conflict. I often encourage adolescents to reflect with a question such as this: "As you go back to last Thursday when you had the argument, can you think about what was going on that day?"

(*d*) A final feature common among people in conflict is that they tend to see the other party entirely in negative terms. The tendency is to dismiss the positive features of the other and concentrate instead solely on the negative. For example, an adolescent dismisses his parents, saying that his father simply "doesn't care at all" about him. Sometimes it is necessary to challenge such negative views. For example: "I really hear you, John, when you say your dad is insensitive and doesn't realize what you are going through. This has hurt you. Yet your view of your dad seems to be entirely negative. Do you really think he doesn't care for you at all?" But we must also hear legitimate complaints; challenging the adolescent's negativity must be done after really listening and responding sensitively to his concern.

Again the caution must be put forward that we cannot alter or control statements made by parents that have contributed to the conflict or have hurt the adolescent. But, in many instances, by helping adolescents see how their own statements and attitudes contribute to family tensions, we can help them to take control of and responsibility for what they say and do, as well as encourage positive behaviors that promote healthy development.

CHAPTER FIVE

Adolescent Stress

Few words have become more popular in the psychological literature than "stress." The father of stress research, Hans Selye, defined stress as "the nonspecific response of the body to any demand made upon it to adapt whether that demand produces pleasure or pain."[1] One should note that stress can be either positive or negative. Positive stress, known as "eustress," is a challenge or positive event; negative stress is termed "distress." Selye formulated a three-stage response of the body to stress that has become known as the general adaptation syndrome (GAS). The first stage is the alarm stage. During this stage, the body recognizes the stressor and mobilizes itself to flee or fight. In the alarm stage the endocrine glands release hormones that increase respiration and heartbeat, slow digestion, and elevate the blood sugar level — all providing a quick burst of energy that is part of the fight or flight response.

As the body continues to confront stressors, it adapts to physiological changes yet resists deterioration. The body manages to resist debilitating illness. This resistance stage, as it is called, can last for days or decades. In other words, depending upon the stressor and the body's capacity for resistance, the body will be capable of withstanding the stress it undergoes.

Eventually, however, without relief from the stressor (e.g., a change in the environmental situation), the body breaks down and illness results (e.g., an ulcer). When this happens, the stage of exhaustion has occurred.[2] A large body of research has now documented the adverse effect that stress has on the immune system.[3]

Interest in stress has spawned a significant body of research literature that has expanded considerably the original ideas set forth by Selye. Later research has focused more specifically on factors such as actual stressors that adversely affect the body, the appraisal the person makes of the stressor, and the individual's coping capacity to resist the stressor's adverse effects. Attempting to incorporate various research findings, two leading researchers define stress as "a particular relationship between the person and the environment that is appraised by the person as taxing or exceeding his or her resources and endangering his or her well being."[4]

More recently, psychologist Stevan Hobfoll has set forth a model of stress that attempts to incorporate both the realities of actual stressors and the cognitive evaluations that individuals give to stressful events. It is called the model of conservation of resources. He defines stress as

> a reaction to the environment in which there is (*a*) the threat of a net loss of resources, (*b*) the net loss of resources, or (*c*) a lack of resources gain following the investment of resources. Both perceived and actual loss or lack of gain are envisaged as sufficient for producing stress.[5]

To further elaborate on the definition, "resources" are defined as what "I value." In this model, there are four categories of resources: Object resources are physical things one values or objects that take on status because of financial expenditure (in the adolescent's case, for example, a car or stereo system). Condition resources are what one seeks: marriage, friendship, job advancement. The third category, personal characteristic resources, refers to personal resources that enable one to master effectively and negotiate successfully everyday life. The final category is energies. These include time, money, and knowledge. "These resources are typified not by their intrinsic value so much as their value in aiding the acquisition of other kind of resources."[6] Hobfoll views stress as the loss of any of the above resources, though he notes that when one experiences loss, one is apt to remedy the situation by replacing lost resources with other desired resources.

Hobfoll's model also places emphasis on one's cognitive understanding (appraisal) of a situation. For example, if a student fails an examination, he might attempt to salvage his threatened loss of self-esteem by devaluing education. The adolescent who is rejected in friendship might reinterpret the situation as an opportunity to meet other people.

I find Hobfoll's model intriguing and helpful. Adolescents are continually confronted with loss. Our goal should be to help them negotiate and deal with loss in terms of Christian values and healthy human growth.

The Adolescent Experience of Stress

We all know what happens when we are stressed for any length of time: we react. Some of the signs of stress are the following:

Physical: high blood pressure, nausea, frequent urination, perspiration, headaches, insomnia, oversleeping, digestive problems, chest pains, heart palpitations, loss of appetite, dizzy spells, back problems, fatigue.

Emotional: concentration difficulties, crying, being easily upset, anger, impatience, overactivity, moodiness, oversensitivity, restlessness, irritability.

Behavioral: nail biting, smoking, alcohol use, lessened productivity, psychomotor movements (e.g., foot shaking, finger tapping), overeating.

Adolescence offers some unique insights into stress: how it is perceived, experienced, and coped with. Below we present some major research findings in this area with an eye toward understanding adolescents' experience of stress and how concerned adults might help them come to terms with the stressors they experience.

Adolescence is a period of transition. The adolescent is experiencing new freedom and renegotiating power and control with parents. Physical and developmental changes take place that generate questions about self. Relationship issues take on an emotional intensity heretofore not experienced. In addition, societal pressures demand new behaviors and increasing accountability. All in all, these changes set the stage for a large number of life events, many of which can appear or are indeed stressful. It is unclear exactly how negative life events influence the adolescent's emotional functioning; there are many factors that must be considered. The event itself (its severity) and how it relates to other events in the adolescent's life is a factor. There are questions regarding the number of negative life events. Further, the specific strengths and weaknesses of the adolescent and the specific family system and cultural environment must be considered. For every adolescent certain specific events will prove stressful, are likely to cause emotional and behavioral upheaval (though not necessarily debilitating), and if of a sufficient intensity can impair future functioning.

Addressing the question of gender, psychologist Jeanne Brooks-Gunn asks: "How stressful is the transition to adolescence for girls?" The number of negative life events is a factor, as are relationship issues, particularly aspects of the mother-daughter bond that might lead to conflict.[7] Clearly, what is stressful for adolescent boys and adolescent girls can differ. Adolescent girls report more stressful events than males, but the impact of such events might be limited to specific outcomes, such as psychological symptoms (but not, for example, lower grades or deviant behavior).[8] Stress appears to have the same effect on different racial groups; stressful events operate in a similar pattern and increase the likelihood of negative outcome for all adolescents.[9]

Research has indicated that changes in environment (e.g., entrance into high school) that mark entry into adolescence can adversely affect behavior and mood state. Further, early adolescents manifest significantly more negative emotions, such as anger and worry, than they did in their childhood years. Their moodiness might well be explained by their deepening awareness of the world's complexity and others' feelings; in effect, early adolescents have more awareness of what can and does go wrong, thereby subjecting themselves to more hurt and disappointment.[10]

Stressful Life Events in Adolescents' Lives

Physician R. Dean Coddington has developed a life-events scale of adolescent stressors.[11] The list includes:

1. the death of a parent
2. the death of a brother or sister
3. divorce of parents
4. marital separation of parents
5. the death of a grandparent
6. hospitalization of a parent
7. remarriage of a parent to a step-parent
8. birth of a brother or sister
9. hospitalization of a brother or sister
10. loss of a job by father or mother
11. major increase in parents' income
12. major decrease in parents' income
13. start of a new problem between parents
14. end of a problem between parents
15. change in father's job so he has less time home
16. a new adult moving into the home
17. mother beginning to work outside the home
18. being told you are very attractive by a friend
19. going on the first date
20. finding a new dating partner
21. breaking up with a boyfriend/girlfriend
22. being told to break up with a boyfriend/girlfriend
23. start of a new problem with parents
24. end of a problem with parents

25. beginning the first year of senior high school
26. move to a new school district
27. failing a grade in school
28. suspension from school
29. graduating from high school
30. being accepted at college
31. recognition for excelling in a sport or other activity
32. getting a driver's license
33. being responsible for an automobile accident
34. becoming an adult member of a church
35. being invited to join a social organization
36. being invited by a friend to break the law
37. appearance in juvenile court
38. failing to achieve something very much wanted
39. getting a summer job
40. getting a first permanent job
41. deciding to leave home
42. being sent away from home
43. being hospitalized for illness or injury
44. death of a close friend
45. becoming involved with drugs
46. stopping the use of drugs
47. finding an adult who really respects you
48. getting pregnant or fathering a child
49. getting married
50. outstanding personal achievement (special prize)

The above list of life events reminds us of the diverse experiences adolescents undergo. The number of potential stressors in an adolescent's life is immense. Some life events can be violent and underscore the "at-risk" nature of adolescence, e.g., witnessing violence or a death, gang involvement, or acquiring a sexually transmitted disease. One psychology instructor who applied Coddington's scale to his urban high school concluded that the "typical" student led a life that could easily be characterized as highly stressed.[12]

Adolescents often complain of physical problems for which there is no organic cause. Adolescents who fit this category, according to one study, have often experienced a wide range of negative life events that differentiate them from other adolescents who complain of symptoms with a physical cause.[13] In other words, the study suggests a relationship between stressful events and complaints of physical illness. In this study, adolescents complaining of physical problems (whether their cause was attributable to an illness or not) reported the following negative life events most frequently (in order of decreasing frequency).

1. failing report card grades
2. arguments between parents
3. serious family illness
4. breaking up with boyfriend/girlfriend
5. death in the family
6. problems with siblings
7. arguments with parents
8. failed year in school
9. loss of a close friend
10. personal illness or injury
11. change in the family financial status
12. problems with classmates
13. change to a new school
14. teacher problems
15. divorce of parents
16. loss of job of mother or father
17. serious illness of a friend
18. brother or sister leaving home
19. moving to new home
20. death of close friend

My own pastoral and clinical experience confirm that this study along with Coddington's listing accurately portray many of the problems that youth find stressful. At the same time, adults should add other events that are specific to the adolescent population to whom one is ministering (e.g., the special concerns of minority youth or factors arising from a specific environmental setting).

College-age young adults face events and situations that are often similar to those of younger adolescents, but the nature of these experiences is such that they deserve separate discussion. One nationwide survey of stress factors in college students discovered the following.[14] Stressful events could be placed in one of four categories: home and community, school, personal issues, and relationships. Reported scores were sufficiently different for men and women students that separate listings were warranted; women's scores were higher than men's. In a table listing events cited by over 50 percent of the students, the following ten were most often cited as a cause of stress. Not surprisingly, a majority of the most cited stressful events focused on academic concerns.

1. final examination week
2. test anxiety
3. academic workload
4. making plans for the future
5. putting off assignments or responsibilities
6. financial pressures
7. grades
8. guilt for not doing better
9. managing to exercise or worrying about not exercising
10. competitiveness for grades

Other findings of the survey focused on how young adult men and women perceived the stress-level of various events. For women the top ten perceived stress-causers were as follows:

1. death of a parent
2. pregnancy or abortion
3. final exam week
4. loss of a close friend
5. breaking off a relationship
6. loss of an intimate relationship
7. divorce or remarriage of a parent
8. change in schools
9. loss of a close relative
10. test anxiety

For men:

1. death of a parent
2. loss of intimate relationship
3. final exam week
4. breaking off a relationship
5. involvement in pregnancy or abortion

6. divorce or remarriage of parents

7. selecting or changing major

8. career opportunities after marriage

9. change in schools

10. loss of close friend

The early years of college undergraduates can be a particularly stressful time. Reasons for this stress include:

1. Students (especially dorm students) have new freedoms. Students who developmentally have not acquired age-appropriate behaviors might lack the maturity to handle the freedoms that the college environment provides.

2. Academic competitiveness increases. Competition for grades can be tremendously unsettling for many students, particularly first-year students who might not be used to such an intensely competitive atmosphere or who found high school to be unchallenging. Some students realize that for the first time they are not at the top of their class. Grade competition can be especially problematic for the perfectionistic student. The ascendance of academic concerns as a major cause of stress for older adolescents can be understood developmentally. Early and middle adolescents are more invested in family and peer group whereas older adolescents increasingly define themselves by future possibilities. Moreover, youth entering college are on the whole more academically focused than the average early or middle adolescents and invest more of themselves in academic pursuits.[15]

3. Undergraduates often bring to college unnegotiated conflicts with parents or yet-to-be resolved family issues. Such conflicts can adversely influence successful adjustment to college.[16]

4. Some late adolescents clearly should not even be in college or need a period of time (e.g., a year off) before going to college. Other young adults find difficulty admitting that college or a certain major was more their parents' idea than their own.

5. Happiness in a college atmosphere necessitates getting along with others (e.g., residence hall living). Some late adolescents have deficiencies in the necessary social skills.

6. Some undergraduates are very conflicted over life goals or personal issues and display their conflicts through irritability, incessant criticism, or withdrawal.

7. Some adolescents enter young adulthood with anger. Often this is the result of family dysfunction or increasing societal pressures. Regardless of its cause, it is carried over into the college years and leads to problems in relationships.

116

8. Because of the lack of secure attachments and healthy models, some young adults have tremendous problems making and sustaining healthy relationships.

9. Drug use, particularly alcohol consumption, is always a temptation during the college years. With increased drug abuse by early and middle adolescents, these young people often enter college lacking the internal psychological resources to deal adequately with stress and relationship-building; they find the college atmosphere an all-too-easy resource for continuing such dysfunctional behavior. These young adults often evidence deficiencies in working through identity and intimacy needs and find alcohol or other drugs a distraction from healthy development.

10. Since college undergraduates are now preparing for entrance into the adult world, wider concerns, such as economic conditions, must be given greater consideration. Thus economic difficulties, most acutely perceived when employment possibilities are grim, weigh heavy on some undergraduates' shoulders, causing fear for the future.

The Pastoral Response

1. Social support has been found to be a particularly strong factor in mitigating stress. One question that adults must ask themselves is: "Does this adolescent have a bond with an adult who provides encouragement and support?" As the Carnegie Council has noted, "Every student needs at least one thoughtful adult who has the time and takes the trouble to talk with the student about academic matters, personal problems, and the importance of performing well."[17]

2. Adolescents are often prone to develop a "negative bias"; that is, they overgeneralize, viewing all events in negative ways and committing numerous cognitive distortions, e.g., magnification (see chapter 3). Adults should both challenge such negative thinking and also expand the adolescents' horizon so that they can view positive life events as well as negative ones, thus fostering a more balanced view of life.

3. Stress is very much tied to everyday behaviors. An adult can be quite helpful to an adolescent by doing an "inventory" with him regarding his everyday life. Dietary habits, exercise, social support, and prayer should all be addressed. I have found it useful to discuss an adolescent's life with her in terms of her various selves. The person is made up of a physical self, a spiritual self, an intellectual self, a relational self, etc. Go over each of these selves and reflect on how each of them is attended to and whether it is healthy. Suggest ways

that are positive and growthful to attend to each self. Another approach is to explore what "buffers" the adolescent possesses. Just as problem areas in the inventory should be identified, the adult should also aid the adolescent in discovering what positive events or actions mitigate the impact of stressful events or foster more positive feelings. Encourage the adolescent to think of the buffers she has or can acquire (e.g., other relationships, a hobby, positive use of time).

4. Sometimes a very general question such as "What concerns do you have about _____?" is helpful. Try to frame the concern in terms of the wider context of developmental needs. For example, if an adolescent finds a particular relationship stressful, talk about the problems involved in the relationship but link them to broader concerns, such as identity and intimacy. In this way the relationship becomes a source for fostering the adolescent's self-discovery.

5. Adolescents are often highly idealistic about their potential for success. This might lead them to overvalue their own abilities, believing that they can master certain situations or change certain things that in reality cannot be changed. The result is needless stress. It is important to reflect with the adolescent on what can and cannot be altered in his or her life.

6. I have found it helpful to use Hobfoll's stress model (presented earlier in this chapter) as a way to discuss issues in the adolescent's life. For example, the various "resources" that Hobfoll presents (e.g., object resources, condition resources, etc.) can be presented to the adolescent so that she might get an overview of the losses that are taking place in her life. After naming the losses or potential losses, you can reflect with the adolescent on how she deals with loss or the threat of loss (e.g., a condition resource such as a valued friendship).

CHAPTER SIX

Divorce and the Adolescent

In modern industrial societies divorce has become commonplace. "In 1990, 1,175,000 couples were divorced, and 1,045,750 children were involved in these divorces. Over the past 20 years, the proportion of people who marry three or more times increased from 4 percent of marriages to 8 percent of the total. Preliminary data indicate that children of divorce, particularly women, have a higher chance of getting divorced themselves than children of intact families."[1] For the more than one million children of divorce there is the lingering reality of the divorce's consequences. Many children suffer long-term effects from divorce, even decades after the divorce has taken place. They grow up in families where parents remain angry and so the children feel ongoing rejection. The family as commonly understood no longer exists for such children, and they must carry with them the burden of these lingering negative feelings.

Of equal concern to mental health experts are the long-term trends of family life. Demographers are divided about trends in marriage stability and marriage itself. Some believe that the number of divorces has peaked and that adult children of divorce will be more selective and committed to their marriage relationship. On the other hand, other experts maintain that adult children of divorce are themselves more likely to divorce and since these adults are now marrying, we will soon witness an even greater divorce rate. Further, one way some adult children of divorce are harmonizing their painful childhoods with their current desires to have children is, simply, to have children without marrying.[2] Regardless of what trend materializes, experts note "that by the beginning of the next decade the majority of youngsters under 18 will spend part of their childhood in single-parent families, many of them created by divorce."[3] This phenomenon has enormous sociological and psychological consequences. Equally important, divorce touches directly the young person's emerging sense of self and growing capacity for commitment. For all these reasons we need to examine the experience of divorce in the young person's life.

Reactions to Divorce

Over the past several decades social scientists have examined divorce and its effects on children, adolescents, and young adults. Let us look at these findings.[4]

1. A sense of abandonment can overtake the young child. Preschool children often feel responsible for their parents' divorce. This self-blame is associated with the child's inability to analyze accurately either the family's situation or the quality of their parent's marital relationship. Young children are powerless. As a consequence, they need the security of all-powerful parents and cannot attribute to them blame for difficulties; instead they find solace in taking responsibility for family disruption. At the time of the divorce and soon afterward regressive behaviors often appear, such as clinging to the remaining parent, sleep problems, and bedwetting.

2. Divorce is disruptive in the lives of elementary-school-age children. School-age children are more realistic and objective than their preschool peers. They respond to such loss with sadness and a variety of behavioral and emotional problems. They wonder if they will permanently lose the parent who has left. Symptoms found in such children include bedwetting, temper tantrums, moodiness, nightmares, anger. Older school-age children can also experience feelings of loneliness, heightened experiences of loss and embarrassment, and growing anger and resentment toward one or both parents. A common feeling among school-age children is fear about their well-being. Will they be abandoned by the remaining parent? What will the future hold? Preadolescent children will often display erratic behavior and become increasingly irritable.

3. A common occurrence among school-age children is academic problems. School-age children must cope with a wide variety of negative emotions that can interfere with the learning process.

4. A consensus has emerged among mental health professionals that staying together for "the sake of the children" is unwise. Children who live in highly conflicted homes are at risk of emotional damage regardless of whether the parents divorce. In some cases, divorce must be viewed as the preferred alternative to ongoing exposure to emotionally damaging discord. Nonetheless, divorce cannot be viewed as benign. Divorce is virtually always painful for all involved, and for some children the effects remain crippling for years to come.

5. How any child copes with divorce depends upon a wide range of mediating factors. When assessing the outcome of a divorce on a child the following factors should be considered: (*a*) the age of the child; (*b*) the sex of the child; (*c*) the quality of the child's re-

lationship with the custodial parent; (d) the quality of the child's relationship with the noncustodial parent; (e) the level of conflict between the parents; (f) both parents' interest in and commitment to the child's welfare; (g) the level of economic security the child can expect; (h) the psychological functioning of the parents — specifically the capacity of the parents to carry on normal parental duties and provide an emotionally secure environment for their children; (i) presence of other concerned caregivers in the child's life (e.g., teachers, grandparents).

6. The mother, who is usually the custodial parent, often experiences an increasingly burdensome state as a result of the divorce. Frequently there is an economic slide resulting in financial problems. She must often work as well as be an available mother. Often she experiences loneliness and anger and at times is unable to meet appropriately her own adult developmental needs. Increasingly under stress from disruption on so many fronts, she experiences what some psychologists call "task overload." In such circumstances the capacity to parent adequately is often impaired, leading in turn to guilt and further anxieties.

7. Earlier studies had concluded that boys, on average, suffered more from divorce than girls. This conclusion is no longer held by researchers. More recent studies have revealed that differences do exist but are a function of age and circumstance. Initially, it appears that school-age boys suffer more from the family's divorce. Boys often become disruptive and aggressive, exhibit a variety of behavior problems in the classroom, and experience increased conflict with mothers. For most boys these behaviors usually diminish with time. The mother's remarriage often has a beneficial effect on her son. The presence of an adult male figure proves advantageous. In contrast, the daughter's behavior usually does not parallel her brother's initially disruptive behavior. However, later problems can surface. Some adolescent girls experience depression and problems in their sexual relationships. Studies have found that girls from divorced homes often fear rejection from men, become involved earlier than girls from intact families in sexual relationships that are short lived, have children at an earlier age, and more frequently divorce. "Among white American women whose childhoods were marred by divorce, the divorce rate is 60 percent higher than for the general population."[5] Another finding is that while for boys the mother's remarriage and the entrance of another adult male figure usually proves beneficial, for girls this new family member often appears to foster a disruption in the mother-daughter bond, often with friction and conflict developing.

Divorce can emerge as a significant factor affecting adolescent functioning. There are several research findings that prove relevant. First, adolescents' most adverse reactions to divorce occur in the years immediately following the family breakup. Time brings about a diminution in behavioral problems, though difficulties continue to exist for many adolescents. As already noted, a growing consensus among mental health professionals is that during childhood boys are apt to experience more adverse effects of divorce, but that during adolescence girls manifest more unfavorable symptoms. "Most research has concluded that adolescent girls are affected more negatively by divorce than are their male counterparts."[6] Among the negative symptoms shown by girls are behavioral problems, diminished self-esteem, greater anxiety, and depression. Even though girls appear to be at particular risk, all adolescents are vulnerable to the emotional distress arising from family breakup.[7] In particular, serious behavior problems can emerge: drug abuse, truancy, academic problems, sexual acting out, anti-social behaviors (e.g., stealing), and negative emotional experience (anxiety and depression).

In the transition from the adolescent to the young adult years (the twenties) the findings are variable. Though it is true that divorce exerts lingering negative effects for some young adults, this cannot be said to be the case for all youth; indeed, many exhibit adequate psychological functioning.[8]

Nonetheless, divorce is painful, even for the older adolescent or young adult. In a perceptive interview with fifty young adult college students whose parents were undergoing divorce, psychologist Barbara Cain captures the trauma of this experience for late adolescents/young adults whose paths down the roads of identity and intimacy are more solidified than those of high school teens. The students reported that they were "shocked" at hearing of the divorce. One reaction was a weakening of their trust of others. "Because the divorce represented the first sobering crisis in their young adult lives, many in the study believed it marked the end of an era of trust and ushered in a new apprehension about life's unforeseen calamities. They reported an unprecedented preoccupation with death, disease and crippling disabilities."[9] Many of the students interviewed wondered aloud if they could themselves marry and avoid the mistakes of their parents, though it should be noted that most saw marriage in their future. Friendship, sibling communication, and religion emerged as the primary social supports for these students.

Of all the researchers in the area of divorce, none has achieved more prominence than psychologist Judith S. Wallerstein. Wallerstein has conducted a long-term study to measure the effects of divorce on children and (along with co-author Sandra Blakeslee) has reported her most recent findings in her well-received book *Second Chances*.

This work documents the effects of divorce on sixty families with a total of 131 children ten years after the marital breakup. Many of these subjects are now adolescents and young adults. The results of Wallerstein's findings are sobering. Over a third of the children were clearly not doing well a decade after the divorce had taken place.

One significant finding was the presence of the "sleeper effect" that many girls suffer. She writes:

> The sleeper effect primarily affects young women, in part because girls seem to fare much better psychologically immediately after divorce than boys. Because girls appear so much better adjusted socially, academically, and emotionally every step of the way after divorce, much of the research about the effects of divorce on children emphasizes the good recovery of girls compared with the more troubled experience of boys.[10]

The sleeper effect is most readily seen in the adolescent and young adult girl's inability to make a commitment or in her experiencing heightened feelings of betrayal. These young women fear commitment, for it exposes them to reliving the mistakes of their parents.

A second finding in their follow-up study was the continued impairing effects that the divorce had upon many parents' capacity to parent adequately. "The diminished parenting continued, permanently disrupting the child-rearing functions of the family. These parents were chronically disorganized and, unable to meet the challenges of being a parent, often leaned heavily on their children."[11] In such families there was often a role-reversal in which the child parents the parent. Such children became "overburdened" and lacked the normal experiences associated with happy and healthy childhoods.

Wallerstein notes that adolescence presents a particularly difficult stage for children as they attempt to address pressing developmental needs within a painful emotional environment:

> Our study shows that adolescence is a period of particularly grave risk for children in divorced families. Through rigorous analysis, statistical and otherwise, we were able to see clearly that we weren't dealing simply with the routine angst of young people going through transition but rather that, for most of them, divorce was the single most important cause of enduring pain and anomie in their lives. The young people told us time and again how much they needed a family structure, how much they wanted to be protected, and how much they yearned for clear guidelines for moral behavior. An alarming number of teenagers felt abandoned, physically and emotionally.[12]

A particularly troubling psychological effect that many adolescents experience in the aftermath of divorce is low self-esteem.

Though all adolescents experience self-esteem problems at some point during this developmental stage, adolescents from divorced homes are especially vulnerable. We quote Wallerstein and Blakeslee at length in order to understand this phenomenon and the specific role that father-absence plays in determining the adolescent's feelings:

> Low self-esteem in late adolescence is often related to unresolved psychological issues between divorced fathers and their children, in which the major strand is that the young people feel rejected, unloved, and undervalued. Children long for their fathers in the years after divorce, and those who are close to their fathers beforehand are especially preoccupied with the notion of restoring the closeness that they remember or fantasize. One of the saddest realities of the divorced family is the difficulty (although not the impossibility) of continuing earlier relationships. And one of our major discoveries ten years after divorce is that this longing is infused with new intensity at adolescence. For girls, the intensity rises during early adolescence. For boys, the need for the father crests somewhat later — at age sixteen, seventeen, or eighteen. Some young people physically search for their fathers, while others psychologically search for some explanation of why their fathers let them down. In so doing, they often interpret their fathers' neutral indifference, passivity, or insensitivity as outright rejection. Just as they are forming a separate identity in adolescence, just when they most need support and approval their self-esteem is injured by someone they love. With wings clipped, it is no wonder they cannot fly.[13]

Adolescent Coping and Divorce

The adolescent who experiences divorce faces experiences that can compromise the attempts at normal maturation. One psychiatrist notes:

> The tasks of adolescence include coping effectively with aggressive and sexual drives, the development of a stable ego and sexual identity, the development of ego autonomy, appropriate separation-individuation, establishment of a stable moral code, vocational choice, and, eventually, heterosexual object choice. Related issues concern development of peer acceptance with a sense of social belonging and comfort in heterosexual relationships.[14]

Though the above menu of tasks is written from a psychoanalytic perspective, it is helpful in pointing out the significant "agenda" that confronts every young person during this developmental phase. The adolescent must come to grips with internal needs and pressures, negotiate or redefine relationships with various individuals, and increasingly take into account societal demands for accountability on the adolescent's part.

The family breakup is problematic for the adolescent because, in the midst of carrying out these many tasks, significant psychic energy must be diverted to accommodate and work through the negative feelings associated with the divorce. In traditional psychoanalytic terms, the adolescent carries out a partial withdrawal of attachment to parents and becomes self-preoccupied. With time, this self-investment is rechanneled toward appropriate "objects" of affection (e.g., boyfriends/girlfriends, peer groups) and a reworked, more mature relationship with parents.[15] The discord of the parental divorce and the accompanying negative feelings make such developmental progressions as outlined above difficult. Loyalty conflicts, anger, and feelings of betrayal often engulf the adolescent, precluding the achievement of normal adolescent goals.

When the adolescent's family is undergoing divorce, or even when she is several years removed from a divorce that took place in her childhood years, goals to insure her healthy functioning need to be considered. Among these goals are the following:

1. The adolescent might need to acknowledge and deal with a variety of negative feelings. Some adolescents feel "used" by parents or resent what they perceive as subtle pressures to "take sides." The adolescent, on his or her own initiative, might ally with one parent against the other; this alliance is often forged with the custodial parent against the parent who has departed. Feelings of betrayal, embarrassment, and anger also frequently occur. Though the adolescent might harbor such feelings they are not necessarily acknowledged. Negative feelings might also arise from the consequences of the divorce, such as lessened family income or relocation to a new neighborhood and school.

2. Some adolescents cling to the fantasy that their parents might be reunited. Obviously such fantasies serve to allay feelings of rejection and accompanying insecurities. They serve childhood desires for security and acceptance. Adolescents need to acknowledge that the breakup is irreversible.

3. Adolescents need also to disengage as much as they can from parental conflict. A common problem for many adolescents is that they possess neither the psychological resources nor the skills to establish adequate boundaries to parental disputes. Emotionally they are drawn into parental conflicts and end up becoming upset, frustrated, and hurt over their inability to abstain from these battles.

4. Another need for adolescents is to invest in normal everyday tasks. There is a need to provide as much stability as possible as they

attempt to cope with the emotional turmoil surrounding the divorce. Help them to see what is stable and secure in their lives.

5. There also is need to encourage adolescents to be "hopeful" regarding current and future relationships. As we have seen, some adolescents wonder whether they can ever trust or be committed within a relationship after watching their own family breakup.

6. The ending of the adolescent's family also raises the issue of how the adolescent handles "loss." Adolescence itself is a time of loss as the security of childhood is shed for the yet-to-be determined adult life. In the midst of such transition, the effects of divorce can be tremendously unsettling.

In my clinical work with adolescents who have undergone the family trauma of divorce I have observed a variety of ways to cope, some healthier than others. I share these "clinical impressions."

The Quiet Adolescent: This adolescent becomes remarkably reserved, hesitant, withdrawn, and disengaged. The typical spontaneity of adolescence is not forthcoming as the young person retreats inward.

The Acting-Out Adolescent: This adolescent acts out his or her anger and upset. Truancy, drug-taking, and "risky" behaviors are often evident. Antisocial tendencies might also be displayed (e.g., breaking school rules, stealing). One gets the impression that the adolescent is trying to displace negative feelings as well as find ways to distract the self from such painful affect.

Mr./Ms. "Cool": This adolescent constructs a sometimes elaborate veneer to shield the self from the pain of family divorce. This adolescent's self-presentation is one of imperturbability. Nothing is unsettling and everything is fine.

The Attention-Seeking Adolescent: The disruptive feelings that affect adolescent-parental ties sometimes lead the adolescent to seek out other significant people to obtain affirmation. This can lead to an upsurge in boastful and attention-seeking behaviors. Such adolescents are often seeking the reassurance that they are still loveable and worthy of another's time and interest as they wrestle with feelings of parental rejection.

The Distracted Adolescent: This adolescent is best described as looking for any distraction that might come along. Attention to appropriate tasks (e.g., school assignments) is often difficult for them. They appear to be unduly influenced by novelty and the personalities of stronger peers. Thus fads and any new group activity are likely to attract their interest.

The Chip-on-the-Shoulders Approach: Some adolescents grow sullen and irritable as a result of family conflict and divorce. These young people are always "on edge." They often are hypersensitive and treat any adult intervention with suspicion. Establishing trust with such adolescents is often difficult.

Though the adolescent might employ a variety of behavioral styles as a way to handle the stresses of divorce, most adolescents, with time, are able to acknowledge at least some of the attending emotions and conflicts that accompany the divorce.

Pastoral Responses

1. Some adolescents still harbor the "perfect world fantasy," believing either that their parents will reunite or that the marriage breakup never "should" have happened. A helpful way to challenge gently this dynamic is simply to reflect with the adolescent on the existence of life's inadequacies and the imperfect nature of so many events in the world. Discussion of imperfection and disappointment provides an opening that allows the adolescent to consider that his family is also human and not perfect.

2. Allow the adolescent to express her feelings about the divorce and reassure her that having ambivalent and divided feelings is normal. The third-person technique is nonthreatening and very helpful. "Clare, when divorce happens many children have a lot of feelings, and some of them can be painful or hurtful. I wonder how it is for you?"

3. With older adolescents I sometimes ask, "What do you do with your hurt?" It is important to help adolescents realize that negative feelings affect their functioning. Encourage them to consider how anger and hurt might be affecting other areas of their lives. Pay particular attention to changes in behavior on the adolescent's part. If you notice certain behavior, provide feedback and suggest that it could be related to the divorce.

4. When divorce strikes, it can become so consuming in the adolescent's life that other events are eclipsed. Reflect with the adolescent on what is going well in her life. Encourage healthy behavior and activities that invite connection and bonding with others in healthy ways.

5. Always reassure the adolescent of your own connection to him. Explicitly state that you are there for him and are available.

6. Trusting others can often be difficult for adolescents from divorced families. Reflect with adolescents on whom they trust and why they confide in and rely on certain people. If possible, reflect with the adolescent on how trust issues might arise in future relationships because of the betrayal and hurt felt from the broken home environment or how even now the adolescent might be finding difficulty in trusting.

7. When divorce splits a family, many adolescents' hurt translates into confusion regarding the possibility for commitment, fidelity, and love in their own lives. Reflect with them on the meaning of love. I find it especially helpful to discuss love in terms of its fragile nature, its need for support, and its mystery. Allow the adolescent to be confused and perplexed, because what is happening *is* genuinely confusing and perplexing.

8. Pay particular attention to adolescent behavior and the level of pain and anger. If serious problems are resulting from either behavior or feelings, referral should be considered.

9. Parents loom large as powerful figures in the adolescent's life. When a family splits up, there is often tremendous ambivalence toward one or both parents. The adolescent desires connection with the parent, yet possesses negative feelings toward him or her. At times feelings toward one of the parents might be mostly negative. The adult might suggest that such anger is itself a sign of love. That is, we experience strong and intense feelings toward those important to us, and when such a person has hurt us, we respond negatively. Do not try to remove the adolescent's anger; rather view it as an attempt to stay connected to a significant figure who is causing the adolescent immense pain.

10. Some adults mistakenly attempt to take away the hurt and anger the adolescent feels or to rescue him from the pain of the divorce. The adult must make sure to maintain adequate boundaries. There are no "quick fix" solutions to the adolescent's acutely felt pain and hurt (or its long-term effects). Healing must be allowed to happen at its own pace. The adult's role is to be a supportive and connecting presence whose relationship with the adolescent provides security and trust. Through this bond and the dialogue that proceeds from it, the adolescent derives self-awareness, understanding of his feelings and behavior, and the hope that commitment and fidelity are possible, even in the midst of current struggles.

Single-Parent Families

One of the stark effects of divorce is the single-parent family. A large number of ill effects are associated with broken homes. In a provocative lead article on the nature of family values, *Newsweek* magazine details a wide variety of psychological and social problems associated with single parenting. These include psychiatric disorders among adolescents, suicide, violent crime and burglary, adult criminal records, impaired learning (especially noticeable for boys with absent fathers), physical sickness, and accident proneness.[16]

The adolescent is not able to work out lingering problems with the absent parent and lacks as well the modeling influences and extra care and attention that the second parent can provide.

Furthermore, the custodial parent is often under great stress and unable to provide adequate parental care. Single parents often must take over a wide array of tasks, and their emotional, physical, and financial resources can be depleted in the process. For example, most single parents have less time, less money, and less social support than two-parent households. Sometimes the adolescent's problems can be used as a diversion to help adults avoid facing issues in their own lives, e.g., a mother becomes so wrapped up in her child's problems that she avoids dealing with her own negative feelings toward her absent husband.[17]

It is not the pastoral counselor's role to center attention on the single parent. However, gentle inquiry can be made about how the parent is doing. One helpful suggestion is to encourage single parents to take care of themselves. Often single parents are so focused on the problems and needs of their children that they avoid taking inventory of their own psychological state. A parent who is under significant stress will find difficulty parenting adequately, no matter how well-intentioned. Encourage the parent to seek out support groups or classes that offer assistance to the single parent. A single parent often needs to network with other adults who provide encouragement and peer support. Adult friendships often fall by the wayside either because of the divorce itself (not being part of a couple, the single parent no longer socializes with other couples) or lack of time and energy. Involvement with other adults is vital for healthy adult emotional functioning.

The Remarried Family

Remarried families pose special questions and deserve some comment.[18] Remarried families are becoming one of the dominant forms of family structure in the United States. Pastoral ministers and mental health professionals will increasingly encounter adolescents who are part of remarried families and are attempting to work through related issues. Second marriages are as likely to fail as first marriages — if not more so. Given the large number of divorces in the United States, more and more divorced men and women remarry. "One of every six American children under 18 years old lives in a stepfamily, according to a 1984 Census Bureau study. By 2000, that proportion will grow to about one in four, Government studies estimate."[19]

Often simply being aware of the issues that remarried families must confront and directing the adolescent's conversation toward them proves helpful. Psychologist William Walsh has described a wide range of such issues:

- name for the new parent
- affection for the new parent and the absent parent
- loss of the natural parent
- affection for new family members
- the fantasy about the old family structure
- discipline issues associated with the new parent
- confusion over the role that each member takes in the remarried family
- conflicts with siblings
- competition for other family members' time.
- negotiating the extended kinship network (the many relatives the adolescent now has)
- developing an adequate self-concept for the new family
- developing an adequate self-concept for each individual family member
- conflicts over parenting issues
- ongoing or new financial concerns
- ongoing conflicts with previous spouses[20]

The adult should also be aware that remarried families have higher rates of sexual abuse than intact families.

Researchers and clinicians have also noted that there are many "myths" that members of remarried families must actively confront and disown, e.g., that the "new" family will easily be formed. Loyalty conflicts, personal uncertainties over the future and the unknown, shifting alliances, and adjusting to new family members are all challenges that members of a newly constructed remarried family must confront. Resolution of problems happens gradually and can take several years.[21]

Given the wide range of issues present in remarried families, the adult can choose any number of these topic areas and reflect on them with the adolescent. Let the adolescent know that remarried families have specific and important issues to work out. Confusion, frustration, or disappointment is understandable. Again, if the adolescent's behavior or feelings impair functioning, then serious consideration should be given to a referral.

CHAPTER SEVEN
Eating Disorders

It is ironic that in a country with such abundance, malnutrition and starvation resulting from eating disorders have become a serious health problem. The desire to be "thin" places enormous pressure on adolescents, particularly females, who make up the overwhelming number of eating disorder cases.

A large nationwide survey conducted by the federal government makes evident the craze for thinness. Twice as many high school girls as boys view themselves as overweight, and many of those whose weight is normal still attempt to shed what they erroneously perceive as excess pounds. The survey noted that

> 44 percent of high school girls are trying to lose weight — including 27 percent of those who think they're the right weight already.... Among all girls surveyed in grades nine to 12, 80 percent said they had, in the past, gone on exercise regimens in an attempt to lose weight; 21 percent said they'd taken diet pills; and 14 percent said they'd vomited to lose pounds. Among the girls who perceived themselves as overweight, 95 percent had tried exercise, 34 percent tried diet pills; and 23 percent tried vomiting.[1]

Researchers found that girls were much more apt than boys to have distorted body images. Most teenage boys, according to this survey, were attempting to gain weight in order to develop the physique of an adult male. Those boys who were dieting were generally obese. In the case of the teenage girls, the findings were markedly different. Many of the teenage girls who were trying to lose weight could be classified as possessing normal weight. In effect, teenage girls misinterpret their own body weight, fostering in turn serious self-concept issues and self-image problems.

The preoccupation that many women have with cosmetic surgery suggests that there are enormous pressures to define self-worth in terms of physical attributes rather than interior qualities. It is estimated that until the recent controversies over breast implant surgery, at least 150,000 women a year underwent this procedure. Indeed, the two most common cosmetic surgeries performed in 1990 were liposuction (a procedure to remove body fat) and breast augmentation. Advertising plays a significant role in skewing women's self-perceptions regarding body image. Women models are 9 percent taller and 16 percent thinner than the average, creating unrealistic ideals for women, particularly adolescent girls who are very sensitive to physical changes and body image. Studies show that girls appear self-confident until their pubertal years and then their self-esteem plunges. Bodily changes coupled with cultural pressures for thinness fuel this decline.[2]

In a provocative article in *American Psychologist*, a group of Yale researchers pose several questions, including: Why are women prone to eating disorders? Which women in particular are prone to develop such a disorder? and, Why are eating disorders such as bulimia appearing with such frequency? The answers to these questions will help to frame our discussion for anorexia nervosa and bulimia that follows.[3]

As we have already stated, eating disorders are overwhelmingly a women's problem. So many women are now or have been on diets, that dieting must be considered a normative behavior for women. Thinness and beauty are highly prized by society and women tend to internalize these attitudes. This internalization is especially true among women of middle- and upper-class status, and, not surprisingly, a higher number of these women tend to suffer from eating disorders. College environments in particular tend to "breed" eating disorders such as bulimia. To be sure, the notion of what constitutes beauty varies with time and the culture, but American culture today clearly equates beauty with thinness.

From early childhood, girls are socialized to focus on their appearance. They are praised for attributes such as neatness, whereas boys tend to be praised more for their actual accomplishments (e.g., school success). Children's books and the popular media teach girls the "singular feminine ideal of thinness, beauty, and youth, set against a world in which men are more competent and also more diverse in appearance."[4] Studies of children's toy preferences find that boys prefer toys that require physical and mechanical activity, but girls choose toys that relate to aesthetic qualities and caretaking. Finally, even during grade school there is a relationship between a girl's thinness and self-concept. "Studies have found that even as children, females are more dissatisfied with their bodies than are males."[5]

The frequency with which adolescent girls develop eating disorders is not unrelated to the pubertal changes taking place and the developmental issues of "Who am I?" that so preoccupy the adolescent years. Adolescent girls have more body fat than boys. "After puberty girls have almost twice as much fat as boys."[6] Weight gain in adolescent boys is primarily in the form of muscle whereas for girls the weight gain is in body fat. The physiological changes taking place in boys foster the masculine ideal of muscular development and lean physique, but for girls such weight gain becomes the very antithesis of their personal goal and the cultural ideal: thin and beautiful. As a consequence, it is not surprising that adolescent girls express significantly more body dissatisfaction than adolescent boys. In addition, a number of researchers argue that while child and adolescent male development is fostered by successful separation and personal accomplishments, young girls' maturation centers on interpersonal issues and connection with others. Girls more than boys "seem to worry more about what other people think of them, care more about being liked, and try to avoid negative reactions from others."[7] As might be expected,

> the strong message to teenage girls regarding the importance of beauty and thinness (as evidenced, for example, in the teen fashion magazines) thus intersects with heightened sensitivity to sociocultural mandates as well as to personal opinions of others. It is not surprising, then, that the adolescent girl becomes concerned with and unhappy about her pubertal increase in fat.[8]

Anorexia Nervosa

Historically, evidence for self-starvation among women dates back to the Middle Ages. Speculation as to why women embarked on self-induced starvation centers on their experience of powerlessness. Devoid of any political leverage in a patriarchal society, women could protest their precarious social standing by taking control of their bodies and determining for themselves their dietary habits. In the late 1800s the term "anorexia nervosa" was introduced to describe a medical condition associated with adolescent females characterized by indifference to weight loss or pride in such loss and dismissal of medical advice to increase caloric intake.[9]

Though such disorders were previously considered rare, the last two decades have spawned such a large number of these cases that there is serious concern among parents, educators, and mental health professionals. In order to dramatize the adolescent experience of anorexia nervosa I summarize the following case study of psychologist Joseph White; it helpfully captures the symptoms and behavior of the anorexic teen:

> Clara is a 14-year-old, female eighth-grade junior high school student, who was referred to an eating-disorder clinic by a clinical social worker at a child guidance clinic....Clara, who is 5'3" tall, has lost

approximately 30 lbs in the past 12 months. Her original weight was 110 lbs, but she now weighs 80 lbs and wants to lose more. Clara says, "I really like being skinny." She thinks "carrying" less weight around makes her a better athlete and "looks better." She detests fat women. Her mother is slightly overweight despite repeated attempts to lose weight by exercising and dieting.

Clara has been dieting for about a year. She originally started dieting because some other girls on her gymnastic team were successfully losing weight by dieting. Clara now eats mostly salads, fruits, vegetables, and breakfast cereals. When she started dieting, her daily limit was approximately 1,100 calories. Clara thinks she is now down to about 500 to 600 calories per day. Despite her skin-and-bones look, Clara exercises daily and denies any fatigue or physical symptoms. Her physician reports menstrual irregularities. Clara does not see any need for treatment at an eating disorder clinic. She claims her only problems are family arguments with her mother about her diet. Clara thinks her mother is "jealous" because she has been unable to lose weight and "can't stay on a diet."

Clara's parents are both professionals....Clara has a 19-year-old brother who is a college sophomore....Clara and her brother are good students. Clara is on the honor roll, the gymnastic team, and plays trumpet in the school band....She says "nobody in my family talks about anything that's real important, except being good, staying out of trouble, and getting good grades....Nobody knows what anybody else is really doing or thinking."[10]

It is estimated that over 90 percent of anorexic cases are female. On the whole, anorexia nervosa is not a common disorder. However, among adolescent girls over age sixteen, the incidence is perhaps one in a hundred.[11] The disorder is most apt to occur among adolescent girls aged thirteen to twenty. The vast majority of anorectics are from white middle- and upper-middle class families. Over the past few years, however, there has been an increase in anorexia in all socioeconomic groups. Likewise, the disorder is now appearing in pre-adolescents and young adult women over twenty with increasing frequency.[12]

Three symptoms are often associated with anorexia. First, the adolescent fears she is gaining weight and will become obese. Second, the anorectic has a distorted body image; even the actual appearance associated with semi-starvation does not contradict the anorectic's view of herself as physically larger than she actually is. Third, there is an ongoing desire to shed weight regardless of actual weight. In other words, even an adolescent who is underweight will set as a goal a desire to lose still more weight.[13] A number of behavioral symptoms are indicators that an adolescent girl might be suffering from anorexia. Below are listed symptoms to look for in determining whether an adolescent is anorectic:

- Loss of significant body weight over a short period of time; the weight loss is not the result of another physical condition (e.g., illness).
- Menstrual irregularities.
- A distorted self-image. The young person believes she is very heavy and becomes excessively focused on her weight and the need to shed pounds, even if she is of normal weight. If she has already lost considerable weight she is unable to see her thinness or even her emaciated condition as inappropriate; she still believes she has more weight to lose.
- Intense preoccupation with dieting.

Sometimes the adolescent's behavior is encouraged by activities in which she is involved. Young women who are in sports competition or other activities demanding thinness (e.g., dancers) can be at risk for developing an eating disorder.[14]

Mental health professionals Frances Kempley and Wanda Weber have summarized a large number of "signs and symptoms" of anorexia nervosa:

Psychological: poor self-esteem; suicidal thoughts; distorted body image; compliance; perfectionism; rigidity; fear of food and weight gain; depression; denial of the problem; overachieving; anxiety; feelings of control over body; apathy; mood swings.

Behavioral: extreme physical activity; fatigue; fights with family; self-isolation from family and friends; compulsive exercise; overuse of laxatives or diuretics; eating alone; overeating (may cook and control family's eating); sleep disturbances.

Physical: excessive weight loss (15 percent or more of total body weight); malnutrition; sensitivity to cold; diminished capacity to think; cardiac arrest; lassitude (fatigue); cavities and gum disease; growth of facial and body hair; hair, skin, and nail problems; misperception of hunger, satiety, and other bodily sensations; electrolyte imbalance (weakness); joint pain (difficulty walking and sitting).[15]

There is no one cause of anorexia, and the disorder probably has different causes in different women. Clinicians have noted that anorectics often manifest some distinctive psychological features. Often they are described as "good girls," and exhibit a high degree of responsibility. They appear in control of most areas of their lives (eating and dieting excluded). Often they are model students, manifesting perfectionistic tendencies. Some fall into the "good student" category, the type that teachers enjoy in the classroom; they tend to be reliable, studious, and attentive. "They are usually shy, serious, neat, quiet, conscientious, perfectionistic, hypersensitive to rejection, and inclined to irrational guilt and obsessive worrying."[16] Sadly, this "good girl" image is a mask hiding more deep-seated issues:

> Underlying the well-organized, achievement-oriented, good-little-girl personality features are likely to be deep-seated feelings of inadequacy, low self-esteem, fears of uncertainty related to adolescent transitions, and worries about loss of control. By keeping busy, staying on her diet, and showing physical stamina by constant exercise, the anorexic teenager seeks to demonstrate to herself and others that she is in control. She admires herself for being able to lose more weight than others, eat less, resist urges to overeat, and stay on top of a busy schedule.[17]

Anorexia is also tied to developmental changes that the adolescent girl is undergoing. Puberty brings about bodily changes that can prove unsettling. Adolescent girls show dramatic increases in body fat at the very time that they receive the cultural message that "being thin" is the only acceptable way to be. The answer to the question "Who am I?," a question difficult to answer in its own right, is complicated by these biological changes. Further, the pursuit of thinness can be a defense against maturation and development as a sexual person. For many adolescents this denial is apt to be aggravated by home environments where family dynamics are hostile to their growing independence and sexual development.

Social factors suspected to be culprits in the development of anorexia include the pervasive cultural obsession with thinness. An excellent example is described in a study done by several psychological researchers. These investigators studied *Playboy* centerfolds and Miss America contestants over a twenty-year period (1959–78). Not only did these women weigh less than average American women, but over these two decades there was a continuing decline in these women's body weights. The researchers also discovered that after 1970 the body weights of Miss America finalists were significantly below that of other contestants. The mass media were emphasizing that "beautiful women" were increasingly thinner. Over these same two decades, the average weight of American women was increasing. In other words, adolescent and young adult women were being held captive to a cultural ideal that was more and more difficult to achieve![18]

Bulimia Nervosa

Bulimic behaviors have been observed since ancient times. The Romans were notorious for their food orgies and subsequent purging through vomiting. The word "bulimia" is derived from the Greek word *boulimia*, which means extreme hunger (literally, "ox-hunger"). The binging and purging associated with bulimia has been recorded in medical literature for over a hundred years, though much of this literature discusses bulimia in relation to anorexia nervosa. "The recognition of bulimia as a distinct syndrome did not occur until it became evident that binge-eating and vomiting behavior occurred in individuals who did not have histories of weight disorders such as anorexia nervosa or obesity."[19]

Psychologist Rolf Muus recounts a typical bulimic episode in Mary, a twenty-one-year-old young adult:

> It would start to build in the late morning. By noon, I'd know that I had to binge. I would go out...and buy a gallon...of maple walnut ice cream and a couple of packages of fudge brownie mix — enough to make 72 brownies....On the way home I invariably finished 12 doughnuts....I'd hastily mix up the brownies and get them in the oven....Then, while they were cooking, I'd hit the ice cream. ...Sometimes I'd finish the whole gallon even before the brownies were done, and I'd take the brownies out of the oven while they were still baking....Seventy-two brownies later, the depression would begin to hit.[20]

Bulimia appears considerably more often in the population than anorexia, and is perhaps two to three times as common. There is of course a fine line between strict dieting and bulimia. Many individuals show characteristics of bulimia but do not qualify diagnostically as having the disorder itself. College-age females are particularly apt to show bulimia or bulimic-like behavior.[21] The incidence of bulimia in the college population ranges from roughly 4 percent to 23 percent. Both the incidence and the diversity of behaviors lead "some researchers...to report separate statistics for bulimics, near bulimics, binge eaters, and vomiters."[22] Thus many young adult females show bulimic behaviors without manifesting the behaviors that qualify for an actual diagnosis of bulimia.

A case of true bulimia is identified by the following diagnostic criteria:

1. Recurring episodes of binge eating. A "binge" is defined as consuming a large amount of food in a set time period.
2. The feeling of being out of control while eating.
3. Attempts to nullify eating by self-induced vomiting, the use of laxatives or diuretics, strict fasting or dieting, and exercise.
4. At least two binging episodes a week for three months.
5. Preoccupation with weight or body image.[23]

"Many women suffer from anorexia and bulimia at the same time or alternate between them. About half of anorectic patients also have bulimia, and about 40 percent of severely bulimic patients have a history of anorexia."[24] Bulimia has been found to be related to mood disorder (depression); a large number of bulimics show evidence of depression. In addition, "bulimia is often accompanied by other psychiatric disorders, of which the most common and most important is alcoholism. In one study one-third of bulimic women also had drug or alcohol problems."[25] In general, "bulimic women are more outgoing, impulsive, and emotional than anorectic women, or at least seem to have a greater variety of personalities."[26]

A large number of factors might predispose a woman to suffer from bulimia. The cultural pressure to be or become "thin," mood problems, a history of dieting, biological tendencies to be heavy, and distinctive family dynamics that emphasize being thin might all lead women to be "set up" for bulimia or bulimic-like episodes.[27]

The Pastoral Response

1. Because eating disorders involve serious medical complications, some of which are life-threatening, adolescents suffering from such disorders should be under both medical and psychological care. Adults who are ministering to the youth must be aware of this boundary issue. The need for professional care does not of course preclude the adult from having a relationship with the young person nor from ministering to her spiritual needs.

2. As noted above, a large number of adolescents and young adults engage in anorectic and bulimic-like behaviors such as continuous dieting episodes, constant fear of weight gain, purging, excessive exercise, and constant focus on food. The adult should target these young people and reflect with them on their behavior. One area of concern is simply dietary habits. The adult might engage the adolescent in a discussion of basic food groups and their importance in the daily diet.

3. I have found it helpful to reflect with adolescents in terms of their "service" as disciples called to help build God's reign. One's body and physical health are vital components of this discipleship. Surprisingly, many youth do not take the time to consider how their bodies are integral for living out their Christian calling of mission and service. Two questions can prove quite helpful. First, ask the adolescent a very general question such as, "I'm wondering, Donna, what 'being healthy' means to you?" Explore the answer in terms of behavior, attitudes, and diet. Help the adolescent to *evaluate* how her behavior does or does not contribute to Christian witness and ser-

vice. Strategize together regarding what behavior or attitudes need altering. Second, I have found it profitable to reflect in terms of St. Paul's idea of the body as a "temple of the Holy Spirit." Reflect with the adolescent on the goodness of God's creation and how she is taking responsibility for this vital part (her body) of God's creation. How does she care for her own life, which is part of God's creation?

4. One area where adult presence can prove very valuable is that of cultural values and assumptions. Talk with the adolescent about her favorite television shows, videos, and movies. What values do these media champion? Discuss how cultural messages such as "thin is beautiful" influence the adolescent's behaviors and choices. How do media values relate to the adolescent's own values? How do these messages affect the adolescent's view of self? How do these messages make her feel? What do they do to her self-image?

5. Many adolescents concerned with body image have self-esteem problems. Again, the best way to foster self-esteem is to promote healthy identity growth in the young person. Review again the characteristics of healthy identity formation discussed in chapter 2. Use the suggested questions to foster such growth in the adolescent.

CHAPTER EIGHT
Abuse and the Adolescent

Few experiences are apt to arouse more negative feelings in the caring adult than speaking with an adolescent about the painful experience of abuse. Few topics have gained more media attention than child abuse. There exist no precise figures on the prevalence of child abuse, and there are several reasons for this uncertainty. Definitions of child abuse vary from study to study, thereby complicating attempts to obtain accurate numbers. Though some behaviors, such as genital fondling, are commonly agreed upon as forbidden, other behaviors are more ambiguous, e.g., the type of clothing worn within the family setting. Similarly, families differ on what forms of punishment are tolerated. Is every form of spanking, for example, abusive? Further, abuse itself is often unreported, and the samples used to obtain abuse rates might not accurately represent the population as a whole.

We do know that the reporting of child abuse is increasing. According to the *Harvard Mental Health Letter*, child protection service agencies reported 2.5 million abuse reports in 1989, up 25 percent from 1985. There are probably several reasons for these increases. For one, media publicity has generated high public awareness of abuse. Heretofore, child abuse was thought to be rare; only in the past two decades has attention been drawn to the likelihood that rates of abuse are much higher than previously suspected. Second, with the increased publicity more and more individuals are comfortable with coming forward (though many are still unwilling to speak up). Third, both children and those professionals responsible for their care (e.g., teachers, social workers) are more sensitized to the abuse issue. Is the actual number of child abuse cases increasing? I believe it is because of increased stresses and strains that families are experiencing. We should also note that some reporting might be overzealous and false charges are leveled when indeed no abuse has taken place.

Surveys indicate that anywhere from one-fifth to one-third of adult women have been sexually abused, while 10 percent of adult men suffered abuse as children. Sexual abuse might occur only once or a few times, but a significant minority experience sexual abuse for months or years. Most sexual abuse is committed by someone known by the victim such as a family member, and such abuse is most apt to be repeated when the perpetrator is a family member. Stepchildren are more vulnerable to abuse than biological children. The family system where abuse takes place is apt to manifest significant dysfunction; quite often one or both parents suffer from an addiction, and the parents themselves possess distorted or unreasonable attitudes regarding their children's abilities and behavior.[1]

Counselors Lynn England and Charles Thompson have reported several "myths" of child sex abuse that deserve mention. One is that incest rarely occurs and that when it does it is usually limited to members of lower socioeconomic groups. In reality, as noted above, a significant number of adult men and women were sexually abused as children. Further, sexual abuse occurs in all economic and social groupings. Another myth centers on the erroneous perception that adults who abuse are strangers. In fact, in most cases the child knows the perpetrator. The overwhelming majority of perpetrators are men; fathers and stepfathers are the most common abusers, followed by other men such as brothers, grandfathers, and uncles. In only a small number of cases are the abusers unknown to the child.[2]

Psychological Abuse

Unfortunately, the psychological maltreatment of children has received little attention. Other terms often used for such inappropriate behavior include "mental cruelty," "emotional abuse and neglect," and "emotional maltreatment." Given the wide variety of behaviors possible, there exists no exact definition of psychological maltreatment. However, ridicule, extreme teasing, demeaning name-calling, manipulative behavior, and emotional neglect fall under this category.

It is reasonable to assume that psychological maltreatment is the core issue in all forms of child abuse. It is hard to imagine any physical or sexual abuse of the child that does not at some point lead to psychologically debilitating consequences. Such maltreatment fosters tremendous insecurity and self-image problems for children and adolescents.[3] As a way to understand psychological abuse, the reader might consider families where adolescents have a difficult time feeling good about themselves or even comfortable in the family. What kind of behaviors are commonplace in such homes? How do members within the family relate to one another? What are the consequences of such family behavior for the adolescent? Also, consider families where physical or sexual abuse has taken place. What are the psychological consequences of such abuse for these adolescents?

Physical Abuse

Parents who abuse their children often were abused themselves as children. It is as if they have internalized an image of what a parent must be and subsequently (and tragically) demonstrate such behavior when parenting their own children. Such parents more than likely grew up in homes where emotional neglect or psychological maltreatment was commonplace. Lacking the security of stable emotional attachment in childhood, they are unable to respond to the normal sacrifices and commitments that go with healthy parenting.

Physical abuse by a parent usually takes place within a specific context. First, as noted above, the parent's own upbringing probably caused scars of maltreatment that were as least psychologically debilitating if not physically abusive. Though in many cases such emotionally impoverished parents try hard and successfully to avoid abusive behaviors toward their own children, in other cases parents simply lack the skills, emotions, and attitudes necessary for successful parenting. Second, the parent's own perceptions of the child are distorted. The child might be either unwanted or perceived as unlovable. The parent might have distorted notions of child development. For example, the parent misperceives the child's crying as a conscious attempt on the child's part to punish or "get back" at the parent. Or the parent might assume the child is a "little adult," believing the child to be more responsible for his or her actions than is developmentally appropriate. Third, the parent might have suffered a crisis (e.g., becoming unemployed), leading to high levels of stress and the displacement of personal anger or felt inadequacies onto the child. Fourth, the parent might be isolated, unable to find the support and counsel from others that enables him or her to weather stress.[4]

The consequences of physical abuse on the adolescent can be understood by comparison to the secure attachment discussed in chapter 2. A securely attached child experiences a sense of security. For such a child the world is stable and safe, and in turn such assurance affords the child the possibility of venturing outward, experiencing new relationships and challenges within the context of an emotionally stable environment. In contrast, the emotional life of the abused child is riddled with insecurity and mistrust. The child experiences tremendous ambivalence, drawn toward the parent, who might in many instances be nurturing, while at the same time being repelled by the painful realities of physical injury and emotional betrayal that have taken place.

Adolescents who suffer physical abuse demonstrate a wide range of behavior. Though such behavior does not necessarily mean physical abuse in the home has taken place, these signs may indicate that further inquiry is appropriate:

- various types of bodily injury such as bruises or scars
- desiring not to leave school premises or church functions and return home
- running away from home
- unruly behavior
- distrust of adults
- poor school performance
- fights with peers
- unlawful behavior
- self-esteem problems
- negative emotional reactions toward others
- problems with alcohol and other drugs
- overly compliant behavior

The above behaviors are not limited to victims of physical abuse but also characterize those suffering from sexual abuse. Moreover, a complicating factor is that such behavior can reflect numerous problems in the adolescent's life, not just abuse. There exists no unique "set" of behaviors or feelings that can be classified as a distinct syndrome that clearly differentiate abused adolescents from those suffering from other problems.

Adolescents who are physically abused can be deeply conflicted. They may feel the need to be loyal to the family or a particular parent or sibling. Embarrassment and fear of what might happen also may be present. Such youth are often confused and angry. Coping with very strong feelings, they find difficulty making sense of the traumatic and physically injurious behavior they are undergoing or have undergone. A significant number of youth who are physically abused suffer severe psychological problems. "It is estimated that at least 25 percent of physically abused children have serious psychiatric problems, including chronic anxiety and depression and sometimes neurological damage."[5] In some instances, as the child grows stronger physically and enters adolescence the physical abuse might cease; however, the psychological toll continues to mount and psychological scars remain.

Sexual Abuse

Today the phenomenon of sexual abuse receives wide publicity. Some of the publicity has been fueled by incidents of reported repressed memory, where an alleged victim, many years or even decades later, suddenly remembers incidents of being sexually abused by family members. Heated controversy has arisen over the veracity of such reports, with some experts insisting that such abuse had indeed taken place, while others insisting that some victims, though perhaps well intended, are in fact basing their claims on faulty memory processing.

Regardless of the controversy surrounding repressed memories, no one denies that sexual abuse is a revolting and horrifying occurrence in a child's or adolescent's life.

Like all development, a child's sexual development takes place within the family. As the child matures the healthy family accommodates the child's developmental changes. Behaviors and attitudes are displayed in an appropriate fashion that signals respect for the child and the maintenance of adequate boundaries. For example, the child is granted more privacy and personal space, her questions are encouraged and answered, and affectional displays are genuine yet appropriate. In the sexually abusing family, such patterns of respect and boundary setting are disregarded. Such families fail to appreciate the developmental needs of the child and in fact "use" the child to meet adult needs.[6]

As a result of sexual abuse, the sexual development of the victim is impaired. An all too common consequence for victims of sexual abuse is inappropriate sexual behavior, sexual dysfunction, or sexual satisfaction problems. Inappropriate sexual behavior (sexual acting out) is seen in some children and adolescents. Some maintain that a child develops a premature sexual response and is forced into a sexual life that he is developmentally ill prepared for, as if his sexuality were prematurely "jump started." Others say that a child learns that only through sexual expression can affectional needs be met or that only through sexually acting out can he or she remaster the trauma of being sexually victimized. And some hold that a victim's sexually acting out is a means to gain attention and power that were denied him as a child.[7]

In order to understand the effects of sexual abuse on children, psychologist David Finkelhor, a leading researcher in the area of abuse, suggests that four elements must be taken into consideration: traumatic sexualization, betrayal, stigmatization, and powerlessness. These four elements must be understood within the context of how the child functioned previous to the abuse, the nature of the abuse, and the response of others to the abuse once it is disclosed. These elements influence how the child comes to think and feel about self and world and how he functions subsequent to the abuse.[8]

Boys' and girls' reactions to abuse are, for the most part, similar. Says Finkelhor, "Boys, like girls, show marked impact as a result of sexual abuse both early and long term. Perhaps the major surprise is the relative similarity of the response of boys to that of girls."[9] However, boys will often externalize their reactions in aggressive behavior whereas girls tend to internalize, with resulting feelings of depression. In regards to the abuse itself, boys are more frequently victims of perpetrators outside the family. Their abuse also tends to begin at an earlier age and to end sooner than that of girls. Further, it is known that a majority of perpetrators of abuse are males; as a consequence, boys are more victimized by same-sex abusers. Males are also more likely to minimize the effects of abuse and are less likely to disclose that they have been abused.[10] Yet both sexes are likely to demonstrate most symptoms in a similar way. "It is somewhat remarkable that, given the importance of gender in the realm of sexuality, more differences have not shown up even on the behavioral and symptomatic level."[11]

It should be stated explicitly that adolescents who have suffered abuse in either childhood or adolescence have been traumatized. The degree of the trauma depends on numerous factors. Consequences of sexual or physical abuse often include some type of stress reaction, e.g., disavowal of emotional feeling (numbing), irritability, sleep problems, memory flashbacks, hypervigilance, and avoidance behaviors. In psychiatric terminology this condition is known as Post-Traumatic Stress Disorder. It should be noted, however, that not all experts believe that stress symptoms of child sexual abuse, though very real, can fit precisely in this category.[12] In some instances, the child's reactions to physical or sexual abuse can take the form of some type of dissociative state such as a trance or blocking of memory that allows him to avoid the trauma. Personality changes may emerge that can lead in some instances to the formation of multiple personality disorder.

As common sense would stipulate, children abused by parents are most likely to be the most seriously affected. Such children must cope with being betrayed and helpless in the face of trauma. Sometimes they are told they are bad, suffering as a consequence tremendous guilt. Further, they may have felt some pleasure in the physical relationship, thereby incurring more guilt. Finally, feelings of anger and rage leading to thoughts of revenge might heighten guilt still further. It is difficult to capture the intensity or severity of the child's reactions because the parent looms so large in the child's psychological life that the capacity to sort out and modulate feelings is complicated and impaired. Feelings that abused children have toward their parents are not only complicated but ambivalent. The parent is not always an abuser and can often be a dispenser of favors or the nurturer the child so desperately desires. Because the parent is the source of so much love in the child's life, the child might cling to or idolize the parent while simultaneously harboring intense feelings of rage and hurt.[13] A particularly complicating feature of sexual abuse in adolescence is that the perpetrating parent might manipulatively grant favors to the victimized youth, thereby fostering in the adolescent an ambivalence about disclosing and terminating the abuse.

The *Harvard Mental Health Letter* notes the following about female and male reactions to abuse:

> A woman who was abused as a girl may allow herself to be further abused by men both physically and sexually, accepting degradation as the price of any intimate relationship. When a sexually abused girl has taken the place of her mother entirely, doing the housework, caring for younger children, and listening to her father's complaints about his work, his wife, or his biological family, she is said to be a "parentified child," Eventually she may no longer acknowledge that she has needs of her own. As an adult she maintains the illusion of having had good parents and continues to care for others, including the abusive father, without expecting anything in turn.[14]

For boys the following reactions are possible:

> Boys are even less likely to admit their feelings about having been sexually or physically abused, and families are more likely to blame them or deny any serious effects. They may prefer to see themselves as bad rather than accept the status of victim. By turning their rage outward and attacking others, they make themselves feel powerful instead of helpless. Sexually abused boys may also be confused about sexual identity, especially if they have had the common physiological response of erection or ejaculation. Sometimes they show signs of fear and hatred of all homosexual men.[15]

The vast array of negative feelings generated by abuse, whether physical or sexual, leads some adolescents to attempt escape through body-focused behaviors. Self-soothing through healthy behavior and the completion of appropriate developmental tasks are the natural outgrowths of normal maturation. However, the abused adolescent's feelings of anger, self-degradation, guilt, and betrayal might not find everyday behaviors satisfying or capable of relieving the overpowering feelings of his or her negative emotions. As a consequence, some adolescents resort to a variety of at-risk behaviors to overcome their pain and to create a sense of self-soothing for their currently disruptive emotional experiences.

Psychiatrist Judith Lewis Herman describes these body-focused/at-risk behaviors that prove satisfying for many adolescents.

> Self-injury is perhaps the most spectacular of the pathological soothing mechanisms but it is only one among many. Abused children generally discover at some point in their development that they can produce major, though temporary, alterations in their affective state by voluntarily inducing autonomic crises or extreme autonomic arousal. Purging and vomiting, compulsive sexual behavior, compulsive risk-taking or exposure to danger, and the use of psychoactive drugs become the vehicles by which abused children attempt to regulate their internal emotional states. Through these devices, abused children attempt to obliterate their chronic dysphoria and to stimulate, however briefly, an internal state of well-being and comfort that cannot otherwise be achieved. These self-destructive symptoms are often well established in abused children even before adolescence, and they become much more prominent in the adolescent years.[16]

The Pastoral Response

1. All states have mandatory reporting laws regarding abuse of minors. It is incumbent on adults to know the laws in their state. Failure to do this not only jeopardizes the adolescent but also exposes the adult and the institution to civil and criminal penalties.

2. All adolescents who have been victimized need the opportunity to share their experience with a professional mental health care provider. The adult should have access to several types of referral sources (private providers as well as public agencies) so that every adolescent, regardless of financial resources, is able to connect with someone experienced in therapeutic care. It should again be pointed out that some children are remarkably resilient. This coupled with the varying degrees of abusive behavior might render some adolescents better able to weather an abusive situation. Some adolescents, of course, improve and recover more quickly than other adolescents. Nonetheless, given the serious nature of abuse, nothing should be taken for granted, and all adolescents should be provided some type of referral.

3. Knowledge of abusive situations involving children and adolescents evokes powerful feelings in adults. The adult working with youth must closely monitor her own feelings in order to provide the most objective and helpful information to the adolescent. This is especially true if the adult herself has been a victim of some type of abuse, thereby arousing negative internal reactions that preclude any correct assessment of the adolescent's situation or lead

to boundary problems with the adolescent. Having other adults to talk to, professional staff meetings, or individual therapy often prove helpful.

4. For a variety of reasons some adolescents are unwilling to disclose abusive situations. Sometimes the adolescent might be manifesting specific problem behaviors, but the account he gives of his life does not suggest any abuse. In such cases the adult must first reflect on the following questions: "How do I make sense of the adolescent's problem behavior?" And then: "What evidence leads me to suspect abuse?" If the response to either or both of these questions leads the adult to suspect abuse, then this issue should be pursued with the adolescent. In situations where the adolescent is not forthcoming with information, I find the best approach, at least initially, is to be nondirective. If abuse has taken place, the adolescent's lack of disclosure probably indicates powerful conflicted feelings. Disclosure of abuse usually comes in a relationship of trust; hence establishing such a relationship is vital for any inquiry. To make such an inquiry, statements that address the nature of the information (a secret) and the feelings involved (conflicted and confused) are important. I usually talk to an adolescent in general about how some families have secrets and how keeping secrets can cause significant stress and burdens for an adolescent. A helpful statement might be: "Sometimes families or we ourselves carry secrets that are very difficult to talk about. Sometimes what we know can cause an awful lot of stress and uneasiness in us and become a serious burden." After this discussion questions like the following are often helpful:

- "Mary, we've talked a lot and yet you seem to be experiencing difficulty in *(name the behaviors)*. I'm trying to make sense of why you are behaving this way. Is there something else going on in your life that you'd like to tell me about?"

- "Is there something else I need to know about that you have not yet shared with me?"

- "Is there anything about your relationship with any family members that you find distressing or hurtful that I need to know about?"

Sometimes an adolescent might respond "What do you mean?" In such instances it is best to repeat simply the gist of the statement: "Well, has anyone you know done something to you that is hurtful or distressing?" When asking such questions repeatedly make reference to your concern for the adolescent as the reason you are asking such questions. Also, it is important to empathize with the adolescent's situation, with statements like "I know some things are difficult to talk about," or "It's hard to talk about such personal things, so take your time," or "I'm here for you, so just take your time." Fortunately, in many cases our suspicions prove unfounded. Yet it might also be that the adolescent is not yet ready to talk about the abuse. Always *connect* with the adolescent with a question like, "Mary, if you ever want to talk, you know where to find me," or "I look forward to getting together again soon and talking some more." Of course if the adolescent does acknowledge abuse then the adult should contact other adults he or she works with and seek their advice. At the same time all discussion should take place in accordance with state laws.

5. If an adolescent reports physical or sexual abuse she may be reluctant for such information to be disclosed to others. There are a variety of reasons for such reluctance, fear for self or others (e.g., siblings), embarrassment, guilt. Though these feelings are very understandable, if the adolescent is under eighteen or others are in danger then the question is what is best for the welfare of the child. A child is, after all, a minor. He cannot always be considered the best judge of what is an appropriate response, no matter what emotions or distress are evident. In such instances as the adult you must make the judgment of what is the best course of action. At the same time, you should empathize with the adolescent's concern and let her know that you realize how difficult disclosure is.

6. A relationship with Jesus Christ and the believing community is grounded in trust. The psychological roots for such trust are initially experienced in the security of the family and most significantly in identifying with the values and beliefs of parents. When abuse occurs this trust is sundered; we then must ask how abused youth can acquire the security and trust necessary for nourishing their faith. There is no simple or easy answer to this question. And the journey of faith for many adolescents who have been abused is often warped and confusing. Though a therapeutic relationship with a professional mental health worker is helpful, the adult in pastoral ministry must also see his or her role as pivotal for the adolescent's healing and healthy growth. The adult who reaches out to the adolescent provides an enormously empowering experience that witnesses to the fact that the adolescent can learn to trust again. Healing is a process that takes time, and the adolescent's healing journey might consist in periods of doubt, mistrust, and alienation from adult authorities. At the same time, the adolescent might desire to find an adult with whom she can build a healthy and secure relationship. When relating to the adolescent in a pastoral relationship, a few guidelines are helpful:

149

a. Give the adolescent permission to feel and express whatever feelings he needs to express.

b. Let the adolescent know that you are available for her.

c. Be patient. Trust takes time to build. Respect the adolescent's boundaries.

d. Reflect with the adolescent on healthy activities and behaviors that he can engage in.

e. Reflect with the adolescent on trust levels in various relationships. Talk about healthy relationships and how her relationships include ones that both are and are not healthy. Discuss "criteria" (behaviors) that reflect healthy relationships.

f. Focus on how the adolescent is a loving person or desires to remain a loving person in spite of the trauma that has occurred. Such discussion should take into account the adolescent's need for integrity and healthy boundaries and should avoid compulsive caregiving responses that refuse to meet the adolescent's own legitimate needs.

g. Let the adolescent know that your relationship with her is a stable and reliable one. Demonstrate that you *respect* her by asking her views and opinions on matters and respecting (though not necessarily agreeing with) what she says. This approach can be empowering for the adolescent because abuse is an experience of being "used" and taken advantage of. Adults who by their manner and questions show respect offer the adolescent an alternative experience of adult-adolescent relationship.

7. When an adolescent has been abused either in childhood or during adolescence, one consequence is what I term "impaired-meaning making." That is, the adolescent's ability to interpret his world and find appropriate significance is rendered deficient and in extreme cases even shattered. The arousal of negative feelings, particularly anger and a sense of betrayal, undermines the adolescent's ability to cohere and find purpose. These negative feelings, coupled with an incapacity for advanced cognitive thinking, might lead the adolescent to forestall productive goal-setting through aimless diversions, reckless behavior, or intensely held and often angrily voiced feelings and opinions about God and religious matters. The adolescent might dismiss God or the church or express openly hostile ideas toward anything religious. Such ideas are, after all, understandable inasmuch as the adolescent's rage arises from betrayal by authorities either divine or secular that have failed to protect. (An extreme case of this is of course the adolescent who has been victimized by a cleric or representative of the church.) The position of the adolescent needs

respect. The period of alienation and hurt that the adolescent experiences might last for a considerable time, in some cases even years. In such cases the best antidote is simply a relationship where the adult (who represents the believing community) conveys trust of and respect for the adolescent. The adolescent's capacity to find meaning is aided by an adult who patiently dialogues with him about his beliefs and future and provides a sounding board as he slowly reestablishes connection with the believing community.

8. Victims of abuse, particularly when the abuse occurs in childhood, can exhibit strong feelings of guilt. Because parents loom as such significant figures in the child's life, the child often cannot attribute responsibility to the offending parent. In other words, the child must preserve the image of adult as a safe and secure provider. As a consequence, the child blames herself for the abusive behavior, taking personal responsibility for the abuse. Such a distorted attribution leads the child to paint herself and to *feel* herself as bad.

By developing a contaminated, stigmatized identity,

> the child victim takes the evil of the abuser into herself and thereby preserves her primary attachments to her parents. Because the inner sense of badness preserves a relationship, it is not readily given up even after the abuse has stopped; rather, it becomes a stable part of the child's personality structure.... The profound sense of inner badness becomes the core around which the abused child's identity is formed, and it persists into adult life.[17]

As a result of this core experience of badness, the adolescent might feel intense guilt and develop significant problems centering on poor self-esteem. As the reader might recall, our model of healthy conscience is premised on several traits including a healthy sense of guilt and adequate self-esteem. For the abused adolescent these two traits are significantly distorted. In addition, as a result of this core experience of "badness," the adolescent might engage in a wide variety of compensatory behaviors such as pleasing others or compulsive caregiving. By such actions the adolescent attempts to make amends for her badness and relieve chronic feelings of inadequacy. Naturally such behaviors fall short, leading in turn to more attempts at repair.

For such adolescents the adult's pastoral role is pivotal. The adult might explore with the adolescent, for example, how she respects and appreciates herself. Go over the adolescent's behaviors and the consequences of such behaviors for her own feelings (e.g., does she always please others or exhaust herself helping others?). Another fertile avenue to explore is how she goes about making moral decisions. What are the criteria she uses to determine the course of action she follows? Many abused adolescents possess impaired decision-making skills along with poor images of self. A primary task of the adult is to aid the adolescent in exploring various aspects of her behavior in order to encourage the formation of healthy conscience functioning.

9. Another area often impaired by a history of abuse is healthy relationship formation. Trust, fidelity, and appropriate expressions of affection are often difficult for the adolescent who has been abused. Whom can I trust? Who will offer me security? What is appropriate information to disclose? These are a few of the questions many adolescents have. One of the best approaches here is simply to explore with the adolescent the meaning of healthy relationships (see chapter 9 on sexuality). Discuss the meaning of friendship and the feelings, attitudes, and behaviors that are appropriate in a relationship.

CHAPTER NINE

Sexuality and the Adolescent

A recent issue of the *New York Times* had a front-page story entitled, "On Campuses, AIDS Testing Is Becoming More Common." According to the article, more and more college students are having themselves tested for the HIV virus. Articles such as this highlight the profound changes that have transpired over the past decade regarding adolescent and young adult sexuality. In 1983 in my book *Adolescent Spirituality* I provided what was to my knowledge the first comprehensive statement on a pastoral theology for adolescent sexual behavior.[1] In this book I outlined an approach to adolescent sexuality that took into account the developmental struggles of the adolescent while at the same time encouraging those working with youth to challenge young people to the ideals of Christian discipleship.

Much has happened in the decade since this book's publication. Sociocultural pressures, the stresses on families and the increasing complexity of everyday life continue to influence adolescent sexual behavior. In addition, questions pertaining to cohabitation, AIDS, homosexuality, and teenage pregnancy constantly surface in the media. All of these factors make the moral evaluation of sexual matters, not to mention the direct ministering to adolescents, a challenging undertaking.

In this chapter I set forth a working strategy that adults can utilize in pastorally counseling youth on sexual matters. I write this chapter as a clinical psychologist and academician who has had extensive clinical experience with adolescents and young adults. At the same time, I also write as a ministry professional who brings to the discussion a Christian understanding of sexuality that embraces the notions of fidelity, commitment, and the Lord's loving challenge to Christian discipleship. The key to the success of such an endeavor is providing a coherent message that respects the adolescent yet never fails to provide the challenge of ongoing growth, for, as Paul reminds us, "it is important that we continue on our course no matter what stage we have reached" (Phil. 3:16).

Friendship, Intimacy, and the Adolescent

In our discussion of adolescent sexual behavior we must avoid the common misunderstanding that narrowly defines sexuality as only physical expression. Though genital expression is essential to any understanding of sexuality, a more enriching view understands sexuality as a "way of being" that incorporates attitudes toward self and others, knowledge of one's emotional life history, and the capacity to relate to others in ways that foster developmental growth. All of this is a way of saying, simply, that the best understanding of sexuality takes place in the context of the meaning of friendship and intimacy. This is not surprising, for happily married couples consistently report that their happiness is grounded in their intimate ties with and respect for one another. Jesus' call is essentially an invitation incorporating the richness of intimacy and the obligations of mature friendship. In addition, true friendship and healthy intimacy provide the spiritual and emotional foundation for the Gospel's call to conversion. In order to understand fully adolescent sexual expression we must first consider the role of friendship and intimacy in the adolescent's life.

Psychologist John Conger offers perceptive insights into the crucial role friendship plays during adolescence. Friendships aid the adolescent's self-understanding; friends offer an avenue for sorting out feelings, developing self-insight, and becoming more aware of personal behaviors and attitudes. Friends provide feelings of self-worth, for the adolescent now feels valued and accepted by another; in short, the adolescent has found someone who truly understands.[2]

For younger adolescents, friendship means having someone to do something with. For middle adolescents friends are individuals who offer security and trust. For the most part, it is only in late adolescence that friendship takes on the level of significant sharing and expression associated with intimacy.[3]

Another intriguing question is how the experience of friendship of adolescent males and females differs. Many male adolescents share intimately with close friends, though their communication is usually more limited than that of female adolescents with their close friends. Overall, female friendships are more characterized by understanding, openness, and tolerance. Though many adolescent males share intimacy with their male friends, there is a sizeable number of adolescent males who define close friendship through their activities rather than intimacy. This latter group is likely to be less tolerant, less communicative, and less trusting of their friends. James Youniss and Jacqueline Smollar found that for the majority of adolescents of both sexes, close friendships with persons of the same sex appear to incorporate the qualities of fairness and mutual respect and serve to meet the material needs of the individuals. For most females, this type of relationship also involves mutual intimacy and meets their emotional needs. For many of the males, these aspects are also present; yet for many males, mutual self-disclosure is clearly not an aspect of their relationships. For about 33 percent of the males, it appears that emotional needs are more likely to be met by a friend of the opposite sex than by a friend of the same sex.[4]

Youniss and Smollar's findings support other research efforts that conclude that there is a tendency for female adolescents to self-disclose more and experience their friendships as more oriented toward meeting emotional needs. At the same time, these researchers point out that the responses of nearly half the male adolescents were similar to the most common female responses. Hence, it is not valid to think of clearly defined differences between adolescent male and female friendship patterns.

Finally, most adolescents take their friendships seriously. Close friendships for adolescents are often principled undertakings; they feature care, respect, trust, and reciprocity, which adolescents expect their friends to uphold and practice, even in the face of numerous failings.[5]

There are several reasons why any meaningful conversation on sexuality and the adolescent must be preceded by a discussion regarding friendship. First, true friendship is at the heart of the Gospel, and Christians are called to live in friendship with one another (John 15:12–17). Helping adolescents define the meaning of friendship for their own lives and encouraging the practice of healthy friendship promotes moral as well as human growth.

Second, friendship is a good and positive experience in any person's life. Everyone would agree that having healthy, emotionally significant relationships is vital for personal well-being and maturity.

Third, the world of the adolescent is radically interpersonal. Relationships are the *essence* of adolescence. Young people oftentimes evaluate their well-being by the quality of their relationships. Troubled relationships, loneliness, and unrequited emotional needs emerge as sources for personal dissatisfaction and negative self-image for many young people. To minister effectively to adolescents we must be aware of their interpersonal needs.

Finally, I fear that the advent of the video and electronic age has prevented many youth from accurately discerning the true meaning and importance of relationships. Many young people have developed distorted idealizations of what a relationship is. Several years ago I worked in a psychiatric hospital on an adolescent ward. During the late afternoon the adolescents were given free time, and many chose to watch television. Most of the time they would turn the channel to one of the afternoon talk shows. As the reader well knows talk shows seek publicity and spice up their entertainment with themes of violence, anger, and frustration that often center on family and interpersonal conflicts. As I observed these adolescents I could not help but think how television was helping to form their "ideal" of what a relationship is.

I raise this issue because it is central for adolescent well-being. If the adolescent's ideal of a relationship involves distorted understandings and unrealistic expectations and she evaluates her relationships according to this ideal, she thereby renders herself vulnerable to ongoing frustration and dissatisfaction. Such negative feelings inevitably spill over to moral decision-making as the adolescent's discomfort or need spurs hasty or inappropriate decisions that compromise moral growth. This is why I term such evaluations "distorted idealizations." Unfortunately, for far too many youth these idealizations become the templates through which they assess the health and satisfaction of their relationships. These distorted idealizations undercut not only moral growth and personal satisfaction but also, I fear, sabotage healthy identity development. The question "who am I?" cannot be answered without being-in-relation, and if the very nature of relationship is misconstrued, then the foundational pieces for constructing a sense of self-definition are tenuous.

Another dimension of relationships that needs discussion is intimacy. "The need for intimacy influences all adolescent patterns and habits, especially those related to close friendship and romantic interests."[6] Erik Erikson defines intimacy as one's "capacity to commit himself to concrete affiliations and partnerships and to develop the ethical strength to abide by such commitments, even though they may call for significant sacrifices and compromises."[7] I like Erikson's definition because it points out that commitment is important for intimate relations and that intimacy requires, at times, struggle and perseverance. Generally speaking the term "intimacy" sparks ideas of self-disclosure, sharing, sexual involvement, emotional closeness, and confidentiality. Psychologist Dan McAdams captures many of these notions when he describes intimacy as the sharing of one's innermost feelings with another.[8] One common misunderstanding of intimacy is that it necessarily means a sexual relationship. Sexual expression is often part of intimacy but is not necessarily so. One need only think of close friendships to realize that intimacy is very much part of many nongenital relationships.

Another frequently asked question is how intimacy relates to love. Recall that intimacy implies a high degree of sharing and personal revelation; such an experience is similar to but distinct from love. Love is a more complex experience; there exist several different types of love. For one, there is the experience of affection that the Ancient Greeks termed *storge*. The best example of this type of love is the love of a parent for a child. Such affection tends to grow with time and involves security, trust, protection, and, most of all, familiarity with another. Though intimacy is part of such relationships, its degree is limited by age and circumstance.

A second type of love is friendship, or what the Greeks labeled *philia*. Friends share a mutual interest or goal, and most certainly friendship involves caring and sharing with another. Most important, friendship is freely chosen. One cannot force friendship; it is part of the mystery of friendship that we are friends with one person rather than another. Friendships involve some degree of intimacy and in close friendships the level of intimacy can be extraordinary.

Another type of love is charity, or what is commonly termed *agape*. This type of love is a selfless love that is unconditional. In the Christian tradition, Jesus' love for humankind represents *agape* in its purest form. Mother Teresa, Martin Luther King, Jr., and local community "heroes" who selflessly sacrifice themselves for others are examples of *agape*. Intimacy in the context of *agape* involves concern for others and communicating one's concern to another in need.

A final type of love is *eros*. This is romantic love and is characterized by romantic involvement and often sexual expression. Intimacy, ideally, is a vital part of erotic love, but need not be. Infatuation can exist without intimacy. Further, the immaturity of the partners might preclude the sharing required for intimate involvement. McAdams perceptively notes that in erotic love one abandons oneself to another, while in intimacy the two people keep boundaries and relate to one another as two persons. In romantic love one is passionate, loses boundaries, idealizes the other, and is jealous. Erotic love is an immensely powerful experience that allows one to experience both indescribable joy and emotional heartache.[9]

How do adolescents view the differences between intimate and nonintimate relationships? In one study of late adolescents both males and females viewed intimate relationships as more characterized by trust, openness, sharing, and physical/sexual interaction. The researchers discovered one sex difference in that males viewed sharing and sexual expression as the most distinctive characteristic of intimacy whereas females understood intimate relationships as best characterized by openness and sharing.[10]

Young people's understanding of intimacy changes as they mature. As adolescents grow older they are more apt to view dating as an experience that fosters intimacy. In a study of early (junior high), middle (senior high), and late adolescence (college undergraduates), early and middle adolescents were more apt to view dating as an experience that fosters egocentric needs and gratification whereas late adolescents understood dating as fostering sharing and closeness.[11] As adolescents grow older they are better able to handle the demands of intimacy.

One critical question many adults come up against is whether an adolescent realizes the difference between love and infatuation. Because of developmental needs some adolescents find themselves overwhelmed by their feelings and caught up in a relationship where boundaries are often lost and the desire for physical expression of their feelings becomes overwhelming. How do we help youth to sort out such feelings? The triangular theory of love offered by psychologist Robert Sternberg can be helpful.

For Sternberg, there are three "ingredients" to love: (1) intimacy, (2) passion, and (3) decision/commitment.

Intimacy reflects closeness, sharing, and understanding. When one is intimate one communicates oneself to another at a deep level.

When one is *passionate,* one desires physical closeness or a sexual relationship with another. One is often thinking about the other and is very conscious of the other's presence or absence.

Decision/commitment refers to the determination to begin a relationship with a person as well as to maintain it, even in times of trial and discomfort.

The above three components in various combinations provide for eight "kinds of love" as represented in the accompanying chart.

I have found Sternberg's taxonomy of love to be quite helpful when working with adolescents and young adults. All too caught up in their feelings, adolescents are apt to misconstrue what their feelings really mean and what their behaviors in a relationship are trying to communicate. A discussion of Sternberg's descriptions of love can provide a wonderful teaching moment. Note that each of the components is an idealized category. More often than not, as Sternberg correctly states, relationships have varying intensities and combinations of the above components. Let us look at each of these "kinds of love" in relation to the adolescent and young adult experience.

Nonlove   In this relationship the adolescent has no particular attraction to another or obligation to him or her. When talking about a particular person, however, it is at times helpful to reflect with the adolescent on what it is about that person that prevents a relationship or leads her to shy away from any relationship. Such discussion can

Taxonomy of Love

Kind of Love	Intimacy	Passion	Decision/ commitment
Non-love	−	−	−
Liking	+	−	−
Infatuated love	−	+	−
Empty love	−	−	+
Romantic love	+	+	−
Companionate love	+	−	+
Fatuous love	−	+	+
Consummate love	+	+	+

Note: + = component present; − = component absent. These kinds of love represent idealized cases based on the triangular theory. Most loving relationships will fit between categories, because the components of love occur in varying degrees rather than being simply present or absent.

Reprinted with permission from Robert J. Sternberg, *The Triangle of Love* (New York: Basic Books, 1987), 51.

be profitable for it can aid the adolescent in understanding more fully her perceptions of others and her likes and dislikes.

Liking   The adolescent has some emotional closeness to a peer whom he "likes." Wide latitude exists in the degree of liking another. It can be worthwhile to reflect with an adolescent on why he likes one person so much. In these discussions focus specifically on features, characteristics, and behaviors of the other that the adolescent finds attractive.

Infatuated Love   All too often relationships in youth are based on idealization of the other, possessiveness, sexual involvement, or obsessing about the other, with little attention given to intimacy or commitment. Infatuation, in essence, is passionate love and nothing else. The best strategy here is to explore with the adolescent how well he "knows" the other. A question I sometimes ask is: "What are your feelings built on?" or "What will happen to your feelings over time if they are just feelings?" In other words, try to stretch the limits of the adolescent's notion of love.

Empty Love   Sometimes adolescents will share that their own parents' marriage is based on commitment, with little intimacy and passion in their marriage. A marriage based on "empty love" is a marriage of commitment and little else. When adolescents share such an experience I find it profitable to explore with them how growing up in such a family has affected them and how they wish their own relationships to be different from their parents'.

159

Romantic Love   Many adolescents find themselves in a relationship of passion and intimacy but no commitment. The best approach here is to focus on the couple's emotional and spiritual resources and how these resources will or will not nourish or sustain a commitment. Another important area for discussion is the role of commitment (best expressed as fidelity) in their relationship.

Companionate Love   This is the love most often found in significant friendships. Fruitful avenues here are to discuss with adolescents who their friends are and what it is about these relationships that leads them to classify certain significant others as friends.

Fatuous Love   This love is observed in long-term relationships in which the partners lack sufficient knowledge of the other. Tragically, such relationships all too often are doomed for failure.

Consummate Love   This type of love represents the "ideal" relationship. Most relationships only approximate this ideal.

At this point the reader might be somewhat perplexed by the many facets that make up relationships in adolescence. Friendship, love, romance, intimacy, and sexual feelings are all part of adolescent development. Let us examine several of these terms.

Friendship is a relationship of varying depth and intensity that ranges from what loosely is termed "a peer" to a deep, emotionally close, and confiding relationship of enormous emotional significance (a close or "best" friend). The meaning of friendship changes through adolescence. The most mature friendships are characterized by high degrees of intimacy, mutual support, and care, and focus on dreams and goals that bind the friends together.

Intimacy refers to feelings and behaviors that nurture and sustain interpersonal communication, self-disclosure, and emotional closeness. Intimacy can be present to various degrees in friendship and love.

Love relationships are those of emotional significance that take on distinctive features depending on the "type" of love. When the relationship is a romantic one there is passion that leads to arousal and a high degree of awareness of the other. Passion in love motivates one to physical closeness, touch, and sexual expression. Besides romantic attachments (characterized by passion), love can be present in friendship, parent-child relationships, or as a generalized attitude and stance toward others (*agape*).

Characteristics of a "Healthy" Relationship

In a pastoral and clinical context, I think the best approach to exploring relationships with adolescents is to shift the discussion from "intimacy" or "romance" to the domain of *health*, in other words, to help adolescents discern the characteristics that are sound building blocks for significant relationships in their lives. Whether it be a friendship or romantic attachment, we need to focus on specific criteria that foster ongoing developmental growth.

A theme of this book is that human development and spiritual/ moral growth are allies. Each of us works out our relationship with the Lord within the confines of the experiences and insights of our lives. Grace coheres and provides meaning for our life journey. Grace works within our human experience to create moments in which our decision-making leads to deepening freedom and more profound levels of self-donation modeled on our Lord's life. Developmental maturity and psychological health provide the optimum framework for grace to work; in maturity and health we are most disposed to be open, aware, and free to respond to the Lord's invitation. Of course, whether we choose to respond to the Lord's invitation is another matter, and most certainly maturity and psychological health are no guarantee that we will embrace discipleship.

Further, in each of our lives there are wounds and darkness. The life of every man and woman involves some brokenness and resistance to a total response to the Lord's beckoning. None of us experiences life as totally free when responding to the Lord's invitation. But our own suffering itself can be an enormous offering to the Lord (e.g., witness someone who admits that he or she is powerless over the lure of alcohol). Nonetheless, it is in and through maturity and psychological health that we are apt to be most *free* and possess the greatest capacity to respond; therefore, we must delineate those aspects of our life experience that both promote healthy relationships and nurture Christian self-identity.

A second reason to frame a discussion of relationships under the heading of health is that youth today are exposed to a wide range of social pathologies and human dysfunctions that mitigate against healthy relationship-building. We already mentioned above the "distorted idealizations" that erroneously define for many adolescents their view of what a relationship must be. In addition, far too many adolescents go without sufficient adult attention and feedback or falter under the weight of inadequate attachment bonding (see chapter 2) or the burden of damaged self-image. For many of these adolescents the flight into relationships serves as a distraction from maturity rather than a building block for it.

Finally, there is growing concern about the violence and dysfunction that are part of many adolescent and young adult relationships. Some women find themselves in relationships that are emotionally abusive or where dating violence or date rape has occurred. It is essential that young people explore what it means to be in a healthy relationship as a way to gain some self-understanding regarding their own behavior.

I offer below ten characteristics that one would hope to see span all meaningful relationships in the adolescent's life. These have as their goal the fostering of developmental growth as well as Christian discipleship. They can be used to evaluate significant relationships in young people's lives and as a blueprint for future relationship-building.

These are characteristics of an optimum relationship. Adolescents and young adults as well as adults rarely function on a level that insures all of these characteristics are consistently operating fully. The goal is to help adolescents be increasingly aware of them in their relationships (rather than trying them all at once).

Characteristics That Promote Healthy Relationships

How might we define a healthy relationship? More specifically, what characteristics allow us to speak of Christian relationship — a bond that nourishes psychological health and a life of discipleship during the adolescent and young adult years? Three considerations deserve attention: (1) psychological health, (2) the presence of Gospel values, and (3) the developmental needs of adolescents.

As with the case of healthy identity growth discussed in chapter 2, developing these characteristics is a process. That is, no adolescent simply "has" these characteristics in some neat package. Rather, they are slowly taken on; with time, some characteristics become more prominent than others. Ideally, as the young adult years are well under way (in the twenties) the young person consistently manifests these characteristics in everyday life.

1. Being Oneself   During the early adolescent years youth feel the pressures of conforming to peer expectations and external demands. One healthy sign of relationship-building is the adolescent's growing comfort with being who he or she truly is and finding the other person in the relationship capable of accepting this reality. Thus there is a growing comfort level with one's self-in-relationship.

- In what ways in this relationship can the adolescent be himself?
- In what ways in this relationship does the adolescent find difficulty in being himself?
- Is the adolescent growing in his comfort level with this relationship?

2. Confidence Sharing/Self-disclosure   As one becomes comfortable with another, one naturally eases into a self-disclosure mode.

During the adolescent period this is tremendously empowering, for it offers the opportunity for trusting another. Sharing confidences signals trust and acceptance. An adolescent soon discovers that she is not alone, that another understands, and that security is possible. At the same time, trust requires time to develop. Premature self-disclosure is inappropriate.

- Is the adolescent growing in trust with this relationship?
- In what areas in this relationship is there trust?
- In what areas in this relationship does trust need to grow?
- What level of self-disclosure takes place in the relationship?

3. Growing Value Awareness A healthy relationship includes becoming more aware that the relationship itself stands for something. In a sense, the relationship becomes more sacramental, for it proclaims the values of the two people within the relationship. A close friendship or a romantic attachment is a witness to what each of the adolescents holds dear. Thus the very actions of each toward the other — living life in fidelity, honesty, forgiveness, and care — mirror the faith life of each participant. As this witness grows, what the relationship stands for becomes the touchstone to evaluate personal actions. Often initially in the relationship a person might realistically ask: "What is the right way to treat the other?" But with the maturing of a relationship the young person now asks what she is called to because of the relationship. In some ways it can be said that the relationship takes on the role of a quasi-conscience, beckoning the adolescent to certain actions.

- Can the adolescent articulate what this relationship stands for?
- What does the experience of this relationship call the adolescent to be?

4. Respect for Boundaries As the adolescent deepens his relationship with another, an increasing mutuality transpires. Oftentimes the two youths share thoughts, feelings, and attitudes. Yet, as we have noted above, true intimacy with another means two different individuals-in-relationship. When the relationship is truly healthy, each adolescent can express many levels of feelings without fearing rejection. Each partner can be influenced by the expectations of the other but not have to conform to them. Nor do the feelings one has for the other become reactive. To be sure, the actions of the other elicit feelings, but they are measured and appropriate, lacking that knee-jerk quality that all too often is unreasonable, harsh, or blind in its response.

- Does the closeness the adolescent feels in this relationship still allow for a sense of separateness?
- How do the two young people in this relationship feel similar?
- How do they view themselves as different?
- How do they respond to differences in preference, attitudes, etc.?
- How do they respond to perceived and actual limitations and shortcomings of the other?
- How reactive are they to the actions of the other? Are their reactions appropriate?

5. Self-discovery   In chapter 2 we discussed one healthy identity characteristic termed "inner complexity." In the context of relationships, it means that the relationship augments self-understanding. I am constantly struck by the way adolescents use their relationships to increase self-knowledge, for example, in terms of emotions. In relationships the adolescent begins to discern an ever expanding and richer set of emotions. These emotional experiences, when lived out in the context of a healthy relationship, spawn a more complete sense of self, an inner sturdiness, so to speak, that enriches one's emotional life. If asked, the adolescent will describe herself as feeling "more complete" or of having "learned something" about herself because of the relationship. This affective undercurrent, stimulated through interpersonal attraction and dialogue, emerges as an essential building block for self-identity and healthy functioning. Ask the adolescent the following questions:

- "What have you learned about yourself from your relationship with _____?"
- "Have you thought about what you still have to learn?"
- "How are you different because of this relationship?" Discuss the differences she experiences.

6. Greater Ethical Sensitivity   This characteristic of a healthy relationship is best viewed as a growing consciousness of the moral dimensions of relational experiences. Keeping confidence, being honest, and doing what is "right" in the relationship increasingly occupy center stage. The adolescent is moving from self-gratification and personal interest as the touchstone for "what to do" in the relationship to a focus on values beyond the self. For example, whether to betray a trust is evaluated more by a commitment to a set of moral principles than by self-gratification.

- Is the adolescent more able to base how to act in the relationship on moral principles (e.g., life of Jesus, Gospel values) rather than on self-interest or self-gratification.

164

- Because of this relationship does the adolescent appear to be more ethically sensitive?

- How is Jesus part of this adolescent's life? How is Jesus part of this adolescent's relationship?

7. Wishing the Good of the Other   With this characteristic the adolescent increasingly desires what is "good" for the other. Even if this good demands sacrifice on the adolescent's part, it is acceptable. Such a stance is obviously the result of a developmental process, and even in late adolescence the natural pulls for possessiveness and self-gratification often override it. Sadly, and often painfully, in some instances this "good" might even lead the relationship to be terminated.

- Ask the adolescent: "What do you really desire for _____ in your relationship with her?"

- Inquire from the adolescent what he believes is best for the other person in the relationship, using the criteria of actions, attitudes, and future behaviors. What is best for himself?

- Can the adolescent see this friend as a "gift" from God?

- How is this adolescent grateful for this friendship?

8. Deepening Level of Commitment   In its fullest sense commitment represents a willingness to remain invested in a relationship even when difficulties arise. True commitment implies self-knowledge and awareness of the other. Further, it means a realistic assessment of the future as well as a hopeful stance regarding events to come.

- Is there a growing sense in the relationship that the adolescents wish it to continue over time?

- Are the adolescents growing more aware of what this particular relationship represents to them as well as what it means for their future-in-relationship?

- Are the adolescents realistic about the future?

9. Increasing Awareness of Other   As research has shown, relationships during the adolescent years are typified by an expanding awareness of another's needs. On average, late adolescents are more apt to be attentive and knowledgeable about one another's needs than early adolescents.

- Does the adolescent appear to be growing in attentiveness and sensitivity to the needs of the other?

165

- Is the adolescent better able to recognize selfish attitudes and behavior in the relationship? Is he able to balance another's rights with his own legitimate needs in the relationship? Is he growing in his awareness of his needs in the relationship?

10. Appropriate Display of Emotions   Significant relationships in the adolescent's life trigger a wide range of emotional responses. Adolescent emotional responses not only demonstrate the significance of the other person; they also reflect the adolescent's discovery of her own deepening affective life. Emotions must be tried out and grown into; through significant relationships the adolescent learns to be comfortable with emotions of various depth and intensity.

- Are the adolescent's emotional displays appropriate?
- How have the feelings of the adolescent led to deepening self-insight?
- How aware is the adolescent of the variety of feelings she might have about this relationship? Can the adolescent express reasons for the various feelings she has?
- What is the range of emotions displayed by this adolescent?

These ten characteristics define an "ideal" healthy Christian relationship. Even the healthiest and most meaningful relationships will at times fall short of realizing all the above qualities. Moreover, the vast majority of adult relationships only approximate these characteristics. Living the life of discipleship is a never-ending journey toward the ideal. What remains essential is the desire and striving to make *more* real by word, thought, and action the living of the Christian life in one's current situation. Concretely, what does this mean? For the adolescent it requires focusing on significant relationships and examining them in a thoughtful and reflective manner. My own pastoral and clinical experience lead me to conclude that the adolescent or young adult is often unable by himself or herself to discern fully whether a relationship is healthy and growthful. As is so often the case adults intervening in adolescents' lives in reflective and respectful ways and engaging in dialogue with them about their relationships offer the best hope that they will acquire a discerning vision in regard to their relationships.

Adolescent Sexual Behavior

Adolescents today are bombarded by the media with messages about sex. Not surprisingly, our culture's obsession with sex, as well as other psychological and sociological factors, encourage sexual activity in youth. Not only are more young people sexually active, but they are sexually active at younger ages. Further, increasing sexual activity is more pronounced among girls; that is, girls' level of sexual involvement is approaching that of boys.[12]

Specialists in human development still have much to learn regarding adolescent sexual behavior; indeed, the study of adolescent sexuality might well be considered to be in its infancy. From their summary of the available literature, social scientists Brent Miller, Cynthia Christopherson, and Pamela King offer the following understanding of adolescent sexual behavior.[13] Not surprisingly, age is positively related to sexual intercourse. That is, the older the adolescent is, the more likely he or she is to have had intercourse. Race is also a factor, with African-American adolescent males having their first experience of intercourse before white or Hispanic males. "Stated differently, black males are about 2 years ahead of white and Hispanic males in the proportion who report having sexual intercourse by a given age."[14] Sexual intercourse at an early age tends to be associated with deviant behaviors such as delinquency and drug abuse; however this trend does not hold up for older adolescents inasmuch as sexual involvement for older adolescents becomes the normative experience. Early age for first intercourse is also associated with higher numbers of sexual partners for both sexes. By age nineteen over half of adolescent females and over three-fourths of adolescent boys report having had sexual intercourse. Though a majority of both sexes have had sexual intercourse, adolescents vary in the amount of sexual activity they engage in. Many adolescents have had few sexual encounters whereas for others sexual activity occurs often.

Adolescents appear to have some type of quasi-moral or commitment stance. For most adolescents, sexual activity is confined to the person they are attached to at the moment; no doubt, most such relationships are emotional attachments with high degrees of infatuation — with sexual involvement lacking intimacy and accompanied by only minimal commitment. It is also a minority of youth (though it is growing) who have multiple sexual partners.

Increased sexual activity among young people has left many parents confused and bewildered. One unfortunate consequence of such behavior is the increasing tendency of some parents to allow sexual activity by their children in the home. Some parents have the attitude that if their child is going to be sexually active it might as well be in the home where he or she is safe from AIDS. Though I can understand parental concern, I do believe that such thinking is woefully misguided. Adolescent sexual desires and urges can be experienced as overwhelmingly powerful during these developing years. As in other areas of the adolescent's life, there is often the need to provide safe environments that offer structure and guidance for these impulses. To state this matter differently, adolescents need places and periods where their impulses are contained and boundaries clearly delineated. Such structure nourishes the adolescent's psyche to seek other forms of developmental growth and offers convenient refuge from the internal and social pressures so commonplace during this period. More than anywhere else, the family environment should provide such a structure. I am afraid the message given from such parental permissiveness is that "no place is safe from your impulses" and that for most adolescents this lack of safety proves both emotionally and developmentally burdensome. In making this statement I do not by any means wish to denigrate or dismiss adolescent sexual desires. Having such impulses and feelings is a normal part of any adolescent's experience. What I do maintain is that the proper channeling and appropriate expression of such feelings in the context of healthy environments offers the optimal experience for mature integration of the adolescent's moral and emotional selves. Parental attitudes and guidance are vital for insuring that such healthy environments exist.

Pastoral Practice and Adolescent Sexuality

In discussing a pastoral practice with youth I first want to affirm the Christian notion that links sexual union with marriage. The mystery and wonder of sexual intimacy is realized most fully through marital union. I believe that sexual involvement outside of marriage always lacks something. The essential linkage between sexual intimacy and marriage as expressed in Christian tradition can be understood on several levels.

1. Meaning-making   It is true that humans have diverse needs. The need for food and water is never far from our consciousness; like all other animals humans seek to satisfy these most basic needs. Deficiencies render us vulnerable, thereby leading to extraordinary efforts to satisfy our hunger and thirst. But as humans we possess capacities other than those we share with animals. Our capacity for reflection leads us to construct meanings for, patterns to, and evaluations of our behavior. Through reflection and the accrued wisdom gathered over the centuries, the Christian tradition has understood sexual expression as mirroring Christ's love for his church. Only the marriage union provides the context that allows sexual intercourse to capture most fully the profound significance of the innermost bond of the Lord's fidelity to and love for the believing community. The love of husband and wife in a committed relationship symbolizes most fully this fidelity and love of the Lord.

In another sense this symbolization underscores the profound level of meaning-making that is unique to personhood. Human beings are meaning-makers who construct meaning by what they say and do. Sexual intercourse is an enormously pleasurable experience, yet this experience is fraught with meaning. Sexual intercourse within marriage signifies the love of one spouse for the other that is a total giving of self, and it occurs within the context of stability and the proper environment for the raising of children. As the moralist Lisa Sowle Cahill notes, there is an essential linkage among sex, love, and procreation. She writes that marriage in the Catholic Christian context is understood

> as an ongoing nexus of social and personal relationships in which sexuality's positive potential is best protected and realized. The message is: sexual pleasure is good, but it is not the whole meaning of sexuality; sex is an unparalleled avenue of intimacy and bonding; and, in addition to enhancing the relationship of the sexual couple, sex has in parenthood and family a distinctive creative power by which it extends and enlivens the couple's own relationship and reinforces the dialectic of their social identity and contribution. In other words, there is a radical and enriching unity to sex's several dimensions: physical pleasure, interpersonal intimacy, and shared parenthood. It is through all of these that a couple's relationship takes on its moral and sacramental character.[15]

In the marriage covenant man and woman publicly proclaim their fidelity and commitment; outside of it the meaning of sexual intercourse is compromised and to some degree rendered impaired. Sexual intercourse outside of marriage occurs outside the context that best insures mutual intimacy and adequate parenting. The profound nature of the meaning of sexual intimacy is reflected in the community's acknowledgment of the sacramental union. Thus for the adolescent there must be discussion of what their sexual behavior *means* to them. Yes, it offers pleasure, provides security, and serves the need for self-understanding. But what does it *mean*? How does it reflect what is most significant for the adolescent — the Lord's intimate relationship? Marriage offers the best assurance that one's sexual behavior will be responsible, nurturing, and creative. Only in marriage does sexual intercourse symbolize the deepest meaning of assent — the "yes" to permanent fidelity through public witness, the "yes" of Jesus whose life was always proclaimed faithfulness.

I do not for a moment believe that expressing this truth to adolescents and young adults will be easy. Indeed, given our culture, the personal histories of many young people, and the lack of guidance in their lives, it will be very difficult for them to understand themselves as meaning-makers, particularly in the area of sexuality. But obstacles must be viewed as a hindrance rather than an excuse. It is incumbent on adults who represent the church in pastoral roles to inquire of adolescents how their actions and behaviors, including those in the area of sexuality, reflect the life of Jesus and the discipleship he calls us to.

2. Frailty   Sexual expression can be a profoundly enriching experience that sustains and nourishes a couple's relationship. Yet sexual intimacy in far too many instances masks emotional and developmental problems. Deceit, possessiveness, manipulation, and unacknowledged feelings such as anger undermine the true meaning of human sexual expression. Unfortunately, some people use sexual expression not as a reflection of closeness and union but as a way to fool themselves regarding their level of commitment or distract themselves from underlying problems in the relationship that need to be addressed. Further, countless people are hurt and rendered vulnerable by the transient nature or instability of their relationships. As a priest and a psychologist I have encountered numerous instances where sexual expression was a mask that covered underlying problems that a couple, because of their own immaturity or unrecognized feelings, were unable to work through. If such frailty is characteristic of many adult relationships, it is not difficult to understand the extreme vulnerability of the adolescent's experience. Developmental issues and overpowering sexual urges cloud the adolescent's decision-making regarding sexual expression.

3. Societal Need   An issue of enormous social and psychological significance is the growing number of unwed mothers and single-parent families. The wider community has a vital stake in upholding the marital union as the proper state for sexual expression. Several decades ago having a child out of wedlock was viewed as a deviant form of behavior and met with much social disapproval. Over this past decade, however, the deviant has more and more become the norm. Today roughly 30 percent of children in America are born to unmarried women. One research institute reports that a million adolescents become pregnant each year. Sadly, more and more teens view having a child as a personal decision and do not reflect on the adverse consequences of such a decision.[16]

Reasons for Adolescent Sexual Behavior

In ministering to adolescents, the first step must be to try to understand the *reasons* that underlie sexual activity. In *Adolescent Spirituality* I discussed a number of reasons for adolescent sexual behavior. In our current discussion I restate these reasons with a more pastoral/clinical emphasis for them.

1. Intimacy   As an adolescent becomes emotionally close to someone there is the desire to express such closeness not only through sharing but through physical expressions such as kissing, petting, and sexual intercourse. Emotional involvement is associated with increased sexual activity for many adolescents and young adults.

- What does sexual activity signify for this adolescent? What is this adolescent trying "to say" by his or her sexual expression?

2. Belonging   Adolescents feel a need to belong. Social interactions with peers lead to increased familiarity and bonding. Over time such involvement might eventuate in sexual expression.

- How does this adolescent feel secure? Is sexual expression a way for this adolescent to feel secure?

3. Dominance   Some youth, particularly male adolescents, feel the need to dominate. Sexual expression provides an experience of power.

- Does this adolescent feel the need to dominate others? Does sexual expression for this youth enhance feelings of being powerful?

4. Submissiveness   Some youth, on the other hand, find their sexual experience as a way to remain dependent on their partner.

- How does this adolescent handle dependency feelings? What purpose does being dependent serve in this adolescent's life?

5. Natural Curiosity   Fascination with sex is understandable, given adolescent developmental changes as well as the emphasis placed on sex by our culture. An adolescent is expected to perform well sexually; there is enormous pressure from peers and the culture to "have it together" and to be "sexually experienced."

- To what extent is this adolescent's sexual behavior motivated by an attempt to understand his or her sexual feelings? How much pressure is there on this adolescent to perform sexually?

6. Passion and Intensity   Sexual expression is an enormously powerful experience in a person's life. As the psychologist John Mitchell notes, "Passion is especially important as a source of psychological rejuvenation, serving to uplift the person, giving a sense of validation, and reinforcing the sense of personal identity."[17]

- What does this sexual relationship "do" for this adolescent? Is it a source of fulfillment, joy, rejuvenation? Is sexual activity a way for the adolescent to distract herself from painful or negative feelings?

171

7. Identification and Imitation   Images in modern culture convey the insidious message that we must always be totally satisfied. We must take and "fill up." On the other hand, we are given the message that critical self-reflection and discernment are to be avoided for they conjure up the notion that our life might be incomplete. Many adolescents succumb to manipulative cultural icons that eschew personal reflection and self-scrutiny. They emulate instead glorified figures who portray hedonistic and consumeristic models.

- How captive is this youth to cultural stereotypes? To what degree is this young person capable of interior reflection and self-scrutiny?

8. Rebelliousness and Negative Identity   Adolescent behavior conveys many messages to the adult world. Challenging adult authority or flouting rules or the adult's expectations are commonplace in most adolescents' lives. When the adolescent becomes preoccupied with being contrary or rebellious then he is said to have adopted a "negative identity." With a negative identity the adolescent scripts a self-definition based on defiance and obstruction rather than the working through of developmental issues. Sexual behavior is one vehicle for the adolescent to announce "no" to the adult world.

- What message is this sexually active adolescent attempting to give adults? What is the quality of this adolescent's relationships with adults (particularly parents). Is sexual behavior a way for this adolescent to defy or provoke parents or other significant adults?

9. Peer Approval   The adolescent who remains chaste can all too easily be perceived as "odd" or view herself as "weird" or "not with it." Isolation and loneliness result. For boys, not being sexually active may convey the impression that they are homosexual. Sexual intercourse, then, might help a boy prove his heterosexual orientation.

- How does this adolescent deal with peer pressure and disapproval? Does the adolescent have sources of support besides a group of peers that might be disapproving of his actions?

10. Escape   Tragically, an increasing number of adolescents use sex as a means to escape difficult and emotionally painful home situations.

- Is this adolescent's sexual behavior a way she escapes from painful feelings? Does sexual involvement help distract this adolescent from emotional burdens?

11. A Cry for Help   Promiscuous behavior signals psychological pain. Some adolescents become overwhelmed by their hurt and emotional distress and know no way to ask for help other than to act out sexually. (Drug taking and other deviant behavior might also be cries for help.)

- Could there be a link between this adolescent's severe emotional distress and her sexual behavior?

12. Fear of Intimacy   Though sexual expression ideally signifies commitment and a profound level of knowing, in some instances adolescents engage in sexual behavior as a way to avoid intimacy. If one's identity is diffuse, then intimacy proves difficult to achieve. In such instances sexual expression becomes a substitute for true intimacy. The adolescent more or less unconsciously says, "I'll prove that I can be intimate. I'll have sex." The adolescent erroneously equates sex and intimacy.

- To what degree does this adolescent experience the characteristics of a healthy relationship presented earlier in this chapter? How capable is this adolescent of intimacy?

13. Pleasure   The pleasurable experience of sexual intercourse is itself reinforcing. Sexual behavior becomes all the more tempting when the adolescent lacks other experiences of joy, pleasure, or gratification.

- What sources of joy and pleasure does this adolescent have in his life besides sexual expression?

14. Love   As the adolescent matures it is increasingly possible for sexual expression genuinely to express loving care and commitment for the future (though it probably expresses other needs as listed above as well).

- Reflect with the adolescent on what she means by love. How does she know this relationship is built on love? What other needs (from the above list) does this relationship fulfill? How is Jesus Christ part of this relationship?

A Pastoral Approach to Adolescent Sexuality

1. Compassionate Care   In helping adolescents to understand their sexuality we must begin with a fundamental premise of pastoral ministry: compassionate care and loving challenge. These twin themes highlight what we so often encounter in the Gospels — Jesus' openness and acceptance of others and his constant desire to challenge others to grow in efforts to build the Kingdom. We must be accepting of where the adolescent is developmentally and offer him or her compassionate care. At the same time, as adult Christians we must challenge adolescents to further Christian growth. Questioning techniques provide the best approach to helping adolescents deal with their relationships and the meaning they give to their own sexual expression.

The first duty of the pastoral minister is to try to understand the importance of the relationship in the adolescent's life. Young peoples' relationships, whether they be sexually active or not, are of enormous significance. Find out from the adolescent how the relationship has helped him to grow. What is different about the adolescent because of this relationship? What has the adolescent found out about himself through this relationship? Adolescent relationships provide one of the most important avenues for self-discovery, a building block for identity growth that fosters self-knowledge and self-esteem. When reflecting with the adolescent questions to keep in mind include:

a. What are the developmental issues that underlie this adolescent's sexual behavior?

b. In what ways is this sexual behavior leading to growth and integration in the adolescent's emotional and spiritual life? How much awareness does the adolescent have of the growth that is taking place in herself?

c. To what extent is the adolescent deepening his insight into his own self and his relationships with others?

d. Does this relationship lead the adolescent to seek more growth in her relationships — a growth characterized by responsibility and commitment?

e. What is the level of commitment expressed in this relationship? Can the adolescent reflect on and talk about this commitment?

f. Does the adolescent have a realistic assessment of her relationship with the other?

In a discussion of the significance of a relationship I have found it helpful to incorporate the "reasons" for adolescent sexual behavior discussed above. At this point I stress the more positive reasons, such as the need for intimacy, in order to avoid defensiveness on the adolescent's part.

Adolescents need to feel that they can discuss their experience on their own terms and have their experience respected. Any pastorally effective approach must include respect and understanding.

2. Loving Challenge   Having demonstrated caring and compassion, it is incumbent upon the adult to provide the means for the adolescent's growth through loving challenge. There are several ways to bring this about.

(*a*) The adult can reflect with the adolescent on how he views a particular relationship as "healthy." The characteristics discussed earlier in this chapter provide some concrete points for discussion. Since no adolescent relationship will realize all of the characteristics, fruitful time can be spent discussing them. Few adolescents will have explored the dimension of "health" in their relationships, and it can be beneficial to do so.

(*b*) It is safe to assume that there are multiple reasons for an adolescent's sexual involvement. Often these reasons are tied to unresolved developmental issues or psychological conflicts. Thus an adolescent, because of need or hurt (both of which are often unconscious), might find sexual expression to be an escape from conflicts in her life. For example, Megan's father is an alcoholic and verbally abusive; her mother is co-dependent on her father and continually criticizing Megan's behavior. In such a family how is Megan to develop the self-esteem and discerning reflection necessary for healthy decision-making? Might she not seek out compensatory experiences that provide her solace and security in an emotional world she finds cold and hurtful? For too many adolescents such as Megan, premature sexual involvement becomes a ready substitute for an emotionally deprived family. With cultural pressures increasing and social mores inhibiting sexual expression on the decline, large numbers of adolescents will continue, mistakenly, to attempt to find through their sexual behavior the care and nurture that should be provided by a well-functioning family system and healthy peer relationships.

The above example points to the power of one's affective intensity to blur and frustrate healthy moral decision-making. In effect, such affective turmoil makes one less free and less able to discern options. If the adult knows the adolescent well or at least is aware of the adolescent's situation, then it is important that the adult widen the discussion and help the adolescent to view how family situations and hurts from other relationships (e.g., breakups) are affecting the current relationship. A helpful way to explore the adolescent's affective life and sexual behavior is to call attention to the family situation or other relationship. Name the feelings the adolescent feels as a consequence of his family situation and relationships. Then explore how he is dealing with these feelings and ask an open-ended question such as: "Do you think, Jack, that there is any way you are dealing with these feelings through your involvement with Elaine?" "Have you thought about this?" Gently probe with these questions. With older adolescents it might also be helpful to frame the discussion in terms of freedom and how negative feelings can make us unfree by clouding our decision-making.

(c) In all relationships there are many opportunities for deceit, dishonesty, possessiveness, jealousy, etc. A way to approach these issues is, again, to first establish what the adolescent experiences in the relationship, focusing on its positive features. Then point out that rarely is anything of just one dimension. For example, even our closest relationships are at times experiences of hurt and disappointment. Use examples from the adolescent's own life. Then ask a question such as, "Kristy, you have spoken about so many positive features of your relationship with Jim. I appreciate what you have said, and I am now wondering if you could talk about your relationship with Jim in terms of the areas that still need to grow and develop? Or what areas are not so wonderful and need to be looked at?" Any adolescent who takes offense at such questions or refuses to examine her relationship critically is probably one whose sexual involvement is the result of need and psychological conflicts rather than a growthful, maturing love. One mark of maturity is the capacity to examine openly and honestly what we value and hold dear. "Loving challenge," of course, must be preceded by "compassionate care," which fosters the trust and openness that allows loving challenge to be accepted and bear fruit.

(d) A fourth approach to loving challenge might be termed "social." As already noted, we live in a culture in which the message is clearly how each of us deserves to be "filled up." The Christian message of fidelity and commitment that allows for forgiveness and critical examination of our actions is shunned and displaced by a message of immediate gratification and superficial relationships. As the religious educator James DiGiacomo notes, "Seldom do the media portray sexuality as linked with commitment, stable family relationships and child bearing. Instead, it is associated with romance, with casual encounters or temporary relationships, with the unspoken premise that fidelity or permanence are not to be expected and may even be undesirable."[18] Often it is helpful to discuss with adolescents how such cultural messages have affected their relationships. Reflect with them on the assumptions and premises that are operative when they relate with peers and how these assumptions and premises have been affected by the wider cultural milieu.

(e) A final point under the loving challenge approach is perhaps the one most directly related to the Christian message. It involves the person of Jesus. I sometimes ask couples or adolescents how Jesus is part of their relationship. Questions such as "How are you showing yourself a friend of Jesus in your relationship?" or "What do you think Jesus would say to you?" are disarming yet fruitful sources for stimulating reflections on adolescent relationships. Discussion of the meaning of "commitment" can also be helpful. (Adults must of course have some understanding of the meaning of this term for themselves.) Finally, I have found it helpful to explore the adolescent's own meaning-making. Helpful questions include: "What are you trying to say by your relationship with one another?" "What does your relationship convey about you?" "What meaning does your sexual relationship provide?" "Have you thought about what you still need for your relationship in terms of being a Christian?"

In chapter 1 we discussed the need for adults who minister to youth to maintain their integrity. Sexual relationships within the sacramental union of marriage have the potential for a profoundly enriching experience. Yet even in marriage the union of a couple also has the potential for harm, because of the existential condition for the partners, their life histories, sin, or psychological immaturity. This is even truer of the sexual involvement of adolescents. There are times when adults for their own *integrity* must speak honestly and openly about the sin, the immaturity, or the psychological problems involved in the adolescent's sexual or emotional involvement with another adolescent. Such challenges are not easy, but adults must exercise their Christian witness with integrity as adult members of the Christian community. Some adolescents need the active intervention of adults to focus on actions or areas of their lives that are harmful. Such "forceful" loving challenge is pastorally most effective when presented *after* "compassionate care" has been demonstrated. The adult must never be far from the question: "Where is my integrity?" or "What does my integrity call me to do in this pastoral situation?" But the living out of this integrity most reflects the Gospel when it is done within the wider context of compassionate care.

The Use of Birth Control in Adolescence

One of the most complex pastoral encounters for adults ministering to adolescents involves the question of premarital use of birth control. What is the adult to do? We know that as adolescents advance in age they are more likely to be sexually active. Further, we know that one million teenagers become pregnant every year. The psychological and economic harm resulting from such pregnancies is well documented. Close to half end in abortion. Nearly half of adolescents fail to use contraceptive devices at the time of their first sexual encounter and a "substantial" number of adolescents fail to use contraceptives in their later sexual relationships.[19] "It is generally recognized that the high rate of adolescent pregnancy in American society relative to other developed nations is attributable to the relatively infrequent and ineffective use of contraception among sexually active adolescents."[20] Tragically, as the data suggest, the stage is set for unplanned pregnancies, a social (and moral) problem that some have labeled an "epidemic."

I believe that religious institutions must publicly oppose contraceptive use by adolescents. Given the collapse and breakdown of so many social structures in our society, churches remain one of the few forces that can provide guidance and structure in the area of sexual behavior. Society is desperately in need of the church's moral stance proclaiming chastity and sexual fidelity as viable alternatives to today's consumer-oriented sexual lifestyle.

Moving from the institutional to the individual level, however, we still face the dilemma of the adult who ministers to the adolescent on a one-on-one basis. In such situations a pastorally sound position is the following. The adult should reflect with the adolescent on Christian values and sexuality and health in relationships, using the "loving challenge" approach discussed above. The adult should not encourage the sexual behavior but should help the adolescent understand the behavior in light of Christian discipleship. If it is clear that the adolescent will remain sexually active, then as a practical pastoral judgment the adult should introduce a discussion of contraceptive usage.

Some might say that discussing contraceptives encourages adolescent sexual behavior. I understand the concern behind such a statement, but we must consider the issue in a wider context.

First, we must address the integrity of the adult who is ministering to the adolescent. By discussion of such factors as "health" and by using a "loving challenge" approach, the adult is maintaining integrity. In effect, by offering an invitation to dialogue the adult is calling the adolescent to Christian discipleship. This is the heart of pastoral ministry and the essence of Christian integrity.

Second, as already noted, one goal of pastoral counseling is the development of self-insight in order that the adolescent might better recognize the Lord's invitation. Deepening self-knowledge includes the question: "How do I take responsibility for my actions?" The adult must minister to the adolescent where that young person *is*, both developmentally and morally. In short, where you are is where you are. To be sure, each of us is called to ongoing growth to more fully realize the discipleship we are called to. But if active sexual involvement is where the adolescent is, then any growth must of necessity start from this current experience. And a key factor in growth is the adolescent's acceptance of responsibility for his or her actions.

A starting point for discussion is a question like this: "Given your sexual involvement, have you thought about how you are taking responsibility for your behavior?" Answers to this question can lend insight into the adolescent's self-perception as a responsible person as well as how the partner in the relationship is viewed. Discussion of pregnancy is also warranted. Having a child out of wedlock or a premature commitment to marriage because of a pregnancy involve very serious moral, social, and psychological issues that need to be addressed. Such discussions should always end with questions for the adolescent to leave with and reflect on. Posing questions helps adolescents to see that where they are is part of a longer process of growth in discipleship and that this process must be reflected upon. The framework for the discussions should be one of loving challenge, reflecting with the adolescent on what is required for a healthy Christian relationship.

Third, in discussing contraceptive usage, the adult should express this possibility with concern and regret. Phrases such as "I am concerned about suggesting this..." or "This troubles me but..." convey to the adolescent that the adult's statements are serious and challenging. Such nuanced statements also maintain the adult's own integrity.

Related to contraceptive usage is the changing status of couples in modern society. Though marriage remains extremely popular and most people do marry, the number of individuals who remain single or have childless marriages is increasing. Likewise, the number of unmarried couples living together continues to rise as does the number of single-parent families and the number of unmarried mothers. Such changing demographics do not go unnoticed by adolescents and can easily influence impressionable youth.

It also appears that many unmarried Americans have opted for sexual relationships in the context of less than permanent commitment. After analyzing survey data, sociologist Andrew Greeley notes

> it would appear that an emergent ethic among many single Americans regards sex as designed for monogamous bonding in quasi-permanent and quasi-committed relationships, which differ from married relationships only in that a public commitment to fidelity and permanency has not (yet) been made.[21]

My own pastoral experience leads me to support Greeley's conclusion. Many young adults in their twenties and thirties have opted for some type of "quasi" relationship that proclaims some type of specialness and exclusivity about the relationship but also eschews any statement of permanency. When pastorally ministering to such couples I again recommend (a) focusing on the "healthy" characteristics of the relationship as well as (*b*) utilizing the approaches of compassionate care and loving challenge mentioned earlier in this chapter. When such couples indicate a willingness to marry, have them consider something like the following: "Why marry now, why not six months ago or six months from now? What has happened in your relationship to make you desire marriage at this time?" Focusing on "what has happened" is an ideal way to begin a discussion of growth and commitment — where the relationship was, where it is going, and how it still needs to grow.

Sexually Transmitted Diseases

A recent headline in the local newspaper announced: "HIV Set to Spread among Area Teens." The increase in HIV/AIDS infection is a major cause of concern among health professionals. The figures are frightening. AIDS now ranks as the sixth leading cause of death among young people aged fifteen to twenty-four. The number of adolescents with AIDS has increased 77 percent in the past three years.[22] Because the lag time between HIV infection and full-blown AIDS can be ten years, many young adults showing symptoms in their twenties were probably infected in their teen years. Around 4 percent of AIDS cases fall into the twenty-to-twenty-four-year-old age range and nearly 16 percent are found among twenty-five-to-twenty-nine-year olds.[23] According to one estimate "nationwide, the rate of teenagers with HIV increases 100 percent every 14 months."[24] A recent study of students on college campuses indicates that perhaps one in five hundred has become infected with the HIV virus. Though college students in general are well informed about HIV/AIDS, many students refuse to practice safe sex.[25] There are other features of HIV infection among adolescents that vary from findings among adults. According to the Center for Disease Control, 6 percent of adult AIDS cases are accounted for by heterosexual contact, but for the adolescent population this figure is 12 percent. AIDS occurs nine times more in men than women in the United States, but among thirteen-to-twenty-four-year-olds the ratio is just four to one.[26] Adolescents at especially high risk for HIV infection include poor, homeless, gay, and runaway youths.

Why are adolescents who are sexually active not practicing safe sex? There are a variety of reasons. We have already touched on cultural messages promoting casual sex and the prevailing ethos in the media of sex with "no consequences." Young people have a desire to experiment and find out about themselves, which includes discovering themselves sexually; often such experimentation is unplanned. Peer pressure undermines efforts at self-control and is reinforced by media messages. Those most at risk for HIV infection — e.g., run-aways, the homeless — focus on simply surviving day by day, and the possibility of HIV infection is far down on their list of concerns.[27]

We have already noted the adolescent tendency to take risks. Generally speaking, adolescents weigh risk and make decisions just as adults do, yet for some there might well be a self-focus that promotes a feeling of invincibility and an "it-can't-happen-to-me" mentality. Many adolescents are focused on the present and sim-ply don't consider long-term consequences. Teenage smoking is an example. Teens do not consider the long-term consequences such as lung cancer or heart disease; rather, they live for the present sensa-tion. Youth for the most part are not exposed to the "saliency" of the consequences of HIV infection. Because of the long incubation pe-riod for HIV, most youth do not see full-blown AIDS cases and thus are deprived of firsthand witness to the disease's lethality. This fos-ters a lack-of-consequences mentality. Also, sexual expression can be a statement to the adult world that the adolescent is his or her own person. The struggle for independence drowns out messages of absti-nence and safe sex. Finally, ignorance of the disease or contraceptive use might be a factor for some youth.[28]

AIDS is not the only sexually transmitted disease that is a threat to the health of youth. According to one research institute, one in five Americans is infected with a sexually transmitted disease (STD). It is estimated that "12 million new sexually transmitted infections occur each year, two-thirds of them to people under 25, and one-quarter to teen-agers."[29] Adolescents and young adults are particularly suscep-tible to STD infection because they are most likely to be unmarried and to have had several sexual partners. The most common STD (with an estimated four million new infections every year) is chlamy-dia, which is widespread among sexually active adolescents and young adults. Chlamydia can lead to urinary, rectal, or vaginal in-fection as well as other serious illnesses. Infertility can also result if chlamydia remains untreated. Unfortunately, the disease often re-mains undetected because many people (particularly women) have no symptoms. Other STDs include gonorrhea, genital warts, geni-tal herpes, and syphilis. STDs, excluding AIDS, account for seven thousand deaths every year.[30]

Given the potential lethal consequences of AIDS and the health problems associated with other sexually transmitted diseases, what should be the stance of the adult pastorally ministering to youth?

Bishop Francis Quinn has addressed this issue directly. The church has consistently stated that genital sexual activity should be reserved for marriage. The church's stance, I believe, has been vindicated by the rampant spread of sexually transmitted disease.

Abstinence remains the only certain way to avoid a sexually transmitted disease. Many fault the church's position as impractical, yet it remains the only certain way to avoid consequences that can be life-threatening.

This brings us directly to the question of condom usage. One problem with promoting condom usage among youth is that it conveys the message that casual sex is the norm and there is no need for self-control. It is frightening that such advice is being offered to youth who are already inundated by cultural messages that casual sex is acceptable and commitment, self-control, and fidelity are not valued in relationships.

> Could it be that the routine distribution of condoms to young people sends the message that casual sex is inevitable, sends the message that one really cannot control the sexual drive and that recreational sex is perfectly acceptable and the norm? That message being received defeats the original purpose of the distribution of the condoms by perhaps increasing rather than reducing the bottom line numbers of AIDS cases.

Bishop Quinn further asks: "Could it not be true that because of the resulting increased incidence of general promiscuity that the total number of HIV cases is greatly increased?"[31]

Questions must also be asked about the safety of condom usage. Use of condoms does greatly lessen the chances of HIV infection, but it does not eliminate this possibility. Condoms do fail. Failures can be the result of slippage, breakage, or not following instructions. Since adolescent sexual intercourse is often experienced under the influence of alcohol and other drugs or in the passion of the moment, following instructions is a matter of serious concern. Furthermore, some condoms are defective and therefore not safe. And the virus for HIV is significantly smaller than the smallest detectable hole in a condom. Because of the problems with condom usage, the more sexual intercourse is engaged in, the more likely an HIV-infected person is to infect a partner. Because AIDS is always fatal, serious moral problems arise from the uncritical acceptance of condom distribution as a form of "safe" sex. Condom usage, in short, does *not* necessarily produce safe sex and might in fact lead to AIDS and eventual death. One commentator noted that providing adolescents with condoms is like using small caliber bullets when playing Russian roulette.[32] In sum, the use of condoms reduces the risk of HIV transmission but does not eliminate it. Because of the lethality of AIDS, the church's stance on abstinence and marital fidelity makes good moral and medical sense!

Plans to distribute condoms in schools give the erroneous impression that in today's climate casual sex can be made safe. I agree with John Quinn, who asserts that with condom distribution in schools and health clinics

> the message comes through clearly that there is no real concern about the wholesome psychosexual development and integration of youth and about the effect of extramarital, adolescent sexual activity on that development. Absent is any real concern about the young person's growth in self-esteem, or growth in understanding and respecting the sacredness of sex and the importance of a genuine sense of responsibility in regard to sex.[33]

Condom distribution in schools and public health agencies is well-intended but misguided. I am afraid it gives license to adolescents involved in transient or infatuated relationships and succumbs to the current cultural milieu that promotes casual, recreational sex devoid of respect and responsibility. Simply stated, it teaches youth the wrong message. Given the misguided messages of the entertainment industry, it is imperative that society have social institutions that counter the casual sex mentality with messages of fidelity, commitment, and integrity. Religious institutions undermine the message they wish to convey when they allow condom distribution.

> It is the burden and inalienable responsibility of the church to call society as a whole to challenge the current normative environment in the hope and belief that many of the ills that characterize that environment can be lessened: the openness to pre-marital sex that so often leads to teen-age pregnancy; the abuse of alcohol and drugs; the overemphasis on competition in sports and academics that leaves so many of our youth overburdened or feeling like failures; the prejudices against people of other ethnic or racial groups.[34]

A prudent pastoral approach with a sexually active adolescent is for the adult to bring up the issue of condom usage in private conversation, framing the discussion within the context of responsibility and respect for the adolescent's own self as well as for his or her partner. However, as always the adult must be grounded in integrity. To achieve such integrity the adult should:

1. tell the adolescent that condom usage is safer sex but *not* safe sex; condom usage reduces but does not eliminate the chances of HIV infection;
2. express concerns regarding the adolescent's sexual behavior and regrets for having to bring up the issue of condom usage;
3. reflect with the adolescent on the meaning of responsibility in a sexual relationship;
4. engage the adolescent in terms of "compassionate care" and "loving challenge" that attempt to understand the adolescent

yet challenge her to moral growth; loving challenge might include reflecting with the adolescent on reasons for his sexual behavior, on the meaning of love and how it differs from infatuation, on the meaning of commitment, on the moral nature of his action, and on the "health" of the relationship.

I realize that the position I have taken will be challenged by individuals on both sides of the issue. Nonetheless, the essence of pastoral care is to respond to the person in a way that is sensitive and inviting while at the same time challenging and growth-oriented. Given the seriousness of AIDS and the realities of adolescent behavior, the above approach best insures appreciation of the urgencies at hand while focusing on attempting to expand youth's moral horizon.

Homosexuality in Adolescence

Another issue that has received much attention is that of sexual orientation. The reasons for homosexuality are a matter of intense debate in the scientific community as well as among the wider public. Recent evidence suggests that genetic and biological factors play a role in developing a homosexual orientation, but the extent of biology's contribution is a matter of dispute.[35] The development of a homosexual orientation probably incorporates a complex interplay of biological and psychological variables.

The actual number of gay men and lesbians is also a matter of intense debate. Findings differ because of different survey and interview methods (e.g., face-to-face interview or anonymous survey) and also because of different definitions of homosexuality. The number of men and women whose sexual orientation is exclusively homosexual is probably several percentage points in the population. However, for many people sexual attraction is not exclusively heterosexual or homosexual. Although the vast majority of people are exclusively heterosexual in their orientation,[36] there are also people whose orientation is generally heterosexual but who also are attracted to members of their own sex. There are also those whose orientation is generally homosexual but who also maintain some attraction to the opposite sex.

This issue is further complicated in the adolescent period. As the adolescent becomes aware of his or her sexual attraction during early and middle adolescence, there can be a rather undifferentiated process toward sexual self-awareness that, at least initially, can include sexual attraction toward same-sex adolescents. Examples include intense same-sex friendships. For the vast majority of adolescents, their focus becomes solidified in opposite-sex attraction, but for a distinct minority it is a same-sex attraction.

The Development of Adolescent Gay and Lesbian Identity

From my own pastoral and clinical experience I would have to say that there is no single developmental process that adequately explains every gay male and lesbian's identity development. Some individuals know from childhood that they are "different." Others come upon this self-awareness gradually during their adolescent or young adult years. Still others live in denial into adulthood. With the more public discussion of gay and lesbian lifestyles, self-awareness among youth with a homosexual orientation has probably increased. On the other hand, I have known young people who believed they were gay or lesbian but who gradually came to realize that they were heterosexual or bisexual but with a predominantly heterosexual orientation.

There are numerous theories of homosexual identity development. Though no one model explains all identity development among gay and lesbian youth, I have found Richard Troiden's homosexual identity development model to be helpful in my own pastoral and clinical work.[37] Troiden sets forth an "ideal" model of how gay and lesbian youth develop their sexual identities. "Ideal" means that no particular youth necessarily goes through this developmental process in exactly this way. The ideal model is a device that provides guidelines for adults to make sense and develop an understanding of youth's experience in the process of establishing sexual identity. The four stages are described below.

1. *Sensitization*   Before puberty a majority of homosexuals tend to see themselves as different from their same-sex peers. They recall memories of "feeling different" and having interests that varied from the stereotypical behaviors associated with boys and girls. Usually there was no sense of feeling "sexually different" before puberty.

2. *Identity Confusion*   Most gay males and lesbians come to understand themselves as homosexual during their adolescent years. Such self-awareness produces confusing thoughts as well as feelings of distress, anxiety, and shame. Research findings indicate that on average gay males are both aware of their sexual feelings and act on these feelings at earlier ages than lesbians. The confusion and distress associated with growing self-awareness of their homosexual identity leads youth to a variety of responses, including denying their feelings, seeking counseling in order to find a "cure," avoiding conversation or information regarding homosexuality, developing

a homophobic attitude, and attempting to act heterosexual. Other strategies include "redefinition," an example of which is the adolescent who experiments with homosexual activity and rationalizes the experience as "just a stage I'm going through."

3. *Identity Assumption*   In this stage homosexuality is incorporated into one's self-definition. One becomes comfortable with defining oneself as homosexual and tolerant of sexual feelings. During this stage one has contact and association with other homosexuals.

4. *Commitment*   In the commitment stage homosexuality is adopted as a "way of life." Self-disclosure is increasingly made to nonhomosexuals.

Each of these stages is an "ideal" type that might not correspond the experience of any one person. Moreover, the stages themselves might blur together.

Because identity acquisition is so fundamental to adolescent development, sexual identity occupies a pivotal role in the well-being of gay and lesbian youth. As noted in an earlier chapter, the expectations, responsibilities, and roles that society encourages and champions are crucial for healthy identity formation. Given the hostility with which many people in society view homosexuality, the adolescent with homosexual feelings will find difficulty in integrating significant aspects of the self. This fosters a chronic sense of dissatisfaction, anxiety, and low self-esteem.

> When homosexuality is blocked from identity in youth, individuals may experience a chronic sense of self-dissatisfaction and feelings of not being accepted for themselves by others. They may adapt their behavior to accommodate to the expectations of others and to obtain peer group validation. Achievement of ego integrity and a genuine sense of self-respect, and the development of a capacity for intimate and authentic interpersonal relationships are difficult when significant aspects of personal identity remain hidden or are regarded as contemptible.[38]

The pastoral question of course is how to minister to the gay or lesbian adolescent in light of church teaching. A prudent pastoral approach is the following. As we have already stated sexual intercourse realizes its fullest meaning in the context of a publicly committed relationship, that is, marriage. This marital commitment expresses the intent of the couple to faithfully nurture each other's love and provides the optimal environment for caring for a child. Marital union assures spiritual and emotional growth for the couple as well as the child. The Christian notion of sexuality views sexual behavior as a *meaning*, a complex unity that incorporates aspects of fidelity, commitment, growth, and procreation. This understanding of sexuality is normative for the Christian community.

Yet in a pastoral encounter, how does an adult help a gay or lesbian adolescent to grow both humanly and spiritually when the norm is a committed heterosexual relationship? There are several issues involved.

First, many gay and lesbian youth suffer from self-esteem problems, anxiety, or chronic self-dissatisfaction. Many of these youth employ unhealthy defense mechanisms such as denial or repression and live a false self. Such adolescents truncate their identity acquisition process. The final result is a chronic state of affective disequilibrium (see chapter 2). The long-term effects of such emotional discomfort for youth are often impaired moral decision-making, problematic interpersonal relationships, and an inability to complete developmental tasks. This psychological injury adversely affects their moral and spiritual lives. How does a young person grow spiritually and make healthy moral decisions when her experience is ongoing alienation, chronic dissatisfaction, and little self-appreciation? If grace indeed works through nature, then how does the Lord's invitation to love take root and grow in a nature that at times can be so psychologically injured?

A second question involves alternatives for a gay or lesbian youth. The affective equilibrium we discussed in chapter 2 requires some level of affection and healthy human connection. Practically speaking, for most people this includes affectionate display and human touch. Are we to tell gay and lesbian youth that the next fifty years of their lives are to remain devoid of such connection? If the gift of celibacy is indeed a grace given by the Lord, is it realistic to believe that the Lord has called every gay and lesbian youth to the celibate state? What are the psychological consequences and human toll that such a perspective would exact? Are such consequences consonant with healthy Christian development? What options are open to the homosexual not endowed with the charism of celibacy?

1. One of the first questions for an adult is to determine whether a young person is gay or lesbian. If a youth makes a statement such as "I'm gay," I believe it wise to accept it at face value. The adolescent might be well aware of his or her sexual orientation. In other instances, as the discussion proceeds one can note and discuss questions regarding fantasy life, attraction, and sexual arousal. The adult should respect the adolescent's privacy and not intrusively probe in these areas. Offer various criteria as "guides" the adolescent might use. Sometimes a general question might be warranted, such as "Are these helpful for you in understanding yourself?" Or the adult might say: "Sometimes these guides enable people to define themselves

better, but for some it takes more time. Understanding ourselves sometimes takes a while and that is okay."

2. Another question that arises is with whom the gay or lesbian adolescent shares information regarding his or her sexual orientation. This can be a complex issue. On the one hand there is a need for self-communication that fosters intimacy, and sharing interpersonally is vital for identity formation. On the other hand, such disclosure has the potential for rendering the adolescent vulnerable to negative reactions and ostracism. Sharing such information in a family can trigger negative reactions and family turmoil. I ask adolescents whom they have told and comment on the natural desire to share personal information with others. Also, it is helpful to delineate who might be told: friends (which friends in particular), siblings, parents. I then discuss the positive and negative consequences of each disclosure. How is it helpful to the adolescent? What will it do for the relationship? I *always* remind adolescents that once information is disclosed they have no more control over whom the other person might tell.

Self-disclosure (or what some term "coming out") is the task of middle or late adolescence (more often the latter). The development of a healthy identity necessitates interpersonal sharing, so a gay or lesbian youth should have as a goal self-disclosure to others. The role of the adult is to aid in determining the most feasible way to accomplish the goal. It is important to understand that self-disclosure is a process that takes time and must be realistically appraised in light of each adolescent's particular situation, family life, relationship patterns, and developmental level.

3. Many gay and lesbian youth have confused feelings and self-esteem problems, often quite serious. Though it is difficult to document, some mental health workers report that gay and lesbian youth have disproportionately high suicide rates. Homosexual youth are not only fearful of being found out but struggling with alienation. Adults should assume a *listening* stance that enables the adolescent to sort out and share feelings of confusion, loneliness, and hurt. When appropriate, the adult should make a professional referral.

4. Adults working with gay and lesbian adolescents should be especially concerned with conscience functioning. Pastoral care of homosexual youth should aid the adolescent in making healthy moral decisions. Gay and lesbian youth are faced with numerous lifestyle questions and moral decisions. They need to come to terms with developmental and relationship issues, with their particular situation, and with the way their personal spiritual journey can be lived in connection with the faith community. In order to integrate

these various dimensions, healthy moral decision-making should be a significant focus for the adult-adolescent dialogue. The adult should refer to the discussion of conscience functioning in chapter 1 for guidelines in aiding the adolescent (see above p. 21).

5. The normative understanding of Christian sexual behavior — with its interwoven network of meaning that proclaims fidelity, commitment, growth, and procreation — does not allow for sacramental marriage between gay or lesbian couples. Nonetheless, the committed relationship of two homosexuals most certainly can express loving commitment and mutual fidelity, which are values championed by the believing community. Such committed relationships can further the spiritual and psychological growth of the couple. They also openly challenge the casual sexual practices and promiscuity that are so often taken for granted today. Prudent pastoral practice must consider the viability of such relationships in concrete situations. My intent is not to endorse such relationships but to apply Christian ideals to the actual experience of individuals who struggle to live as creatures of God.

This pastoral approach is appropriate for couples that are committed in mutual fidelity to one another. There are also many relationships that show only limited commitment or no commitment. I speak here of short-term or casual sexual relationships, group sexual activity, cruising, and promiscuity. Even the most compassionate understanding of the Gospels, moral teaching, and church tradition is not consistent with such behavior. Indeed, such behavior contradicts and undermines the very *meaning-making* of Christian sexual expression, which is the living out of the Lord's faithful commitment. Sound pastoral practice in the face of such behavior includes loving challenge that looks at identity growth, healthy relationship-building, and the reasons behind the behavior. Because such behavior can cause psychological harm and physical injury (e.g., STDs, AIDS), professional referral must also be considered.

Terminating Relationships in Adolescence

One very common experience for most adolescents is disruption and termination of relationships. Adolescents develop intense friendships and romantic relationships without realizing that all too frequently such relationships are subject to misunderstanding, conflict, and termination. During these developmental years relationships serve as vital allies in self-discovery and provide enormous security. Relationships generate positive feelings of soothing and trust, thereby leading to self-disclosure and the sharing of intimacies. The wounded feelings caused by disruption of such relationships lead to anger, jealousy, and resentment — thus undermining a sense of God's presence. Moreover, such reactions can frustrate moral growth, for adolescents often act out their hurts and anger in unhealthy ways. Common reactions include negative self-statements, displacement of anger to others, self-injurious behavior (e.g., alcohol abuse), and manipulation of others (e.g., taking advantage of someone sexually as a way to find distraction and avoid hurtful feelings).

Because of their growing need for intimacy and their capacity for more deeply felt feelings, adolescents, especially those in the early and middle period who possess less life experience to draw upon, are capable of developing rather quickly what to them are meaningful and significant relationships. Adults working with youth too often dismiss the pain adolescents experience from terminated relationships as simply a "typical" experience or something the adolescent will "get over eventually." Adults need to be sensitive to the adolescent's grief and the hurt emanating from such loss.[39] The following suggestions may prove helpful.

1. The first priority is to give the adolescent the opportunity simply to talk about the lost relationship. Topics include how the relationship began, what the relationship was like, how the relationship changed over time, and positive experiences in the relationship. In other words, simply let the adolescent tell her "story" of the relationship. Sometimes this might take more than one session. Retelling the story is an excellent method for beginning the journey to healing.

2. Get the adolescent's perspective on what went "wrong" that led to the relationship's demise. Encourage him to be the other person in the relationship and take the other's perspective. What insights does he have about the other? Is he capable of taking the other's perspective?

3. Reflect on the ways she is hurting. Help her to become aware of her grief and loss. Reflect on her reactions to the end of the relationship. What type of reactions has she had, e.g., withdrawal, arguments with significant others such as family members or friends? Reflect on what behavioral changes have taken place. Help the adolescent to focus on specific behaviors, on what she is doing and feeling because of the loss.

After reflecting on the consequences of the loss aid the young person in understanding where his behaviors or feelings are leading him. Are their experiences causing unhealthy consequences or impeding his living a Christian life? Sometimes a general question is helpful, like "How do you think your hurt is affecting you?" If the adult has observed certain behaviors, make them known to the adolescent. Adolescents are often unaware of how the hurt from disrupted relationships affects them.

4. After the adolescent is able to share her story and reflect on her reactions and hurts, it becomes the adult's task to aid her to find meaning in the experience. The best question is one such as "Audrey, we've talked a lot about the relationship and I am wondering now how you are different because of it?" or, "What have you learned from the relationship?" Follow this up with, "What will you take from this experience that will help you in your future relationships and in your life?" Such questions help adolescents to find meaning in their experience and to integrate their experience with their goals.

Questions that relate the adolescent's experience to Christian themes can also be asked, for example: "How is your hurt affecting your ability to be a loving person?" "Have you thought about how this experience might make you a more loving and caring person?" "As a Christian, have you thought about how this experience influences you now and for the future?" The purpose of these questions is to encourage meaning-making on the adolescent's part and to integrate conscious awareness of Gospel values into the meaning-making process.

CHAPTER TEN

Depression and Adolescence

Mental health officials have grown increasingly concerned about the number of young people suffering from depression. Generally speaking, the adolescent period is a time of moodiness, and most adolescents display a wide range of moods during these years. But some youth develop serious, longer lasting depressive moods that do not go away; such youths often suffer from a depressive disorder. Some types of depressive illness impede everyday functioning. The most severe forms are incapacitating.

Depression is best understood as a complex interplay of biological, psychological, and social variables (the biopsychosocial approach). Research indicates that the biological variable most associated with depression is a neurotransmitter deficiency. Neurotransmitters are chemical messengers in the brain, and a deficiency in the neurotransmitter serotonin has been linked to depression.

Other research has focused on the role that psychological variables play in depression. Family dysfunction (caregivers who are unavailable or hostile), substance dependence, and sexual abuse are just a few of the adverse experiences that have been linked to depressive feelings. Other researchers have focused on the role of thought patterns. For example, depressed individuals have been found to have a negative style of thinking; that is, they view their world and their experiences in negative ways.

Social factors are also considered significant in depressive illnesses. Unemployment, racism, and other forms of discrimination have the capacity to debilitate their victims, creating self-esteem problems, anger, or intense rage.

In adults and adolescents there are various symptoms associated with depressive illnesses. Among these are the following:

1. lack of appetite or increased appetite (overeating)
2. sleep problems manifested in either too little or too much sleep
3. feelings of fatigue or low-energy level
4. self-esteem problems

5. difficulty concentrating or difficulty in decision-making
6. feelings of hopelessness[1]

Recently, more attention has been given to adolescent depression because of the publicity surrounding adolescent suicide. There are a variety of reasons why adolescents are prone to depression. Their new capacity for advanced cognitive thinking (formal thought) allows them to become self-critical. As they reflect on their lives adolescents may compare themselves with their peers, and negative evaluations of their own home life compared to their perception of that of their peers can lead to depressive feelings. As discussed in previous chapters, adolescents value relationships, and those adolescents who feel disconnected from peers, who are experiencing relationship conflicts, or who have few friends often find themselves feeling lonely and isolated. Loneliness in particular can be a terribly tormenting experience during the adolescent years. Further, some adolescents suffer emotional deficits from never having formed adequate attachment bonds with parents, and these negative feelings begin to surface during adolescence.

Unlike children who define themselves by means of physical features (e.g., "I am tall") and what they do ("I am in third grade"), adolescent self-understanding centers on psychological conceptions. Thus adolescents become sensitive to feelings such as sadness, guilt, and loneliness, and often these feelings are acute. In addition, with the advent of adolescence, youth experience higher levels of stress associated with numerous physical, emotional, and social changes. These negative life events (stressors) can take their toll on emotional functioning. At the same time, youth differ in the number of supports and protective buffers they have at their disposal to deal with stressful life events.[2] Some adolescents, even if they face serious adversity in their early years, are able to weather such difficulties because of protective factors that serve to insulate them from the difficulties. Examples include having a special talent or some healthy relationships in one's life.

Depressed adolescents can have other psychological problems in addition to their depression. Two conditions associated with depressive feelings are acting out and disruptive behaviors commonly associated with juvenile delinquency and drug abuse.[3]

Research consistently finds that women report levels of depression two to three times that of men. Differences in male and female depression are also seen in adolescence, with adolescent girls reporting more depression than boys. Researchers believe that a significant factor in depression among female adolescents is body image. As we saw in our discussion of eating disorders, relationships and physical appearance are emphases in the socialization of women. Biological changes (the adolescent female's increased body fat) and relationship problems render female adolescents more vulnerable to depressive moods. There are also distinct differences between how female and male adolescents cope with depressive feelings. Adolescent girls are apt to view themselves in critical ways (with statements like "I look terrible"), to evaluate their experiences negatively, to view themselves as inadequate, and to eat less; boys are more apt to withdraw from others, be irritable (verbally abusive), and perform poorly in school.[4]

Suicide and the Adolescent

Suicide, following accidents and homicides, is the third leading cause of death among young people (ages 15–24). National attention has increasingly focused on the suicide risk among youth. Recently, multiple suicides among youth ("copy-cat suicides") have received wide publicity.

Each year five thousand young people ages fifteen to twenty-four succeed in killing themselves. It is estimated that as many as four hundred thousand youth attempt suicide yearly.[5] Some experts believe there might be as many as a hundred attempted suicides for every successful one and that several million youth have attempted suicide at some point during their adolescent and young adult years. Further it is likely that some fatal accidents (e.g., auto crashes) might well be masked suicides. In the last thirty years the rate of suicide among youth has grown over 300 percent, with the rate higher for youth fifteen to nineteen than twenty to twenty-four. White males represent the group with the highest rate of suicide, though there has been a dramatic rise in suicide-related deaths among African-American males. There is also evidence that Native American adolescents are a particularly vulnerable group "at risk" for suicide. Though studies are not as extensive for Native Americans as other groups, one report noted that one out of six Native American teens had attempted suicide.[6] Rates for white and African-American adolescent females have also increased, but not as fast as for males. Females are three times more likely to attempt suicide than males, but males are several times more likely to succeed. It is speculated that the higher death rate among males is due to the use of more lethal means. Adolescent males tend to use methods such as hanging and firearms whereas females are more inclined to less violent (and therefore less successful) methods such as pills. Although there are indications that female adolescents are beginning to use more lethal means,[7] the "typical" teenager who attempts suicide is a white female who uses pills. Suicide among youth has received publicity because of the alarming rate increase, but in fact the highest suicide rate is found among the elderly.[8]

Risk Factors for Suicide in Adolescence

Research indicates a number of risk factors for suicide. The major ones are as follows.[9]

1. *Depression*   As might be expected, depression is related to a significant number of adolescent suicides. Adolescents who are depressed are not, however, necessarily suicidal.

2. *Drug Use*   Drugs are also linked to suicide. Abusing drugs is a way for adolescents to medicate their pain, but it can also cause poor impulse control leading to impulsive actions such as suicide attempts.

3. *Behavioral Problems*   Adolescents who have conduct problems and express anger and hostility are also at risk.

4. *Family Dysfunction*   Family dynamics are believed to be a factor in suicide among the young. Dysfunction in the family system can take the form of parental emotional illness or impaired interpersonal relationships among family members. Youth growing up in families who have a history of emotional disorders are more at risk.

5. *Accessibility of Means*   Adolescents at risk who live in households where firearms are available should be monitored closely. These young people have the means available successfully to act out their impulses.

6. *Past Suicide Attempts*   Adolescents who previously have attempted suicide are much more likely than their peers to attempt suicide again.

7. *Stress Factors*   Incidents that raise anxiety for the at-risk youth should be a concern. The suicide-prone youth struggles with humiliation or failure or anticipates future humiliation or failure. The adolescent can obsess over a failure or rejection (whether actual, perceived, or anticipated) from which suicide becomes the preferred escape.

Adolescents who are successful at suicide usually suffer from emotional illness. However, there are cases of adolescent suicide involving what might be termed "model children." These adolescents are not perceived to be problem cases, and their deaths leave the community in shock. Yet many of these youth might well have been suffering adolescents whose turmoil went unnoticed by concerned adults. Generally speaking, adolescents who commit suicide experience a breakdown in their coping defenses that render them at risk. In contrast, though normal adolescents at times find themselves under significant stress, they possesses adequate coping mechanisms; although they might be hurting, they possess or can find the resources to weather their emotional storms. Adolescents who repeatedly attempt suicide suffer from chronic emotional dysfunction, impaired family situations, and inadequate coping resources.

Questions to Consider

The adult should consider the following questions to determine whether an adolescent is at risk for suicide.

1. What stress is the adolescent under (whether actual or perceived) and what resources does the adolescent have to cope with this stress? Examples of failure include academic problems, serious illness, legal problems, failure in goals or relationships.

2. Does the adolescent have a plan? The more the adolescent speaks about a plan or appears to have thought out the suicide the more concerned the adult should be. In a similar vein, what "method" does the adolescent have for carrying out the suicide? The more lethal the method, the more the youth is at risk. The adult might also consider whether the adolescent has access to some lethal means (e.g., a gun in the house).

3. Does the adolescent experience problems in everyday living or show different behaviors? Is he withdrawing? losing interest in school? becoming more irritable?

4. Has the adolescent hinted or made some reference to not being around in the future or engaged in some behavior that is a cause for concern (e.g., given away her CD collection)? In the majority of cases adolescents who commit suicide give prior warning of their intention.

5. Is the adolescent using drugs?

6. Has the adolescent attempted suicide before?

7. What feelings is the adolescent experiencing? sadness? hopelessness? anxiety?

8. How isolated is the adolescent? To whom is the adolescent connected? Does the adolescent feel understood by anyone or does he feel misunderstood or alone?

9. Has there been some loss in the adolescent's life that she has not been able to cope with (e.g., death in family, breakup in a relationship, illness)?

10. What is the emotional quality of the adolescent's family: supportive? hostile? neglectful? noncommunicative? rejecting? abusive?

Though most adolescents at one time or another think about death and many adolescents will have some thought of suicide, fortunately, most do not act on their thoughts. Nonetheless, all suicidal thoughts, feelings, and gestures must be taken *seriously*. Even if an adolescent's apparently suicidal behavior is simply attention-seeking or manipulative, it represents a psychological dysfunction in need of intervention.

The Adolescent in Crisis

There is probably no greater fear for adults who minister to youth than to encounter the suicidal adolescent. In such cases what should the adult do? The following are guidelines.

1. Stay calm. Consider the adolescent's coming to you as a sign of your value in her life. Be grateful for this opportunity to be a source of support. At the same time, be aware of possible anxiety over the adolescent's crisis and understand that such feelings are natural. Being overanxious will not help.

2. Do not try to solve the adolescent's problem. Unless you are a licensed mental health professional, you should see your role as a source of support whose goal is to connect the adolescent with a professional. (You must of course be aware of your own issues. For example, do you feel the need to "rescue" the adolescent? What are your feelings about referring the adolescent to a mental health professional? Do you feel inadequate when a referral is made? Recall from the first chapter that the adult-adolescent relationship is for the welfare of the adolescent.)

3. Connect and empathize with the adolescent. Listen carefully and express your concern. Let the adolescent know you are there for him.

A person who seriously contemplates suicide and has the avowed intention of ending his or her life is probably experiencing the following. The *feeling* is one of hopelessness. The person also is in considerable *pain* (and may well not realize how hurting he is). Suicide, then, is the option. It is the way to solve the problem — the problem of pain. Why not utilize another option or find an answer other than suicide? For the suicidal person there are *no* other options. The thinking processes of the suicidal adolescent are constricted and she believes that there is no choice but to kill herself. Suicide, in effect, is *the* solution — the only solution available.[10] Though this way of thinking might strike us as "odd," it must be respected and taken seriously.

1. If an adult suspects an adolescent might be suicidal, the following approach is recommended. Reflect with the adolescent on her life concerns. "Mary, you have spoken about some serious concerns and I am wondering how you are dealing with them because it sounds to me like a lot to have to deal with."

2. The adult should either question Mary or review in his own mind the questions listed above to determine if she is at risk of suicide.

3. Many people erroneously think that bringing up the question of suicide can implant the idea in a person's mind. The consensus of mental health professionals, however, is that this is not the case. Rather, introducing the question of suicide can bring a sense of relief that allows the adolescent to ventilate and talk over her feelings. In addition, not bringing up the subject can signal to the adolescent that such talk is "forbidden"; in effect, she is left to her own resources and misperceives the adult as uninterested in her predicament.

4. I usually bring up the subject with a question like the following: "Some people who are going through what you are think about hurting themselves. I'm wondering if you have ever had such thoughts?" Obviously, many people at one point or another have thoughts about suicide. Having ideas does not mean that one will act them out. However, having the ideas should be a cause of concern. If some of the risk factors discussed above are present (e.g., substance use), then such ideas should be of significant concern. I always let the adolescent know that the reason for my question is my care for her. "The reason I'm asking this question, Mary, is that I care for you."

5. Inquire if the adolescent has a plan. As noted above, the more elaborate and thought out the plan, the more there is cause for concern.

6. If the adolescent appears suicidal, I go back to the concerns she has expressed and ask, "I sense you are in a lot of pain and I am wondering how you are dealing with your hurt?" Another question, simply, is: "How do you hurt?" Other comments include: "It seems that killing yourself might be a way to solve the issues we have talked about"; "I'm wondering if you're seeing suicide as the solution"; "It sounds like your hurting a lot, and suicide is the way to take away your hurt."

7. Strategize with the adolescent about *alternatives*. Help him to see that there are other options. The goal here is to generate some alternatives to suicide. The suicidal adolescent suffers from tunnel vision and dichotomous thinking in which the only choices are (*a*) feel pain or (*b*) kill myself. Explore options together.

8. The *goal* of any discussion should be to connect the adolescent with a professional. Do *not* try to help the adolescent alone. A strategy is to summarize the problems the adolescent is experiencing and say something like, "Mary, I really care for you, and because I care for you it is important, I think, that we find a trained professional for you to talk to." Be understanding, yet firm. If the adolescent balks at speaking with someone else, gently reiterate your care for her and

assure her that your own relationship with her will not end. Let her know that you are insisting that she see a professional because of your care and concern. Be willing to go with her to speak with others or to enlist the aid of others.

On a personal note, as a clinical psychologist I have worked with a number of suicidal clients. Even though I have training in clinical matters, I always worry about any client who is showing at-risk behavior for suicide. Working with an adolescent at risk for suicide can be tremendously disconcerting for the adult. There might be a tendency to avoid the issue. On the other hand, the adult might become so upset that he doesn't gather enough information or fails to be present in order to "hear" the adolescent in need. Adults should take special efforts to monitor their feelings and reactions. In our care for youth we are called to be on the "front line," to connect with them and aid them in finding the help they need. We should share our concerns with other caring adults who can provide feedback. In-service workshops also are helpful. In sum, be there for the adolescent but be aware of your own feelings and your limitations.

CHAPTER ELEVEN

Drug Abuse and the Adolescent

Surveying nearly fifty thousand junior and senior high students, a recent study found increased usage of marijuana and LSD among students and a less critical attitude toward those who use drugs; the survey has prompted some to wonder whether drug usage among youth is beginning to rise again after declining in recent years.[1]

For youth, alcohol remains by far the most popular drug, and so alcohol use, abuse, and dependence will be the main focus of this chapter. Alcohol affects the entire body. It is readily absorbed into the bloodstream and, in a pregnant woman, passes through the placenta to the fetus. Alcohol is a depressant that affects mental functioning. Though moderate drinking is generally not considered harmful for adults, chronic heavy drinking is associated with numerous illnesses and medical conditions. One result of heavy drinking is often the development of tolerance — the need for more and more alcohol to produce the same "high." Heavy drinking is known to cause liver damage, neurological impairment, intestinal problems, and cardiac illnesses such as hypertension and heart damage.[2]

Alcohol's effects, however, go well beyond medical infirmities. Close to twenty million Americans abuse alcohol or are alcoholics, and one family in four experiences problems from alcohol. When family members are included one can easily discern the serious emotional toll that alcohol takes on a huge number of lives. The death statistics associated with alcohol are staggering. Over a hundred thousand people die yearly in alcohol-related deaths. Alcohol use is associated with half the murders, accidental deaths, and suicides in the United States. Among youth it is estimated that 5 percent drink daily, and two out of three high school seniors drink alcohol in any given month.[3] Several million youth today abuse alcohol, and this abuse is beginning at younger and younger ages.

Alcohol Abuse and Dependence

Difficulties with alcohol usage are classified as either alcohol abuse or dependence. Alcohol abuse is using the substance during a twelve-month period with one or more of the following consequences: (*a*) failure to fulfill rule obligations (e.g., a student skipping class); (*b*) repeated "at-risk" behaviors (e.g., driving while intoxicated); (*c*) legal problems (e.g., arrests); (*d*) recurring or worsening interpersonal or social problems (e.g., fighting).

A more serious condition is alcohol dependence. Dependence is defined as experiencing three of the following symptoms over a period of one year.

1. Using alcohol in larger amounts or over a longer period of time than intended.

2. Failing to control or diminish the use of alcohol even though one tries or desires to lessen usage.

3. Spending more time on activities that enable the consumption of alcohol (e.g., obtaining money to spend on alcohol).

4. Suffering impairment in carrying out expected obligations (e.g., school work) because of intoxication or withdrawal symptoms.

5. Withdrawing from everyday activities because of alcohol use.

6. Continuing use of alcohol even though one knows it is the cause of or a factor in a recurring physical, psychological, or social problem.

7. Developing tolerance for alcohol with a corresponding need to increase the amount of alcohol consumed in order to get the same effect.

8. Experiencing withdrawal symptoms.

9. Using alcohol to avoid withdrawal symptoms.[4]

The Path to Alcoholism

There exists no one way for becoming an alcoholic; the road to alcoholism involves a complex interplay of biological, psychological, and cultural variables. There are a number of risk factors associated with alcoholism, and these are reviewed briefly below.

1. Sex   Alcoholism appears to be predominantly a male disorder. There exist many more alcohol-dependent males than females though there is evidence that the number of females is increasing.

2. Family History   A child who has a parent who is an alcoholic is several times more likely to develop alcoholism than a child raised in a family where there is no alcoholic parent. Genetic factors play a major role in alcoholism, yet there also exist strong environmental factors that must be taken into consideration. The likelihood that an individual will become an alcoholic probably depends on the interaction of genetic disposition with specific environmental factors. Environmental factors are also shown to be important by cases of alcoholism in individuals who have no family history of alcoholism. Many individuals in treatment centers have no family history of alcoholism.

3. *Psychological Disturbance*   Alcoholism is associated with a wide range of mental disorders, among them depression and behavior problems. Evidence indicates that suicide is often related to alcoholism.

4. *Age*   Generally speaking alcoholism is more likely to appear in the adolescent and young adult years (before forty) than in the later adult years. This trend is especially true for men; in women there is a tendency for a later onset.

5. *Protective Factors*   Many alcoholics report that they tolerate alcohol better than their nonalcoholic peers. In other words, their bodies do not react as negatively (e.g., a serious hangover) to heavy consumption of alcohol. It may be that individuals who suffer more adverse reactions actually have a protective buffer that shields them from alcoholism.

6. *Cultural Factors*   Alcohol abuse and dependence is more likely to be present in certain cultural environments and among certain ethnic groups or where the opportunity for heavy drinking is available and the drinking tolerated.[5]

Current research indicates that there are several different "types" of alcoholism. There is no set pathway for becoming an alcoholic and the progression to alcoholism for each individual involves a complex relationship among biological, psychological, and social factors.

Adolescent Alcohol Use

The vast majority of adolescents and young adults have used alcohol or some other drug at some point in their lives. Because the use of alcohol is so widespread, the fact that a youth has experimented with alcohol should not be a cause for alarm. Some adolescent drinking can be understood as the consequence of peer pressure, curiosity, or the playing out of identity issues. It might well be that experimenting with alcohol is a sign of psychological health, for it signals a youth's openness to "trying out" adult behaviors.[6] Understandably, however, there is cause for concern when experimentation places one in high-risk situations (e.g., drinking while driving) or when experimentation becomes more frequent and leads to regular usage. And even adolescents who simply experiment with alcohol should be drawn into discussion in order to clarify the reasons for their drinking and the possible adverse consequences (legal, psychological, etc.).

The psychologists David Hawkins, Richard Catalano, and Janet Miller have reviewed a large number of studies in order to delineate those factors that lead to and protect against substance abuse. Among the factors associated with substance abuse are what the researchers term "contextual factors." These include lack of legal restrictions, availability of the drug, and low functioning level of the neighborhood. Individual and interpersonal factors include the following: an individual's physiological response to the drug, poor parental practices and family conflict, family use of drugs, low levels of attachment within the family, childhood problem behaviors, academic failure, poor interpersonal relationships, association with drug-using peers, alienation and rebelliousness, favorable attitudes toward drug usage, and early use of drugs.

The factors mentioned above are confirmed by my clinical and pastoral experience. A majority of the factors point to environmental influences that in one way or another frustrate and disrupt normal adolescent growth and encourage a youth's journey down the road to drug abuse. In chapter 2 we noted that the problems associated with the experience of affective disequilibrium frustrate and confound the young person's attempts to live a healthy moral and spiritual life. Many of the risk factors identified above (e.g., family conflict) disrupt healthy emotional experiences. Drinking or other drug usage can become a way for the adolescent to avoid intense levels of affective disruption. The need to distract the self from emotional pain when combined with genetic, social, and other psychological factors (e.g., poor interpersonal skills) renders the adolescent especially vulnerable to developing substance abuse or dependence problems.

Attention must also be given to those "protective" factors that buffer youth from developing alcoholism. The same researchers note that four specific factors (which they term forms of "social bonding") serve to lessen youth's involvement with drugs. These four elements of social bonding are:

1. strong attachment to parents
2. commitment to schooling
3. regular involvement with church activities
4. belief in the norms and values of society

In chapter 2 the case was made for a strong attachment bond as a requirement for healthy functioning. All four of the above factors reflect the need for connection — some form of attachment bonding. The evidence again seems to suggest that a vital ingredient for healthy development in youth is relational investments that orient them toward healthy bonding and productive activities. It is helpful to reflect with young people on "healthy" connections or attachments in their lives.

Signs of Drug Usage among Adolescents

There is a wide array of behavior that can indicate that the adolescent is abusing a substance. Among them are the following:

1. withdrawal from everyday activities
2. relationships with peers who use drugs
3. lack of interest in physical appearance
4. decreased interest in making an impression on others
5. lack of interest in school and school-related activities
6. constant need for money
7. lack of energy or continual fatigue
8. moodiness or impulsive display of angry and hostile feelings
9. accidents while driving
10. involvement in deviant behaviors such as stealing or truancy
11. secretive behaviors or growing communication problems with parents and other adults
12. overall decline in responsibility

Even if an adolescent is able to give up a substance, recent research indicates that preventing relapse is a complex process involving a large number of variables. This is all the more true for adolescents, and relapse rates for young people are extraordinarily high. Part of the reason for this lack of success involves the social nature of drug usage. As we know, adolescents have a strong interpersonal orientation, and relationships occupy a central role in their lives. Adolescents who cluster together and use drugs cement a sturdy bond that provides self-definition. Furthermore, such adolescents sunder ties with both healthy peers and the normal developmental activities crucial for identity building. In a sense, adolescents who abuse drugs create their identity not through normal developmental channels, but through the drug. Stated differently, the drug increasingly becomes the locus of identity for the abusing youth. This adolescent in turn suffers a developmental deficit, i.e., a lack of a firmly rooted and well-defined identity. When the adolescent is able to come "clean," he now confronts a painful reality: the need to play "catch up." Whereas nonabusing peers are proceeding along a normal course developmentally, establishing intimate relationships, and solidifying identity gains, adolescents coming off drugs find themselves having to go back and discover "who am I?" This self-inquiry is all the more painful, for the newly drug-free adolescent must now find a whole new set of friendships; this relationship-building is often aggravated by poor interpersonal skills and other emotional problems. I have worked with a number of young adults in their twenties who have gotten off drugs but who have had to begin the process of self-discovery and relationship-building with rudimentary skills and poor self-esteem.

Numerous studies indicate that psychological factors play a particularly strong role in relapse. Negative emotions such as anger and depression and interpersonal conflicts that the person is unable to handle are significant factors leading to relapse. Unfortunately, such emotions and conflicts often preoccupy youth, rendering them particularly vulnerable to relapse.[7]

Finally, heavy drug usage is tied to a number of emotional and behavioral problems. Thus the adolescent who successfully battles drug use must often address other painful problems like depression or antisocial tendencies. With many this is further complicated by polydrug abuse, that is, abusing more than one substance, e.g., alcohol and cocaine.

The Alcoholic Family

With so many adolescents and young adults affected by alcohol either directly (by their own use/abuse) or by the presence in their home of a substance-abusing or substance-dependent parent, it is important to examine this form of family dysfunction more closely.[8] Psychologist Stephanie Brown, a specialist on alcohol addiction, has offered an incisive analysis of how alcohol influences and impairs the family system as well as the children within the family. According to Brown, denial and rationalization are common defenses employed in alcoholic families. The alcoholic family is chaotic. Usually there is considerable tension within the family as the denial becomes both more absolute and more brittle. Children growing up in alcoholic homes often experience tremendous shame or embarrassment. The alcoholic parent embarrasses or humiliates the child through public drunkenness, emotional outbursts, and inconsistent or erratic behavior. The alcoholic home is often unpredictable, and rule-making is inconsistent.

As a consequence, the child never feels secure within the home.

Rules enforced or statements made one day are ignored or contradicted the next. Because of parental inadequacy children must often switch roles and assume parental responsibilities. Indeed, one common theme voiced by adult children of alcoholics is that they were never allowed an opportunity to be children. As a consequence of these dynamics, children growing up in alcoholic homes commonly employ the following defenses: (*a*) denial, (*b*) emphasis on control, (*c*) all-or-nothing thinking (which allows them to maintain a tight rein on feelings that prove threatening or ambiguous), and (*d*) assumption of responsibility.[9]

Brown's understanding of the alcoholic family is particularly insightful when she explores the dynamics of attachment and identity formation. Because the child has been robbed of a secure childhood on account of parental drinking, the child's attachment is rendered tenuous and impaired. Unable to acknowledge either needs or dependence, the child withdraws emotionally and erects defensive barriers that protect from further hurt and feelings of abandonment. For the child in an alcoholic home, according to Brown, alcohol becomes the central identifying force for identity formation. Children cannot help but identity with their family of origin, and this entails buying into the denial and distortions caused by alcohol. Adolescents in the alcoholic home are heavily burdened. They struggle to reconcile the survival-oriented defenses formed as a product of the family system with newly found needs to identify, attach, and bond with others.

Tremendous loyalty problems can be triggered by the dilemma of protecting a family system the adolescent has identified with and acknowledging legitimate needs that if acted upon will begin a separation process fraught with ambivalence and fear. Fortunately, recent publicity about "dysfunctional families" has lead to greater public awareness of the problems many youth in alcoholic home environments face. Many schools and public organizations have set up group sessions that provide an outlet for children and adolescents to share their struggles and begin the journey toward identity growth in a healthy and productive fashion.

Widespread publicity about dysfunctional families and adult children of alcoholics (ACOAs) has led to much needed interventions to address significant issues of family impairment; it is important, however, to address some of the excesses surrounding what loosely might be termed the "dysfunctional movement." Otherwise, a distorted view emerges that fosters a stereotypical understanding of adolescent experience.

Books and magazines have popularized the notion of a specific set of characteristics associated with children who grow up in alcoholic homes (e.g., low self-esteem). The problems with many of these writings is that they do not qualify as scientific research. This does not mean that they have no merit, but it does mean that they must be carefully examined in order to identify personal projections and biases.

One way to provide criteria for such scrutiny is to examine what research studies in the professional literature say about the effects of parental alcoholism. Psychologists Melissa West and Ronald Prinz, who reviewed scientific studies over a ten-year period, concluded that the findings "taken as a whole support the contention that parental alcoholism is associated with a heightened incidence of child symptomatology."[10] However, these same researchers also noted that many cautions are warranted: "Neither all nor a major portion of the population of children from alcoholic homes are inevitably doomed to psychological disorder."[11] According to the research, the "effects" of parental alcoholism on many children is not of a magnitude that would lead inevitably to psychological problems. As discussed in an earlier chapter, some children are resilient and able to thrive even in the face of adversity. Many factors need to be taken into consideration, including protective buffers a child has and other risk factors (like physical abuse and poverty). In sum, an alcoholic parent in the home does *not* mean that a child or adolescent is inevitably heading down the road toward psychological dysfunction.

One study of college students suggests that the attempt to find a personality profile of adult children of alcoholics is flawed because the descriptions of ACOAs are so vague and general that they can apply to anyone. In other words, both children from alcoholic homes and children from nonalcoholic homes can apply these descriptions to themselves, thus invalidating the belief that ACOAs suffer from a special set of symptoms.[12] For example, a person might say, "I am an adult child of an alcoholic and that is why I have low self-esteem." But since a vague term like "low self-esteem" can be applied to both ACOAs and non-ACOAs, how can one be certain that having an alcoholic parent is the cause of low self-esteem? Still another study of college students found that for a large number of personality measures there appeared to be no difference between ACOAs and non-ACOAs. Differences that did surface between the two groups included a tendency for ACOAs to feel more self-depreciation (especially the female ACOAs), while male ACOAs experienced greater need for autonomy and independence than their non-ACOA male peers.[13] This finding would correspond to other research that suggests that females internalize and males externalize in response to difficult problems. Finally, one major review of temperamental and personality characteristics of children of alcoholics (COAs) and non-

COAs indicate a few but not many differences between these two groups.[14]

How can we make sense of these findings? First of all, more sophisticated studies are being done of alcoholic home environments; as the results of these studies become known, more precise patterns will be determined. On the basis of the literature as it now stands I think we can prudently conclude the following. A child, adolescent, or adult who has experienced an alcoholic home environment in his or her family of origin is vulnerable to certain behavioral and emotional problems, but the long-term effects of such problems might well be reduced by factors in that person's life. In both pastoral and clinical practice I have worked with individuals who have suffered greatly from the emotional ravages of an alcoholic home environment. On the other hand, I know many cases of young people and adults who have weathered quite adequately alcoholic home environments, who function quite well, and who have not needed professional intervention or self-help groups.

Many professionals who work in the recovery movement might find this statement difficult to accept. My response is that those dealing with addiction regularly encounter people who need help or who are suffering seriously as a result of an alcoholic home environment; however, this group is *not* representative of all individuals affected by alcohol. It is known, for example, that many people who have abused alcohol have quit on their own without professional assistance or the aid of self-help groups. Likewise, those in the recovery movement do not come in contact with the many individuals who come from alcoholic homes who have not sought help and who function adequately on their own. I suspect that many recovery specialists, though certainly well-intentioned, have a somewhat biased view.

Another factor is the background of those who work in recovery. Many people in the recovery movement are themselves recovering alcoholics or are products of alcoholic home environments. We must remember that one's own experience is not necessarily normative for all individuals affected by alcohol. It is important to avoid stereotypes according to which a person "has to" be experiencing specific symptoms and to acknowledge the complexity and uniqueness of each individual.

The Pastoral Response

1. As noted above, adults working with the youth in the area of drinking or drugs should first be aware of related issues in their own lives. Without this self-awareness boundary issues inevitably

arise (e.g., becoming too involved, overidentifying with the adolescent's situation, attempting to rescue the adolescent). Some helpful questions for the adult to consider are:

- What are my boundaries with this adolescent?
- If I am a recovering alcoholic, how does this influence my work with this adolescent?
- If I am an adult child of an alcoholic, and how does this influence my work with this adolescent?

2. Sometimes it is helpful to have a set list of questions to get some sense of the adolescent's involvement with alcohol. For example:

- What do you drink?
- How much do you drink in a day? week?
- When do you drink?
- With whom do you drink?
- Have you considered the reasons why you drink?

Ask the adolescent to be *specific* in her answers to each of these questions. The most common defenses of adolescent abusers are denial and rationalization. Gently but firmly provide feedback to the adolescent regarding the behaviors that you have witnessed or are aware of.

3. Drinking in adolescence is not only a personal experience, but usually a group activity as well. Explore with the adolescent who his "friends" are. Reflect together on the role that drinking plays in these friendships. I have often asked adolescents a question like, "Suppose, John, you and your friends had nothing to drink or did not drink. How would this affect the friendships? Would you still be friends? What would you and your friends do?" Reflect with the adolescent on the values that are important to his peer group. Can he name the values? Does he have any values different from the group?

4. I have found the best single way to explain addiction to adolescents and young adults is to use a "friendship model." I start with the question: "What would you do for your best friend?" For a "best friend" one would usually do anything — make great sacrifices and give up other valued resources. After a discussion of the adolescent's responses, I go on to say: "That is exactly what an addict does. In the long run the drug is the best friend and the addict will give up everything else — other friends and love relationships, work, time, money." Because adolescents are so interpersonally oriented, talking about alcohol or other drugs in the terms of friendship allows effective entrance into the adolescent's thinking.

5. The adult should not hesitate to recommend that the young person participate in self-help or support groups such as Alcoholics Anonymous, Al-Anon, or Al-Ateen. It is also helpful for the adult to attend workshops and seminars on adolescent drug usage, co-dependency, and family dysfunction and to have resources and information regarding referral available. If intervention appears necessary, be familiar with specialists in the area of addiction who can assist in such an undertaking.

6. If adolescents are not to be involved in drug abuse, then it remains incumbent on adults to provide and encourage positive, health-promoting behavior for them. Explore with the adolescent what she likes to do that is healthy and growthful. Do an "inventory" of her daily and weekly activities and help her discern what it means to be well-balanced in terms of time commitments, relationships, and activities. Reflect with the adolescent on healthy identity growth (chapter 2) and healthy relationship building (chapter 9).

7. Adolescent drinking and other drug usage affect the young person physically, emotionally, and spiritually. Explore with the adolescent your concerns and ask about how he cares for himself. Reflect with him on how drinking or drug usage fails to show "care" for the self. Speak about how the Christian is called to be a "temple" of the Spirit both in body and in mind and explain how such a vocation is being impaired by drinking and drugging. As in other areas a challenging question might be: "How do you think Christ views your behavior?" or "How is this making or not making you a better Christian?" Other questions might be: "How do you relate drinking to being a loving person?" or "Are there ways your drinking is putting you or others at risk?" Increasingly, adolescents are viewing drug usage as a normal part of everyday life; there is no "moral" question involved. We need to gently but firmly communicate to adolescents that there are serious moral issues involved in drug usage that affect the adolescent personally as well as his relationships with the entire community.

8. Adolescents growing up in homes where family members are substance-abusing or substance-dependent are often filled with negative feelings. Shame, anger, and guilt can be particularly prominent. It is unrealistic to expect the adolescent not to have reactions (such as anger) to addictive behaviors in the home. Fortunately, there is much more awareness of family dysfunction, and many adolescents have been exposed to literature and thinking about the problem. The most important thing the adult can do with the adolescent is to reflect with her on the wide range of feelings she might have toward another family member and the home situation. Help the adolescent make connections between her feelings and her behavior. Often the

adolescent is unaware of exactly how her feelings are influencing her, and the adult can provide valuable feedback about how healthy or unhealthy her behaviors are. As always, encourage positive behaviors. Remind her that though she may not be able to alter the family situation or control the behavior of another family member, she *can* take responsibility for her own actions.

Conclusion

In today's environment adolescents and young adults encounter situations and experiences that most certainly "test" both their will and their capacities to lead a life of discipleship. Current commentators on the contemporary scene have documented the indicators of increasing social pathology that have generated serious obstacles to youth's attempts at living morally and spiritually maturing lives. The "hostile" climate that many young people experience is not going to disappear. Moreover, at best recent trends underscore the serious challenges that adults who minister to youth must address if effective religious education and pastoral ministry programs are going to succeed.

Nonetheless, though the challenges before us are immense, there exist signs of hope. Recent public discussions of values in education and recurrent interest in the stability and health of families are positive signs that serious issues vital to the social and moral health of society are now beginning to be addressed. Furthermore, churches are implementing more sophisticated and professional programs for youth as forms of outreach and catechesis. Finally, we must not dismiss the millions of parents and youth who attempt to and do live lives that reflect Gospel values. In my own role as a lecturer and worship leader I have witnessed in my travels numerous examples of "good" people who do "good" things.

Few experiences that adolescents and young adults undergo are more vital and necessary than a relationship with a concerned and caring adult. What we must keep in mind, and what these pages have pointed out, is that when developing such a relationship we must always be sensitive to the developmental and emotional turmoils and dysfunctions that can impede healthy human and spiritual growth. Such experiences not only rob youth of the opportunity to appreciate most fully their humanness, but also undermine the Lord's ongoing loving invitation to youth to respond more and more freely to his offer of discipleship. More than anything, our relationships with youth must provide them a concrete experience of this "loving invitation." With that end in mind, I have written this book. It is hoped that in these pages the reader has found a resource for a more effective way to offer such an invitation as well as the desire to make this invitation more real.

Notes

Preface

1. Charles M. Shelton, *Adolescent Spirituality: Pastoral Ministry for High School and College Youth* (New York: Crossroad, 1989).

2. Charles M. Shelton, *Morality and the Adolescent: A Pastoral Psychology Approach* (New York: Crossroad, 1989).

3. In this work, "adolescent" refers to the ages twelve to twenty-two — the typical junior/senior high and undergraduate college years. For the sake of variety I intermittently use the term "young adult" for college student and "the young," "young people," "students," or "youth" to refer to adolescence as defined above.

Chapter 1: Adolescent Pastoral Counseling

1. Ken Magid and Carole A. McKelvey, *High Risk: Children without a Conscience* (New York: Bantam, 1988).

2. " 'Teenagers Have It Harder,' according to Adult Survey," *Resource* 2 (Fall 1988): 2.

3. Quoted in Daniel Patrick Moynihan, "Social Justice in the Next Century," *America* 164 (September 14, 1991): 135.

4. Mary Rose McGeady, D.C., "Disconnected Kids: An American Tragedy," *America* 164 (June 15, 1991): 639–45.

5. Quoted in Jim Castelli, "New Campaign Rallying Cry: Put Children First," *National Catholic Reporter* (February 7, 1992): 3.

6. U.S. Bishops, "Putting Children and Families First: A Challenge to Our Church, Nation and World," *Origins* 21 (November 28, 1991): 395–96.

7. Francis A. J. Ianni, *The Search for Structure: A Report on American Youth Today* (New York: The Free Press, 1989), 75.

8. Search Institute, *The Troubled Journey: A Profile of American Youth* (Minneapolis: Search Institute, 1991). The results from this survey were obtained from a population sample of over forty-five thousand students grades six to twelve. Most of these students resided in Midwestern communities whose populations were under a hundred thousand. Hence, the survey is a portrait of "Middle America" youth. One must be cautious in generalizing from this data to other youth populations such as inner-city

215

youth. Nonetheless, the assets listed by the report make excellent sense as foundational for all youth in their quest to become mature, productive, and healthy adults.

9. The adult might find it helpful to use this list as a basic "checklist" when working with an adolescent or young adult. In other words, ask yourself the question: "How many of these assets does this young person have?"

10. Search Institute, *The Troubled Journey*, 2.

11. "2 U.S. Surveys Find Anxiety about the State of Family Life," *New York Times*, November 22, 1991, A12.

12. Ibid.

13. David A. Hamburg and Ruby Takanishi, "Preparing for Life: The Critical Transition of Adolescence," *American Psychologist* 44 (May 1989): 825.

14. Ibid., 825–27.

15. American Psychiatric Association, *A Psychiatric Glossary*, 4th ed. (Washington, D.C.: APA, 1975), 48. Quoted in Armand M. Nicholi, Jr., "The Adolescent," in *The Harvard Guide to Modern Psychiatry*, Armand M. Nicholi, Jr., ed. (Cambridge: Harvard University Press, 1978), 519.

16. For a short summary of these findings see Daniel Goleman, "Outpost of Adolescence Is Found in Adulthood," *New York Times*, November 8, 1988, B1, B10.

17. Ianni, *The Search for Structure*, 17.

18. Anthony W. Jackson and David W. Hornbeck, "Educating Young Adolescents," *American Psychologist* 44 (May 1989): 832.

19. Fred M. Hechinger, *Fateful Choices* (New York: Carnegie Council on Adolescent Development, 1992), 21.

20. For a summary of these findings see Jacquelynne S. Eccles, Carol Midgley, Allan Wigfield, Christy Miller Buchanan, David Reuman, Constance Flanagan, and Douglas Mac Iver, "Development during Adolescence: The Impact of Stage-Environment Fit on Young Adolescents' Experiences in Schools and Families," *American Psychologist* 48 (February 1993): 90–101.

21. Robert L. Hendern, "Stress in Adolescence," in L. Eugene Arnold, ed., *Childhood Stress* (New York: John Wiley, 1990), 251–52.

22. Jay P. Jensen and Allen E. Bergin, "Mental Health Values of Professional Therapists: A Nationwide Interdisciplinary Survey," *Professional Psychology: Research and Practice* 19 (June 1988): 290–97.

23. Judith Viorst, *Necessary Losses* (New York: Fawcett, 1986), 3. I would recommend this work to readers with the caution it is very psychoanalytic and makes numerous assumptions about human development from only the psychoanalytic perspective.

24. These points are eloquently made by the psychiatrist Anthony Storr in his fascinating work, *Solitude: A Return to the Self* (New York: Ballantine Books, 1988). I highly recommend this book.

25. I have outlined elsewhere a "psychology of gratitude" and its role in healthy human functioning and the moral life. See Charles Shelton, *Morality of the Heart: A Psychology for the Christian Moral Life* (New York: Crossroad, 1990), 119–22.

26. Jerome D. Frank, "Therapeutic Components Shared by All Psychotherapies," *The Master Lecture Series: Psychotherapy Research and Behavior Change* (Washington, D.C.: American Psychological Association, 1981), 10.

27. Ibid., 16.

28. For an interesting discussion of these issues see Donald R. Atkinson and Homer M. L. Miller, "Pastoral Counseling and Confidentiality," *Counseling and Values* 31 (October 1986): 89–96.

29. Vernon F. Jones, *Adolescents with Behavior Problems* (Boston: Allyn and Bacon, 1980), 3.

30. Homer U. Ashby, Jr., "Values and the Moral Context of Pastoral Counseling," *Journal of Religion and Health* 20 (Fall 1981): 177.

31. Robert Coles, *Harvard Diary: Reflections on the Sacred and the Secular* (New York: Crossroad, 1988), 93.

32. Frank, "Therapeutic Components," 11.

33. Charles M. Shelton, *Morality and the Adolescent: A Pastoral Psychology Approach* (New York: Crossroad, 1989).

34. I have argued elsewhere that empathy is the "heart" of morality and the foundation for the Christian moral life. See Shelton, *Morality of the Heart.*

35. See Shelton, *Morality and the Adolescent,* 59–134.

Chapter 2: Adolescent Development and Dysfunction

1. Charles M. Shelton, *Adolescent Spirituality: Pastoral Ministry for High School and College Youth* (New York: Crossroad, 1989), 29–120.

2. Jerome Kagan, *Unstable Ideas: Temperament, Cognition, and Self* (Cambridge, Mass.: Harvard University Press, 1989), 92.

3. See David Elkind, "Understanding the Young Adolescent," *Adolescence* 49 (Spring 1978): 129–32.

4. Marilyn Jacobs Quadrel, Baruch Fischhoff, and Wendy Davis, "Adolescent (In)vulnerability," *American Psychologist* 48 (February 1993): 102–16.

5. For discussion of these and other terms see Don E. Hamachek, "The Self's Development and Ego Growth: Conceptual Analysis and Implications for Counselors," *Journal of Counseling and Development* 64 (October 1985): 136–41.

6. Roy F. Baumeister, *Escaping the Self: Alcoholism, Spirituality, Masochism, and Other Flights from the Burden of Selfhood* (New York: Basic Books, 1991), 4.

7. Erik Erikson, *Identity: Youth and Crisis* (New York: W. W. Norton, 1968).

8. James E. Marcia, "Identity in Adolescence," in Joseph Adelson ed., *Handbook of Adolescent Psychology* (New York: John Wiley, 1980), 160.

9. Richard Logan, "Identity Diffusion and Psycho-Social Defense Mechanisms," *Adolescence* 13 (Fall 1978): 503–7.

10. By providing this example I am not trying to reduce the reasons for adolescent suicide solely to a loss of boundaries. Suicide remains a very complex act incorporating biological, psychological, and social/cultural factors.

11. For a general discussion of this issue see Doreen Kimura "Sex Differences in the Brain," *Scientific American* 267 (September 1992): 119–25.

12. Carol Tavris, *The Mismeasure of Women* (New York: Simon & Schuster, 1992), 83. See also Mary Brabeck, "Comment on Scarr," *American Psychologist* 44 (May 1989): 847.

13. Sidney Callahan, *In Good Conscience: Reason and Emotion in Moral Decision Making* (San Francisco: HarperCollins, 1991), 198. A serious critique of and important challenge to a distinct feminine view of morality is raised in Phyllis Grosskurth, "The New Psychology of Women," *New York Review of Books* 38 (October 24, 1991): 25–32.

14. James E. Marcia, "Identity in Adolescence," in Joseph Adelson, ed., *Handbook of Adolescent Psychology* (New York: John Wiley, 1980), 178.

15. Erik H. Erikson, *Identity, Youth and Crisis* (New York: W. W. Norton, 1968), 261–94,

16. Serena J. Patterson, Ingrid Sochting, and James E. Marcia, "The Inner Space and Beyond: Women and Identity," in Gerald R. Adams, Thomas P. Gullotta, and Raymond Montemayor, eds., *Adolescent Identity Formation* (Newbury Park, Calif.: Sage Publications, 1992), 12.

17. Ibid., 17.

18. Sally L. Archer, "A Feminist's Approach to Identity Research," in Adams, Gullotta, and Montemayor, *Adolescent Identity Formation*, 34.

19. For an excellent summary of this research see Nancy J. Cobb, *Adolescence: Continuity, Change, and Diversity* (Mountain View, Calif.: Mayfield Publishing Co., 1992): 422–27.

20. Patricia H. Dyk and Gerald R. Adams, "Identity and Intimacy: An Initial Investigation of Three Theoretical Models Using Cross-Lag Panel Correlations," *Journal of Youth and Adolescence* 19 (November 2, 1990): 91–110; see also Nancy J. Cobb, *Adolescence*, 434–35.

21. Archer, "A Feminist's Approach," 27.

22. Ruthellen Josselson, *Finding Herself: Pathways to Identity Development in Women* (San Francisco: Jossey-Bass, 1987), 10.

23. Ibid., 11.

24. Cobb, *Adolescence*, 427.

25. Ibid., 427–30.

26. Jean S. Phinney and Doreen A. Rosenthal, "Ethnic Identity in Adolescence: Process, Context, and Outcome," in Adams, Gullotta, and Montemayor, *Adolescent Identity Formation*, 165–66. This chapter (145–72) is an excellent introduction to the current research findings on minority youth identity development.

27. For this discussion I rely on the following two sources: Reiko Homma-True, Beverly Greene, Steven R. Lopez, and Joseph E. Trimble, "Ethnocultural Diversity in Clinical Psychology," *Clinical Psychologist* 46 (Spring 1993): 74–87, and Derald Wing Sue and David Sue, *Counseling the Culturally Different* (New York: John Wiley, 1990).

28. Derald Wing Sue and David Sue, *Counseling the Culturally Different*, 229.

29. June M. Tuna, "Mental Health Services for Children," *American Psychologist* 44 (February 1989): 188.

30. Sally I. Powers, Stuart T. Hauser, and Linda A. Kilner, "Adolescent Mental Health," *American Psychologist* 44 (February 1989): 200.

31. Ibid., 201.

32. Ibid., 200–201. See also George W. Albee, "The Answer Is Prevention," *Psychology Today* 19 (February 1985): 60–64, and Darrel A. Regier, William E. Narrow, Donald S. Rae, Ronald W. Manderscheid, Ben Z. Locke, and Frederick K. Goodwin, "The De Facto US Mental and Addictive Disorders Service System," *Archives of General Psychiatry* 50 (February 1993): 85–94.

33. Leonard Saxe, Theodore Cross, and Nancy Silverman, "Children's Mental Health," *American Psychologist* 43 (October 1988): 800.

34. Kathleen O'Malley, Inese Wheeler, Jim Murphey, John O'Connell, and Michael Waldo, "Changes in Levels of Psychopathology Being Treated at College and University Counseling Centers," *Journal of College Student Development* 31 (September 1990): 464–65.

35. Elissa K. Koplik and Anthony J. DeVito, "Problems of Freshmen: Comparison of Classes of 1976 and 1986," *Journal of College Student Personnel* 27 (March 1986): 124–30.

36. Alan Kazdin, "Psychotherapy for Children and Adolescents," *American Psychologist* 48 (June 1993): 652.

37. Fred M. Hechinger, *Fateful Choices* (New York: Carnegie Corporation, 1992), 21–22.

38. For an informed discussion of "temperament" see Jerome Kagan, "Temperamental Contributions to Social Behavior," *American Psychologist* 44 (April 1989): 668–74; and Jerome Kagan, *Unstable Ideas* (Cambridge Mass.: Harvard University Press, 1989).

39. Kagan, "Temperamental Contributions to Social Behavior," 668.

40. Joseph B. Treaster and Mary B. W. Tabor, "Teen-Age Gunslinging Is on Rise, in Search of Protection and Profit," *New York Times*, February 17, 1992, A1.

41. Susan Chira, "Student Poll Finds Wide Use of Guns," *New York Times*, July 20, 1993, A8.

42. Ibid.

43. Philip J. Hilts, "Gunshot Wounds Become Second Leading Cause of Death for Teen-Agers," *New York Times*, June 10, 1992, A14.

44. By discussing "cultural impairment" I do not mean to disparage the many advantages our culture provides (e.g., emphasis on rights and individual liberties). I simply want to stress the impediments that culture brings to any discussion of healthy adolescent development.

45. Quoted in Alan Durning, "How Much Is Enough?" *Technology Review* 94 (May/June 1991): 57.

46. Stuart Ewen, *All Consuming Images: The Politics of Style in Contemporary Culture* (New York: Basic Books, 1988), 271.

47. Alasdair MacIntyre, *After Virtue* (Notre Dame, Ind.: University of Notre Dame Press, 1981), 235.

48. Robert M. Bellah, Richard Madsen, William M. Sullivan, Ann Swidler, Steven M. Tipton, *Habits of the Heart* (Berkeley: University of California Press, 1985), 76.

49. Robert M. Bellah, Richard Madsen, William M. Sullivan, Ann Swidler, Steven M. Tipton, *The Good Society* (New York: Alfred A. Knopf, 1991), 86.

50. David G. Myers, *Psychology*, 3d ed. (New York: Worth Publishers, 1992), 570.

51. L. Rowell Huesmann and Neil M. Malamuth, "Media Violence and Antisocial Behavior: An Overview," *Journal of Social Issues* 42, no. 3 (1986): 1.

52. L. Rowell Huesmann, "Psychological Processes Promoting the Relation between Exposure to Media Violence and Aggressive Behavior by the Viewer," *Journal of Social Issues* 42, no. 3 (1986): 125.

53. Ibid., 136.

54. Based on lecture by Jean Kilbourne given at Regis University, February 26, 1992.

55. Quoted in Lawrence Kutner, "Parent and Child: The More Subtle Shades of Body Dissatisfaction Are Just as Insidious as Anorexia and Bulimia," *New York Times*, March 12, 1992, B2.

56. The discussion of attachment theory that follows and the subsequent model that is presented is derived from the following sources: Mary D. Salter Ainsworth, "Attachments beyond Infancy," *American Psychologist* 44 (April 1989), 709–16; Mary D. Salter Ainsworth, "Infant-Mother Attachment," *American Psychologist* 34 (October 1979), 932–37; Mary D. Salter Ainsworth and John Bowlby, "An Ethological Approach to Personality Development," *American Psychologist* 46 (April 1991), 333–41; John Bowlby, *A Secure Base* (New York: Basic Books, 1988); Jerome Kagan, *Unstable Ideas* (Cambridge, Mass., Harvard University Press, 1989); Jerome Kagan, "Temperamental Contributions to Social Behavior," *American Psychologist* 44 (April 1989), 668–74; Robert Karen, "Becoming Attached," *Atlantic Monthly* (February 1990), 35–70; R. Rogers Kobak and Amy Sceery, "Attachment in Late Adolescence: Working Models, Affect Regulation, and Representations of Self and Others," *Child Development* 59 (1988): 135–46; Irwin Jay Knopf, *Childhood Psychopathology*, 2d ed. (Englewood Cliffs, N.J.: Prentice-Hall, 1984); Vittorio F. Guidano, *Complexity of the Self* (New York: Guilford Press, 1987); Vittorio Guidano and Gianni Liotti, *Cognitive Processes and Emotional Disorders* (New York: Guilford Press, 1983); Ken Magid and Carole A. McKelvey, *High Risk: Children without a Conscience* (New York: Bantam Books, 1988); Patricia H. Miller, *Theories of Developmental Psychology* (San Francisco: W. H. Freeman, 1983); Ross A. Thompson, ed., *Socioemotional Development: Nebraska Symposium on Motivation, 1988* (Lincoln: University of Nebraska Press, 1990).

57. Bowlby, *A Secure Base*, 121.

58. Ibid., 27.

59. Karen, "Becoming Attached," 38.

60. Bowlby, *A Secure Base*, 11.

61. Ibid., 129–30.

62. Daniel K. Lapsley, Kenneth G. Rice, and David P. FitzGerald, "Adolescent Attachment, Identity, and Adjustment to College: Implications for the Continuity of Adaptation Hypothesis," *Journal of Counseling and Development* 68 (May/June 1990): 561.

63. R. Rogers Kobak and Amy Sceery, "Attachment in Late Adolescence: Working Models, Affect Regulation, and Representations of Self and Others," *Child Development* 59 (1988): 135.

64. See Kagan, "Temperamental Contributions to Social Behavior."

65. Judith Stevens-Long and Michael L. Commons, *Adult Life*, 4th ed. (Mountain View, Calif.: Mayfield Publishing, 1992), 148.

66. Emmy E. Werner, "Children of the Garden Island," *Scientific American* 260 (April 1989): 106–11; Emmy E. Werner, "High Risk Children in Young Adulthood: A Longitudinal Study from Birth to 32 Years," *American Journal of Orthopsychiatry* 49 (January 1989): 72–81; Ann S. Masten, Karin M. Best, and Norman Garmezy, "Resilience and Development: Contributions from the Study of Children Who Overcome Adversity," *Development and Psychopathology* 2 (1990): 425–44.

67. Carol Gilligan, Janie Victoria Ward, and Jill McLean Taylor, *Mapping the Moral Domain* (Cambridge, Mass.: Harvard University Press, 1988), xxx.

68. Stevens-Long and Commons, *Adult Life*, 70–72; and Myers, *Psychology*, 120–21.

69. Helen G. Rabichow and Morris A. Sklansky, *Effective Counseling of Adolescents* (Chicago: Association Press, 1980), 49–50.

70. Adult readers might wish to reflect on the degree that they utilize these various defenses. Since defense mechanisms are for the most part unconscious processes, it might be helpful, too, to reflect on these with a friend.

71. The following discussion of adolescent and young adult defenses is based on my own clinical experience as well as the following sources: Knopf, *Childhood Psychopathology*, 98; Rabichow and Sklansky, *Effective Counseling of Adolescents*, 48–59; George E. Valliant, *Adaptation to Life* (Boston: Little, Brown, 1977), 383–86.

72. Rabichow and Sklansky, *Effective Counseling of Adolescents*, 52.

Chapter 3: Counseling: Some Issues and Approaches

1. This discussion is based on my own clinical experience as well as Gerald D. Oster, Janice E. Caro, Daniel R. Eagen, and Margaret H. Lillo, *Assessing Adolescents* (New York: Pergamon Press, 1988).

2. This discussion of anger is based on my own clinical experience as well as Carol Tavris, *Anger: The Misunderstood Emotion* (New York: Simon and Schuster, 1989).

3. Sandra S. Meggert, " 'Who Cares What I Think?': Problems of Low Self-Esteem," in Dave Capuzzi and Douglas R. Gross, eds., *Youth at Risk: A Resource for Counselors, Teachers and Parents* (Alexandria, Va.: American As-

sociation for Counseling and Development, 1989), 102. For an elaboration on these features and a more extensive list see D. Frey and C. J. Carlock, *Enhancing Self-Esteem* (Muncie, Ind.: Accelerated Development, 1984).

4. Peter Freiberg, "Self-Esteem Gender Gap Widens in Adolescence," *APA Monitor* 22 (April 1991): 29.

5. Ibid.

6. James J. Gill, "Indispensable Self-Esteem," *Human Development* 1 (Fall 1980): 34.

7. Albert Ellis, "The Impossibility of Achieving Consistently Good Mental Health," *American Psychologist* 42 (April 1987): 365.

Chapter 4: The Adolescent and the Family

1. Barbara D. Whitehead, "Dan Quayle Was Right," *Atlantic Monthly* 271 (April 1993): 47.

2. Stuart T. Hauser, *Adolescents and Their Families* (New York: The Free Press, 1991), 17.

3. The following discussion of family strengths is based on Michele Burhard Thomas, *An Introduction to Marital and Family Therapy* (New York: Macmillan, 1992), 61–66. See also Nick Stinnet and John DeFrain, *Secrets of Strong Families* (Boston: Little, Brown, 1985).

4. Ibid., 64.

5. Dolores Curran, *Traits of a Healthy Family* (New York: Ballantine Books, 1983), 26–27.

6. Pat Conroy, *The Prince of Tides* (New York: Bantam, 1986), 157.

7. William Damon and Daniel Hart, *Self-Understanding in Childhood and Adolescence* (New York: Cambridge University Press, 1988).

8. Nancy J. Cobb, *Adolescence* (Mountain View, Calif.: Mayfield Publishing, 1992).

9. Stuart T. Hauser, *Adolescents and Their Families* (New York: The Free Press, 1991), 231.

10. Ibid., 233.

11. Judith Smetana, "Adolescents' and Parents' Conceptions of Parental Authority," *Child Development* 59 (April 1988): 321–35.

12. Judith G. Smetana, "Adolescents' and Parents' Reasoning about Actual Family Conflict," *Child Development* 60 (October 1989): 1063.

13. Raymond Montemayor, "Parents and Adolescents in Conflict: All Families Some of the Time and Some Families Most of the Time," *Journal of Early Adolescence* 3, nos. 1–2 (1983): 83–103.

14. James Youniss and Jacqueline Smollar, *Adolescent Relations with Mothers, Fathers, and Friends* (Chicago: University of Chicago Press, 1985), 29–51.

15. David Popenoe, "Scholars Should Worry about the Disintegration of the American Family," *Chronicle of Higher Education* 39 (April 14, 1993): 48.

16. For this discussion of multiculturalism and families I rely upon Cobb, *Adolescence*, and Derald Wing Sue and David Sue, *Counseling the Culturally Different* (New York: John Wiley, 1990).

17. Susan M. Heitler, *From Conflict to Resolution* (New York: W. W. Norton, 1990).

Chapter 5: Adolescent Stress

1. Quoted in Roger J. Allen *Human Stress: Its Nature and Control* (Minneapolis: Burgess Publishing Company, 1983).

2. Ibid., 2–13.

3. Steven F. Maier and Mark Laudenslager, "Stress and Health: Exploring the Links," *Psychology Today* (August 1985): 44–49.

4. Quoted in Stevan E. Hobfoll, "Conservation of Resources: A New Attempt at Conceptualizing Stress," *American Psychologist* 44 (March 1989): 515.

5. Ibid., 516.

6. Ibid., 517.

7. Jeanne Brooks-Gunn, "How Stressful Is the Transition to Adolescence for Girls?" in Mary Ellen Colten and Susan Gore, eds., *Adolescent Stress: Causes and Consequences* (New York: Aldine De Gruyter, 1991), 131–49.

8. Bruce E. Compas and Barry M. Wagner, "Psychosocial Stress during Adolescence: Intrapersonal and Interpersonal Processes," in Colten and Gore, *Adolescent Stress*, 67–85.

9. Sanford M. Dornbusch, Randy Mont-Reynaud, Philip L. Ritter, Zeng-yin Chen, and Laurence Steinberg, "Stressful Events and Their Correlates among Adolescents of Diverse Backgrounds," in *Adolescent Stress*, 111–30.

10. Reed Larson and Linda Asmussen, "Anger, Worry, and Hurt in Early Adolescence: An Enlarging World of Negative Emotions," in Colten and Gore, *Adolescent Stress*, 21–41.

11. I wish to thank R. Dean Coddington for permission to reproduce this list of life events. The complete scale includes a scoring of the events listed. For information on scoring and the complete scale contact R. Dean Coddington, M.D., 116 West Main Street, St. Clairsville, OH 43950.

12. Bob Pettapiece, "Developing a Stress Scale for High School Students," *High School Psychology Teacher* 19 (March/April 1988): 8–10.

13. John W. Green, Lynn S. Walker, Gerald Hickson, and Juliette Thompson, "Stressful Life Events and Somatic Complaints in Adolescents," *Pediatrics* 75 (January 1985): 19–22.

14. Herman S. Bush, Merita Thompson, and Norman Van Tubergen, "Personal Assessment of Stress Factors for College Students," *Journal of School Health* 55 (November 1985): 370–75.

15. Bruce E. Compas and Barry M. Wagner, "Psychosocial Stress during Adolescence: Intrapersonal and Interpersonal Processes," in Colten and Gore, *Adolescent Stress*, 74.

16. See Frederick G. Lopez, "Patterns of Family Conflict and Their Relation to College Student Adjustment," *Journal of Counseling and Development* 69 (January/February 1991): 257–60.

17. Quoted in Benjamin H. Gottlieb, "Social Support in Adolescence," in Colten and Gore, *Adolescent Stress*, 288.

Chapter 6: Divorce and the Adolescent

1. Barbara Kantrowitz, Pat Wingert, Debra Rosenberg, Vicki Quade, and Donna Foote, "Breaking the Divorce Cycle," *Newsweek*, January 13, 1992, 49.

2. Ibid., 52.

3. Ibid., 49.

4. The sources of these findings are the following: L. Eugene Arnold and John A. Carnahan, "Child Divorce Stress," in L. Eugene Arnold, ed., *Childhood Stress* (New York: John Wiley, 1990), 373–403; Jane E. Brody, "Problems of Children: A New Look at Divorce," *New York Times*, June 7, 1991, B1, B13; Jane E. Brody, "Children of Divorce: Actions to Help Can Hurt, Studies Find," *New York Times*, July 23, 1991, B1 B11; Jane E. Brody, "Personal Health: Identifying the Factors That Can Ease the Way for Children Whose Parents Separate," *New York Times*, July 24, 1991, B6; Rebecca L. Drill, "The Effects of Divorce on Children," *High School Psychology Teacher News* 18 (January 1987): 2–3; Robert B. McCall and S. Holly Stocking, *A Summary of Research about the Effects of Divorce on Families* (Boys Town, Neb.: Boys Town, 1988); Judith S. Wallerstein and Sandra Blakeslee, *Second Chances* (New York: Ticknor & Fields, 1989).

5. Brody, "Children of Divorce," B11.

6. Abbie K. Frost and Bilge Pakiz, The Effects of Marital Disruption on Adolescents: Time as a Dynamic," *American Journal of Orthopsychiatry* 60 (October 1990): 545.

7. Ibid.

8. See Sandra F. Allen, Cal D. Stoltenberg, and Charlotte K. Rosko, "Perceived Psychological Separation of Older Adolescents and Young Adults from Their Parents: A Comparison of Divorced versus Intact Families," *Journal of Counseling and Human Development* 69 (September/October 1990): 57–61, and Hillevi M. Aro and Ulla K. Palosaari, "Parental Divorce, Adolescence, and Transition to Young Adulthood: A Follow-Up Study," *American Journal of Orthopsychiatry* 62 (July 1992): 421–29.

9. Barbara S. Cain, "The Price They Pay: Older Children and Divorce," *New York Times Magazine*, February 18, 1990, 50.

10. Wallerstein and Blakeslee, *Second Chances*, 63.

11. Judith S. Wallerstein, "Children After Divorce: Wounds That Don't Heal," *New York Times Magazine*, January 22, 1989, 21.

12. Ibid., 19.

13. Wallerstein and Blakeslee, *Second Chances*, 149.

14. Allan Z. Schwartzberg, "Adolescent Reactions to Divorce," in *Adolescent Psychiatry*, vol. 8, Sherman C. Feinstein, Peter L. Giovacchini, John G. Looney, Allan Z. Schwartzberg, and Arthur D. Sorosky, eds. (Chicago: University of Chicago Press, 1980), 382.

15. For a discussion of this process see Peter Blos, *On Adolescence: A Psychoanalytic Interpretation* (New York: The Free Press, 1962).

16. Joe Klein, "Whose Values?" *Newsweek*, June 8, 1992, 21.

17. Wade Lewis, "Strategic Interventions with Children of Single-Parent Families," *The School Counselor* 33 (May 1986): 375–78.

18. Some professionals prefer the term "remarried" family to "stepfamily."

19. Lawrence Kutner, "Parent and Child: For Children and Stepparents in New Families, War Isn't Inevitable," *New York Times*, June 30, 1988, B3.

20. William M. Walsh, "Twenty Major Issues in Remarriage Families," *Journal of Counseling and Development* 70 (July/August 1992): 709–15.

21. Patsy Skeen, Robert B. Covi, and Bryan E. Robinson, "Stepfamilies: A Review of the Literature with Suggestions for Practitioners," *Journal of Counseling and Development* 64 (October 1985): 121–25.

Chapter 7: Eating Disorders

1. "34 Percent of High School Girls Think They're Overweight," *Rocky Mountain News*, November 1, 1991, 4.

2. Lena Williams, "Girl's Self-Image Is Mother of the Woman," *New York Times*, February 6, 1992, A1, A12.

3. What follows is a summary of Ruth H. Striegel-Moore, Lisa R. Silberstein, and Judith Rodin, "Toward an Understanding of Risk Factors for Bulimia," *American Psychologist* 41 (March 1986): 246–63.

4. Ibid., 249.

5. Ibid., 250.

6. Ibid.

7. Ibid., 250–51.

8. Ibid., 251.

9. Joseph L. White, *The Troubled Adolescent* (New York: Pergamon Press, 1989), 181.

10. Ibid., 180–81.

11. William G. Johnson and April H. Crusco, "Eating Disorders Part I: Anorexia Nervosa," *High School Psychology Teacher* 17 (March 1986): 2. See also "Eating Disorders — Part I," *Harvard Mental Health Letter* 9 (December 1992): 1.

12. White, *The Troubled Adolescent*, 182.

13. Ibid.

14. For stringent diagnostic criteria for anorexia nervosa see American Psychiatric Association, *Diagnostic and Statistical Manual of Mental Disorders IV* (Washington, D.C.: American Psychiatric Association, 1994), 544–45.

15. Frances A. Kempley and Wanda T. Weber, "The Secret and All-consuming Obsessions: Anorexia Nervosa and Bulimia Nervosa," in *Youth at Risk: A Resource for Counselors, Teachers and Parents*, eds. Dave Capuzzi and Douglas R. Gross (Alexandria, Va.: American Association for Counseling and Development), 175.

16. "Eating Disorders — Part I," *Harvard Mental Health Letter*, 3.

17. White, *The Troubled Adolescent*, 185.

18. David M. Garner, Paul E. Garfinkel, Donald Schwartz, and Michael Thompson, "Cultural Expectation of Thinness of Women," *Psychological Reports* 47 (1980): 483–91.

19. Barton J. Blinder and Kristin Cadenhead, "Bulimia: A Historical Overview," in Sherman C. Feinstein, Aaron H. Esman, John G. Looney, Allan Z. Schwartzberg, Arthur D. Sorosky, and Max Sugar, eds., *Adolescent Psychiatry*, vol. 13 (Chicago: University of Chicago Press, 1986), 233.

20. Quoted in P. Chance, "Food Madness," *Psychology Today* 18 (June 1984): 14.

21. "Eating Disorders — Part I," *Harvard Mental Health Letter*, 2.

22. Paula R. Holleran, Joseph Pascale, and James Fraley, "Personality Correlates of College Age Bulimics," *Journal of Counseling and Development* 66 (April 1988): 378.

23. American Psychiatric Association, *Diagnostic and Statistical Manual of Mental Disorders*, 68–69.

24. "Eating Disorders — Part I," *Harvard Mental Health Letter*, 2.

25. Ibid., 4.

26. Ibid., 3.

27. Striegel-Moore et al., "Toward an Understanding of Risk Factors for Bulimia," 254–56.

Chapter 8: Abuse and the Adolescent

1. "Child Abuse — Part I," *Harvard Mental Health Letter* 9 (May 1993): 1–3.

2. Lynn W. England and Charles L. Thompson, "Counseling Child Sexual Abuse Victims: Myths and Realities," *Journal of Counseling and Development* 66 (April 1988): 370–73.

3. For this discussion of "psychological maltreatment" I rely upon Stuart N. Hart and Marla R. Brassard, "A Major Threat to Children's Mental Health: Psychological Maltreatment," *American Psychologist* 42 (February 1987): 160–65.

4. Ruth S. Kempe and C. Henry Kempe, *Child Abuse* (Cambridge Mass.: Harvard University Press, 1978), 10–24.

5. "Child Abuse — Part II," *Harvard Mental Health Letter* 9 (June 1993): 1.

6. Deborah Tharinger, "Impact of Child Sexual Abuse on Developing Sexuality," *Professional Psychology* 21 (October 1990): 332.

7. Ibid., 333.

8. See David Finkelhor, "Early and Long-Term Effects of Child Sexual Abuse: An Update," *Professional Psychology* 21 (October 1990): 329; Deborah Tharinger, "Impact of Child Sexual Abuse on Developing Sexuality," 333.

9. Finkelhor, "Early and Long-Term Effects of Child Sexual Abuse," 325.

10. Diana M. Elliott and John Briere, "The Sexually Abused Boy: Problems in Manhood," *Medical Aspects of Human Sexuality* 26 (February 1992): 68; Finkelhor, "Early and Long-Term Effects of Child Sexual Abuse," 326.

11. Finkelhor, "Early and Long-Term Effects of Child Sexual Abuse," 326.

12. Ibid., 329.

13. "Child Abuse—Part II," 2.

14. Ibid.

15. Ibid.

16. Judith Lewis Herman, *Trauma and Recovery* (New York: Basic Books, 1992), 109–10.

17. Ibid., 105.

Chapter 9: Sexuality and the Adolescent

1. See Charles M. Shelton, *Adolescent Spirituality: Pastoral Ministry for High School and College Youth* (Chicago: Loyola University Press, 1983; paperback edition, New York: Crossroad, 1989), 233–93.

2. John J. Conger, *Adolescence and Youth: Psychological Development in a Changing World* (New York: Harper & Row, 1977), 339–40.

3. John C. Coleman, "Friendship and the Peer Group in Adolescence," in Joseph Adelson, ed., *Handbook of Adolescent Psychology* (New York: John Wiley, 1980), 410.

4. James Youniss and Jacqueline Smollar, *Adolescent Relations with Mothers, Fathers, and Friends* (Chicago: University of Chicago Press, 1985), 122–23.

5. Ibid., 126–27. See pp. 94–139 for an overall view of adolescent friendship patterns.

6. John J. Mitchell, "Adolescent Intimacy," *Adolescence* 11 (Summer 1976): 275.

7. Erik H. Erikson, *Childhood and Society* (New York: W. W. Norton, 1963), 253.

8. Dan P. McAdams, *Intimacy* (New York: Doubleday, 1989).

9. See C. S. Lewis, *The Four Loves* (New York: Harcourt Brace, 1960), and McAdams, *Intimacy*, 40–45.

10. Bruce Roscoe, Donna Kennedy, and Tony Pope, "Adolescents' Views of Intimacy: Distinguishing Intimate from Non-intimate Relationships," *Adolescence* 22 (Fall 1987): 511–16.

11. Bruce Roscoe, Mark S. Diana, and Richard H. Brooks, "Early, Middle, and Late Adolescents' Views on Dating and Factors Influencing Partner Selection," *Adolescence* 22 (Spring 1987): 59–68.

12. For a discussion of adolescent sexual behavior see Thomas P. Gullotta, Gerald R. Adams, and Raymond Montemayor, eds., *Adolescent Sexuality* (Newbury Park, Calif.: Sage Publications, 1993).

13. The following findings are taken from Brent C. Miller, Cynthia R. Christopherson, and Pamela K. King, "Sexual Behavior in Adolescence," in ibid., 57–76.

14. Ibid., 64.

15. Lisa Sowle Cahill, "Marriage: Institution, Relationship, Sacrament," in John A. Coleman, ed., *One Hundred Years of Catholic Social Thought* (Maryknoll N.Y.: Orbis Books, 1991), 111–12.

16. See Vincent Carroll, "The Ills of Illegitimacy," *Rocky Mountain News*, December 19, 1993, 104A; Charles Krauthammer, "Redefining Deviancy,"

Rocky Mountain News, December 5, 1993, 94A; Lena Williams, "Pregnant Teen-Agers Are Outcasts No Longer," *New York Times,* December 2, 1993, B1, B4.

17. John J. Mitchell, "Some Psychological Dimensions of Adolescent Sexuality," *Adolescence* 8 (Winter 1972): 456.

18. James J. DiGiacomo, "All You Need Is Love," *America* (February 14, 1987): 126.

19. Jeanne Brooks-Gunn and Frank F. Furstenber, Jr., "Adolescent Sexual Behavior," *American Psychologist* 44 (February 1989): 252–53.

20. Stephen R. Jorgenson, "Adolescent Pregnancy and Parenting," in Gullotta, Adams, and Montemayor, *Adolescent Sexuality,* 112.

21. Andrew M. Greeley, "Sex and the Single Catholic: The Decline of an Ethic," *America* 167 (November 7, 1992): 347.

22. Barbara Kantrowitz, Mary Hager, Geoffrey Cowley, Lucille Beachy, Melissa Rossi, Brynn Craffey, Peter Annin, and Rebecca Crandall, "Teen-agers and AIDS," *Newsweek,* August 3, 1992, 45.

23. Nina Youngstown, "Warning: Teens at Risk for AIDS," *APA Monitor* 22 (October 1991): 38.

24. Carol Kreck, "HIV Set to Spread among Area Teens," *Denver Post,* December 29, 1991, 12A.

25. See Katherine S. Mangan, "Sexually Active Students Found Failing to Take Precautions Against AIDS," *Chronicle of Higher Education* 35 (September 28, 1988): A32, and Joseph Wakelee-Lynch, "HIV Infection Rate Higher Than Expected among College Students," *Guidepost* 32 (July 13, 1989): 1.

26. Kantrowitz et al. "Teenagers and Aids," 47.

27. Youngstrom, "Warning: Teens at Risk for AIDS," 38.

28. Gary B. Melton, "Adolescents and Prevention of AIDS," *Professional Psychology: Research and Practice* 19 (August 1988): 403–8.

29. Felicity Barringer, "Report Finds 1 in 5 Infected by Viruses Spread Sexually," *New York Times,* April 1, 1993, A1.

30. Warren E. Leary, "Sharp Rise in Rare Sex-Related Diseases," *New York Times,* July 14, 1988, 23.

31. Francis Quinn, "The Church and AIDS Prevention," *Origins* 21 (March 5, 1992): 635.

32. See John A. Leies, "Condoms and AIDS," *Ethics & Medics* 18 (May 1993): 2–4; John R. Quinn, "Distributing Condoms in High Schools," *America* 165 (November 2, 1991): 320; Brian E. Scully, M.D., "Condoms Reduce, but Don't Eliminate, the Risk for AIDS," *New York Times,* January 28, 1993, A14; Beverly Sottile-Malona, "Condoms and Aids," *America* 165 (November 2, 1991): 317–19.

33. Quinn, "Distributing Condoms in High Schools," 320.

34. Ibid.

35. For a short summary of the research that argues for a genetic/ biological basis see Michael Bailey and Richard C. Pillard, "The Innateness of Homosexuality," *Harvard Mental Health Letter* 10 (January 1994): 4–6. For a criticism of the biological approach see William Byne and Bruce Parsons,

"Biology and Human Sexual Orientation," *Harvard Mental Health Letter* 10 (February 1994): 5–7.

36. When using the word "exclusively" I mean an ongoing sexual attraction toward either males or females and an awareness that this is one's orientation. According to this definition an adult might be classified as exclusively heterosexual yet during adolescence have had a homosexual encounter that is most appropriately explained as part of a process of self-discovery. As this example indicates, one's definition of heterosexuality and homosexuality is of critical importance for this discussion.

37. Richard R. Troiden, "Homosexual Identity Development," *Journal of Adolescent Health Care* 9, no. 2 (1988): 105–13.

38. Rosalie L. Cross, "Identity Formation of Gay Adolescents," *Adolinks* 3 (Summer 1985): 1.

39. Margaret G. Kaczmarek and Barbara A. Backlund, "Disenfranchised Grief: The Loss of an Adolescent Romantic Relationship," *Adolescence* 26 (Summer 1991): 253–59. This article contains suggestions for helping adolescents work through loss over their relationships.

Chapter 10: Depression and Adolescence

1. American Psychiatric Association, *Diagnostic and Statistical Manual of Mental Disorders IV* (Washington, D.C.: American Psychiatric Association, 1994), 349.

2. Carol Rubin, Judith Rubenstein, Gerald Stechler, Timothy Heeren, Antonia Halton, Donna Housman, and Linda Kasten, "Depressive Affect in 'Normal' Adolescents: Relationship to Life Stress, Family, and Friends," *American Journal of Orthopsychiatry* 62 (July 1992): 430–41.

3. "Mood Disorders in Childhood and Adolescence — Part I," *Harvard Mental Health Letter* 10 (November 1993): 3–4.

4. For literature on this topic see Betty Allgood-Merton, Peter M. Lewinsohn, and Hyman Hope, "Sex Differences and Adolescent Depression," *Journal of Abnormal Psychology* 99, no. 1 (1990): 55–63; Jack H. Block, Per F. Gjerde, and Jeanne H. Block, "Personality Antecedents of Depressive Tendencies in 18-Year-Olds: A Prospective Study," *Journal of Personality and Social Psychology* 60, no. 5 (1991): 726–38; Daniel Goleman, "Why Girls Are Prone to Depression," *New York Times*, May 10, 1990, 12; Reed W. Larson, Maryse H. Richards, Marcela Raffailli, Mark Ham, and Lisa Jewell, "Ecology of Depression in Late Childhood and Early Adolescence: A Profile of Daily States and Activities," *Journal of Abnormal Psychology* 99, no. 1 (1990): 92–102.

5. "Action Urged to Prevent Suicides by Teen-Agers," *New York Times*, August 30, 1988, 7.

6. "Young Indians Far More Likely Than Others to Attempt Suicide," *New York Times*, March 25, 1992, A8.

7. James R. Rogers, "Female Suicide: The Trend toward Increased Lethality in Method of Choice and Its Implications," *Journal of Counseling & Development* 69 (September/October 1990): 37–38.

8. Many of these statistics were gathered from Alan L. Berman and David A. Jobes, *Adolescent Suicide: Assessment and Intervention* (Washington, D.C.: American Psychological Association, 1991). This is an excellent source book for understanding suicide and the adolescent.

9. Information is taken from Berman and Jobes, *Adolescent Suicide;* Jane E. Brody, "Suicide Myths Cloud Efforts to Save Children," *New York Times,* June 16, 1992, B7–B8; Maria Gispert, Maryellen S. Davis, Loralee Marsh, and Kirk Wheeler, "Predictive Factors in Repeated Suicide Attempts by Adolescents," *Hospital and Community Psychiatry* 38 (April 1987): 390–93.

10. This discussion of suicide dynamics is based on my own clinical experience as well as Edwin Shneidman, *The Definition of Suicide* (New York: John Wiley, 1985). Shneidman's analysis of suicide is in my view the best resource for understanding the nature of suicide.

Chapter 11: Drug Abuse and the Adolescent

1. Joseph B. Treaster, "Survey Finds Marijuana Use Is Up in High Schools," *New York Times,* February 1, 1994, A1, A10.

2. Kathleen McAuliffe, "Small Molecule, Large Effects," *U.S. News & World Report* 103 (November 30, 1987): 60, and James E. Royce, *Alcohol Problems and Alcoholism* (New York: Free Press, 1989).

3. Lewis J. Lord, Erica E. Goode, Ted Gest, Kathleen McAuliffe, Lisa J. Moore, Robert F. Black, and Nancy Linnon, "Coming to Grips with Alcoholism," *U.S. News & World Report* 103 (November 30, 1987): 56–62.

4. The criteria for substance abuse and dependence are taken from American Psychiatric Association, *Diagnostic and Statistical Manual of Mental Disorders IV* (Washington, D.C.: American Psychiatric Association, 1994), 181–83.

5. John E. Helzer, "Epidemiology of Alcoholism," *Journal of Consulting and Clinical Psychology* 55 (June 1987): 284–92, and Marc A. Schuckit, "Biological Vulnerability to Alcoholism," *Journal of Consulting and Clinical Psychology* 55 (June 1987): 301–9. For a critique of the biological approach to alcoholism see Dennis L. Thombs, *Introduction to Addictive Behaviors* (New York: Guilford Press, 1994).

6. For this argument as it relates to marijuana see Jonathan Shedler and Jack Block, "Adolescent Drug Use and Psychological Health: A Longitudinal Inquiry," *American Psychologist* 45 (May 1990): 612–30.

7. Richard R. Bootzin and Joan Ross Acocella, *Abnormal Psychology,* 5th ed. (New York: Random House, 1988), 294–95.

8. Stephanie Brown, *Treating Adult Children of Alcoholics: A Developmental Perspective* (New York: John Wiley, 1988). I rely on Brown's analysis for discussion of the alcoholic family. I strongly recommend this book for an understanding of the effects of alcohol on family functioning.

9. Ibid., 92.

10. Melissa Owings West and Ronald J. Prinz, "Parental Alcoholism and Childhood Psychopathology," *Psychological Bulletin* 102, no. 2 (1987): 204–18.

11. Ibid.

12. Mary Beth Logue, Kenneth J. Sher, and Peter A. Frensch, "Purported Characteristics of Adult Children of Alcoholics: A Possible 'Barnum Effect,'" *Professional Psychology: Research and Practice* 23 (June 1992): 226–32.

13. Alan Berkowitz and H. Wesley Perkins, "Personality Characteristics of Children of Alcoholics," *Journal of Consulting and Clinical Psychology* 56 (April 1988): 206–9.

14. Michael Windle, "Temperamental and Personality Attributes of Children of Alcoholics," in Michael Windle and John S. Searles, eds., *Children of Alcoholics: Critical Perspectives* (New York: Guilford Press, 1990), 129–67.

Index